Marathon Training For Dummies®

Cheat Sheet

Telling Time

From *mile splits* (the time it takes you to run each mile of a marathon) to *finish times* (your overall time for a race) to the speed displayed on your treadmill, marathoners are faced with all sorts of numbers. Read on to see what they mean.

Reading around the colons

When you see 4:02:27, 8:31, or :80, what does it all mean?

- ✔ **Any number with two colons is giving you hours, then minutes, then seconds.** So 4:02:27 means 4 hours, 2 minutes, and 27 seconds.

- ✔ **When you see one colon, the time is in minutes and seconds.** So 8:31 means 8 minutes and 31 seconds.

- ✔ **Times that are over — but close to — a minute or an hour may be converted to hours or minutes or may not.** So you may see 80 seconds as :80 or as 1:20 (1 minute, 20 seconds). If you run a 10K in 65:00 (65 minutes), it may also be written as 1:05:00 (1 hour, 5 minutes).

Figuring your average?

To calculate minutes per mile when you're running one of your measured road routes, use a calculator and do the following:

1. **Round your seconds to minutes and your hours to minutes, too.**

   For example, 36:33 (36 minutes and 33 seconds) becomes 37 minutes, and 1:10:24 — that's 1 hour, 10 minutes, and 24 seconds — becomes 70 minutes.

2. **Divide the minutes by the number of miles.**

3. **Subtract the minutes, so that you're left with just the decimal that represents the number of seconds. Then multiply that decimal by 60.**

   For example, if after you divide your minutes by miles, you're left with 9.27, subtract 9 and multiply .27 by 60 to get 16.2 and round it down to 16.

4. **Put the number of seconds back with the minutes, and you have your pace.**

   Using the previous example, you end up with 9 minutes + 16 seconds = 9:16 minutes per mile.

Marathon Training For Dummies®

Translating Race Lengths

A marathon is measured in miles, but many other races are measured in kilometers. Read on to see what all those lengths mean in miles and kilometers:

- **Marathon:** 26.2 miles
- **30K:** 18.6 miles
- **25K:** 15.5 miles
- **Half-marathon:** 13.1 miles
- **20K:** 12.4 miles
- **15K:** 9.3 miles
- **10K (or 10,000 meters):** 6.2 miles
- **5K (or 5,000 meters):** 3.1 miles
- **1,600 meters:** 1 mile (4 times around a track)
- **1,500 meters:** .93 miles (3¾ times around a track)
- **800 meters:** ½ mile (2 times around a track)
- **400 meters:** ¼ mile (1 time around a track)
- **200 meters:** ⅛ mile (½ time around a track)

Getting from Miles per Hour to Minutes per Mile

If you run on a treadmill, you may want to convert miles per hour to minutes per mile. Follow these numbered steps to see how:

1. **Divide 60 by whatever miles per hour the treadmill displays.**

   For example, if the treadmill says you're running 7.1 miles per hour, divide 60 by 7.1, and you get 8.45 (almost 9 minutes).

2. **Subtract the minutes, so that you're left with just the decimal that represents the number of seconds and then multiply that decimal amount by 60.**

   Subtract 8 and multiply .45 by 60 to get 27.

3. **Add that number back to the minutes, and you have your pace.**

   8 minutes + 27 seconds = 8:27 minutes per mile.

For Dummies: Bestselling Book Series for Beginners

Marathon Training

FOR

DUMMIES®

by Tere Stouffer Drenth

WILEY

Wiley Publishing, Inc.

Marathon Training For Dummies®

Published by
Wiley Publishing, Inc.
909 Third Avenue
New York, NY 10022
www.wiley.com

For general information on our other products and services or to obtain technical support, please contact our Customer Care Department within the U.S. at 800-762-2974, outside the U.S. at 317-572-3993, or fax 317-572-4002.

Wiley also publishes its books in a variety of electronic formats. Some content that appears in print may not be available in electronic books.

Library of Congress Cataloging-in-Publication Data:

Library of Congress Control Number: 2002114831

ISBN: 0-7645-2510-7 3761 3121   5/08

1B/SQ/QS/QT/IN

Manufactured in the United States of America

10 9 8 7

WILEY is a trademark of Wiley Publishing, Inc.

About the Author

Tere Stouffer Drenth started running when she was 9 years old and, except for a few injury-plagued years in college, she has never lost her love of the sport. Tere (which rhymes with "Mary") won four individual state championships in Michigan, earned a full athletic scholarship to the University of Tennessee, and was named a *Harrier Magazine* cross-country All-American.

After graduating from Tennessee with a Bachelor of Science degree in Industrial Engineering, Tere tried the professional running life for a while, but with that high-paying degree burning a hole in her pocket, she decided to pursue a more normal career route and continued running only as a means of staying fit.

It wasn't until years later, when she was encouraged by her husband to co-coach the Franklin Community High School cross-country teams with him (the boys' team won the Indiana state championship in 2001), that Tere considered trying to get back into professional racing. She had, by then, earned an English degree from Indiana University and was working as a freelance writer and editor, which meant her schedule was flexible enough to train and race. In December of 2001, at age 35, she won her first prize money in over 15 years and was hooked on racing all over again. Throughout the last year, Tere has placed in the top 15 at nearly every professional race she has entered, at distances ranging from 3K to the marathon. Her goal is to qualify for the 2004 U.S. Olympic Marathon Trials in St. Louis.

Tere, resides in Charlevoix, Michigan, with her husband, Doug, and two Labrador retrievers. You can reach her at tdrenth@ earthlink.net.

Dedication

To Pete Stouffer and Janet Stouffer Dunn, who joined a track club in the summer of 1975 and didn't mind having their kid sister tag along.

Author's Acknowledgments

Running requires an extraordinary amount of help from others. When I ran as a child and teenager, my parents, Richard and Anne Stouffer, paid for all my equipment, traveled with me across the state and country to attend races, and often massaged my cramped calves after those races were over. To keep me company, my dad rode his bike while I ran, and when my evening runs extended into darkness, my mom came out to find me, drove behind me, and shined the car lights on my path. They were responsible for my early success.

As an adult, I was lucky enough to find another support person: my husband, Doug Drenth, who has made countless sacrifices for me. Doug believes that every dollar spent on running shoes, massage therapy, treadmills, and hotels is both necessary and expected. He holds down the fort while I travel to races, he runs errands (including numerous trips to FedEx boxes) when work and training take longer than I expect, and he schedules our time together around my training runs. Mostly, though, Doug acts as a sounding board and coach, helping me to decide which workouts and races to run and when to run them but without scolding or saying, "I told you so" when those workouts or races don't turn out as I hope they will. It would be an understatement to say that I would never have been able to make a successful return to running without Doug's patience, support, and encouragement.

Writing this book took an entire team of professionals. Acquisitions editor (and good friend) Pam Mourouzis first listened to the idea for this book and presented it to acquisitions director Joyce Pepple and publisher Diane Steele. Chuck Stouffer of Stouffer Graphics (Rochester Hills, MI), who also happens to be my brother, conducted the photo shoot and processed all the wonderful photographs in the book. Friend and fellow marathoner Matt Ebersole, co-owner of The Athletic Annex running store (Indianapolis, IN) served as the technical reviewer for the book and gave excellent feedback. Copy editor Esmeralda St. Clair corrected all my errors and made the text sound 100 percent better. And while project editor Kathleen Dobie, a consummate professional and absolute joy to work with, managed most of the project, editor Chrissy Guthrie stepped in to handle the final details.

I'd also like to thank my high-school running coaches, Lou Miramonti, Doug Bonk, John Dunn, and Kermit Ambrose; post-collegiate coach Walt Drenth; massage therapist Steve Kramer; the Franklin Community High School cross-country teams; and Janet Stouffer Dunn, my sister and biggest supporter.

Publisher's Acknowledgments

We're proud of this book; please send us your comments through our Dummies online registration form located at www.dummies.com/register/.

Some of the people who helped bring this book to market include the following:

Acquisitions, Editorial, and Media Development

Project Editor: Kathleen A. Dobie

Acquisitions Editor: Pam Mourouzis

Copy Editor: Esmeralda St. Clair

Technical Editor: Matt Ebersole

Editorial Manager: Christine Meloy Beck

Editorial Assistant: Melissa Bennett

Special Help: Chrissy Guthrie

Cover Photos: ©Ed Bock/CORBIS

Cartoons: Rich Tennant, www.the5thwave.com

Production

Project Coordinator: Regina Snyder

Layout and Graphics: Melissa Auciello-Brogan, Stephanie D. Jumper, Michael Kruzil

Special Art: Chuck Stouffer, Stouffer Graphics

Proofreaders: John Tyler Connoley, John Greenough, TECHBOOKS Productions Services

Indexer: TECHBOOKS Production Services

Publishing and Editorial for Consumer Dummies

Diane Graves Steele, Vice President and Publisher, Consumer Dummies

Joyce Pepple, Acquisitions Director, Consumer Dummies

Kristin A. Cocks, Product Development Director, Consumer Dummies

Michael Spring, Vice President and Publisher, Travel

Brice Gosnell, Publishing Director, Travel

Suzanne Jannetta, Editorial Director, Travel

Publishing for Technology Dummies

Andy Cummings, Vice President and Publisher, Dummies Technology/General User

Composition Services

Gerry Fahey, Vice President of Production Services

Debbie Stailey, Director of Composition Services

Contents at a Glance

Introduction..1

Part 1: Getting Started with Your Marathon Training 7
Chapter 1: Realizing the Risks and Rewards of Running.....................9
Chapter 2: Choosing Your Running Gear.......................................21
Chapter 3: Figuring Out Where and When to Run.............................39
Chapter 4: Taking Your First Run 53
Chapter 5: Stretching, Warming Up, and Cooling Down.....................73

Part II: Taking Your Running a Stride Farther 95
Chapter 6: Developing a Mileage Base..97
Chapter 7: Adding Strength and Speed......................................109
Chapter 8: Improving Your Running Technique 135
Chapter 9: Eating and Running...151

Part III: Dealing with Running Injuries............169
Chapter 10: Pinpointing the Causes of Injuries 171
Chapter 11: Treating Your Injuries 181
Chapter 12: Cross-Training While You're Injured......................193

Part IV: Planning Racing Strategies 201
Chapter 13: Easing Into Marathon Racing.................................203
Chapter 14: Marathon Countdown: T Minus 24 Hours....................213
Chapter 15: After Your Marathon Is Over...................................225
Chapter 16: Reducing Your Finish Time Next Time 235

Part V: The Part of Tens................................243
Chapter 17: Ten Ways to Keep Running Fun 245
Chapter 18: The Ten Biggest Marathons 251
Chapter 19: Best Tune-Up Races in North America.....................259

Appendix...273
Running Web Sites and Other Resources.................................273

Index..277

Table of Contents

Introduction *1*

    About This Book 1
    Conventions Used in This Book..............................2
    Foolish Assumptions 2
    How This Book Is Organized....................................2
        Part I: Getting Started with Your Marathon Training...3
        Part II: Taking Your Running a Stride Farther 3
        Part III: Dealing with Running Injuries..........................3
        Part IV: Planning Racing Strategies 3
        Part V: The Part of Tens..3
    Icons Used in This Book...4
    Where to Go from Here 4

Part I: Getting Started with
Your Marathon Training.................................. *7*

    Chapter 1: Realizing the Risks
    and Rewards of Running. **9**

        Focusing on the Fundamentals 9
            Knowing what a marathon isn't......................................10
            Finding a marathon to race 10
            Preparing yourself 10
        Discovering the Rewards of a Marathon....................12
            It's incredibly challenging..12
            The training gets you into fantastic shape.................12
            Running relieves stress 13
            You can raise money for charity...................................13
            People think you're a little nuts....................................14
         Investing Yourself, Your Time, and Your Money..................15
            Training time and energy...15
            Extra sleep 16
            Extra calories 16
            Equipment costs 16
            Race entry fees and travel expenses............................17
         Examining Your Marathon Goals 18

    Chapter 2: Choosing Your Running Gear. **21**

        Finding Running Gear 21
        Choosing Shoes to Match Your (Running) Style 22
            Making a happy landing..24
            Listening to the pitter patter of your feet....................25
            Rolling to your toes: Pronating, supinating,
                or staying neutral..26

Knowing How Often to Change Your Shoes....................28
Sporting a Sports Watch 29
Dressing for Fitness and Fashion............................30
    Layering your upper body for comfort.......................31
    Investing in jackets and vests 33
    Draping your million-dollar gams 34
    Covering your head and hands................................36
    Socking it to 'em...37

Chapter 3: Figuring Out Where and When to Run 39

Blazing the Best Trail...39
    Charging through city streets 40
    Sailing through the 'burbs 42
    Bounding down bike paths....................................43
    Winding along country roads.................................43
    Digging dirt trails 45
    Galloping through golf courses,
        cemeteries, and parks 46
    Trotting around tracks 47
    Pacing treadmills 47
Deciding When to Run (and When to Stay Indoors) 49
    Handling hot, humid weather 49
    Cruising through cold, icy weather..........................50
    Singing in the rain...51
    Doing your distance in the dark 52

Chapter 4: Taking Your First Run 53

Pointing Yourself in the Right Direction....................53
    Dressing appropriately 54
    Avoiding blisters...54
    Being sure not to eat and run...............................55
    Running a good route..56
    Taking identification with you 59
    Avoiding antiperspirants 59
    Recording your mileage......................................59
    To snot or not to snot 64
Starting Slowly but Surely...................................64
Taking Care of Aches and Soreness...........................66
Figuring How Far and How Fast to Go the Next Month........66
    Pacing your run...67
    Planning your weekly mileage................................68
Getting a Little Help from Your (Running) Friends...........69
    Signing up for a marathon-training class....................69
    Flocking together with birds of the
        same feather: Running clubs 70
    Drumming up your own band 71
    Hiring a coach or trainer 71

Chapter 5: Stretching, Warming Up, and Cooling Down. **73**

The Great Stretching Debate(s) 73
Understanding Active Isolated Stretching...........................74
Active stretching..75
Isolating the stretch 75
Flexing the benefits 76
Setting up for the stretch..76
Mapping out your bod 76
Extending Yourself..77
Stretching your hams, quads, and hips 79
Gaining flexibility in your calves, shins, and feet........85
Stretching your butt and lower back 89
Warming Up to Your Run..92
Cooling Down After Your Run or Workout.....................93

Part II: Taking Your Running a Stride Farther.....*95*

Chapter 6: Developing a Mileage Base **97**

Getting More for Your Mileage 97
Building your base..97
Increasing strength and speed...................................98
Sharpening before your race......................................98
Doing LSD (Long, Slow Distance).....................................99
Striking a balance 99
Putting yourself through the paces...........................100
Planning a weekly long run......................................101
Planning a weekly short run.....................................103
Taking Days Off — or Not!...103
Creating a Training Plan...105
A 16-week plan for beginners 106
A 16-week plan for experienced runners...................107
If you have more than 16 weeks................................108

Chapter 7: Adding Strength and Speed. **109**

Running Rings Around Your Finish Time 110
Training to the right tempo.......................................113
Recognizing that "fartlek" isn't a dirty word.............114
Running intervals...116
Repeating your runs with repetition 118
Building Strength 119
Running hills: You're not in Kansas anymore...119
Doing circuits 120
Putting Yourself through the Paces on Paper 133

Chapter 8: Improving Your Running Technique 135

Sizing Up Your Posture...135
Carrying Your Arms Correctly.....................................137
Hitting Your Top Stride..139
Dissecting Drills 140
Breathing Easy..148
    Taking a deep breath...148
    Breathing to the beat of your feet 150

Chapter 9: Eating and Running 151

Running to Eat or Eating to Run?................................151
    Considering carbohydrates..................................153
    Packing in protein...160
    Focusing on fats..161
    Supplementing with vitamins and minerals.............163
Licking Your Chops Before a Race.............................164
Drinking to Your Health..165
Fending Off Food Allergies...166

Part III: Dealing with Running Injuries 169

Chapter 10: Pinpointing the Causes of Injuries 171

Focusing on Flexibility 171
Wearing Worn Out — or Just Plain Wrong — Shoes...........172
    Buying more shoes than Imelda Marcos 172
    Finding a fit like Cinderella's 173
Not Getting Enough R & R..173
    Sloughing off sleep 174
    Running yourself into the ground..........................174
    Doing too much, too soon 175
Being Unbalanced 175
Graduating from the School of Hard Knocks.....................177
Dying for a Drink 177
Filling Up with the Wrong Fuel 178
Running Inefficiently...178
Inheriting Bad Genes 178
Falling Down and Other Misfortunes..........................179

Chapter 11: Treating Your Injuries 181

Taking on Do-It-Yourself Treatments 181
    Getting the kinks out: Stretching 181
    Applying ice...182
    "Take two new shoes and call
        me in the morning"...183
    Popping pills...183
    Changing your running surfaces.............................184

Strengthening your muscles.................................184
Taking time off...184
Examining Everyday Injuries.......................................185
Rubbing up against blisters...............................185
Staring at shinsplints..187
Looking at leg cramps.......................................187
Arching away from plantar fasciitis 188
Twisting an ankle...188
Not needing knee pain 189
Holding off hip pain...189
Backing away from back pain...........................190
Fussing about stress fractures.........................190
Knowing When to See a Professional 191
Finding a sports medicine doctor 191
Making the most of massage............................192

Chapter 12: Cross-Training While You're Injured 193

Staying Buff While You're Healing..............................193
Running on water (Or is that "in" water?).................194
Being a tortoise for a while: Walking...........196
Practicing aerobics, yoga, Pilates, or Tae-Bo...........197
Biking, blading, skating, and skiing 197
Missing the mark on a machine 198
Swimming upstream...198
Training with weights.......................................198
Getting physical — therapy, that is...............199
Transitioning Back to Running....................................199

Part IV: Planning Racing Strategies..................201

Chapter 13: Easing Into Marathon Racing 203

Picking and Choosing Your Marathon.......................203
Running with the elites or the locals 203
Finding the right frequency.............................206
Tuning Up with Tune-Up Races.................................206
Getting a Handle on Your Strategy............................207
Going for a goal..207
Writing a race plan 208
Visualizing your race..210
Deciding Whether to Invest in Racing Gear...............211

**Chapter 14: Marathon Countdown:
T Minus 24 Hours 213**

Dining the Day Before...213
Picking Up Your Packet 214
Getting Your Ducks All in a Row 216

Getting Plenty of Shut-Eye 217
    Slumbering long enough 217
    Setting your alarm 218
Skipping a Square Breakfast 219
Warming Up and Stretching..219
Pulling Strings at the Start 220
Guzzling and Gobbling on the Run 221
Knowing What to Think About During Your Marathon......223

Chapter 15: After Your Marathon Is Over 225

Right after Your Race...225
    Cooling down 226
    Rehydrating and refueling 226
    Stretching...227
    Treating blisters..227
    Planning a shake-out run or walk 228
The Week after the Marathon...228
    Dealing with aches and pains.....................................228
    Knowing how much (or whether) to run....................229
    Getting plenty of rest...230
    Eating well 230
The Next Month 230
    Working through the post-race blues.........................231
    Deciding what comes next
        on your racing calendar...232
    Building your base again 232
    Knowing when to add speedwork 233

Chapter 16: Reducing Your Finish Time Next Time. . . 235

Peering into Your Past Training 235
    Adding more speed workouts.....................................236
    Bumping up your mileage..237
Training on Your Last Legs 238
Understanding the One-Percent Theory................................239
Making Peace with Plateaus 240

Part V: The Part of Tens.....................................243

Chapter 17: Ten Ways to Keep Running Fun. 245

Creating a Club...245
Galloping with Your Dog 246
Leaving Your Watch Behind..246
Playing Games 246
Running in the Rain 247
Setting a New Goal 247
Starting Speedwork...247
Taking Days Off...248

Taking the Scenic Route...248
Varying Your Route...249

Chapter 18: The Ten Biggest Marathons........ 251

Flora London Marathon 252
New York City Marathon 252
LaSalle Bank Chicago Marathon.................................252
Paris Marathon..253
Berlin Marathon..253
Honolulu Marathon...253
The City of Los Angeles Marathon.............................253
Marine Corps Marathon..253
Suzuki Rock 'n' Roll Marathon 254
Boston Marathon 254
Other Marathons to Consider 254

Chapter 19: Best Tune-Up Races
in North America............................. 259

Northeast and Mid-Atlantic United States.........................260
Falmouth Road Race 260
Utica Boilermaker 15K Road Race...........................260
Army Ten Miler 260
National Cherry Blossom Festival 10-Mile Run.........261
New Haven 20K Road Race..261
New Bedford Half-Marathon......................................261
Philadelphia Festival of Races 261
Southeast United States 262
Crazy 8's 8K Run 262
Azalea Trail Run 262
The Peachtree Road Race 10K 262
Bank of America Gasparilla Distance Classic...........262
Gate River Run 263
Anheuser-Busch Colonial Half-Marathon 263
Kiawah Island Half-Marathon 263
News and Sentinel Half-Marathon 263
Rock 'n' Roll Half-Marathon......................................263
Walt Disney World Half-Marathon 264
Midwest United States...264
Quad-City Times Bix 7..264
Crim Festival of Races...264
Chicago Half-Marathon 264
Indianapolis Life 500 Festival Mini Marathon 265
Kentucky Derby Festival Half-Marathon..................265
Lincoln Half-Marathon..265
Fifth Third River Bank Run 25K 265
Western United States 266
Wharf to Wharf...266
Celestial Seasonings Bolder Boulder 266

Bay to Breakers 12K 266
Lilac Bloomsday Run...266
Great Aloha Run..266
3M Half-Marathon 267
Gatorade Half-Marathon 267
Race to Robie Creek 267
Canada..267
Grande Course de Montreal 267
Sporting Life 10K DownHill...................................268
Times-Colonist Garden City...................................268
Calgary Herald Stampede 268
Pacific RoadRunners First Half Half-Marathon 268
ScotiaBank Toronto Waterfront Half-Marathon 269
ScotiaBank Vancouver Half-Marathon.......................269
Around the Bay 30K..269
Mexico and the Caribbean..269
Cara Suites 10k...270
Out to Hell 'n' Back 10K 270
Ufukuzo Midnight 10K..270
World's Best 10K...270
Cozumel Half-Marathon 270
Run Barbados Festival, ScotiaBank
Half-Marathon...271

Appendix...**273**

Running Web Sites and Other Resources **273**
Web Sites..273
www.marathonguide.com..273
www.coolrunning.com 273
www.sportscentral.com/marathon.html 273
www.marathontour.com 274
www.usaldr.org..274
Magazines 274
Running Times 274
Runner's World..274

Index **277**

Introduction

● ●

So you want to train for a marathon? Whether you're an old pro at running long distances or you just saw a brochure for a marathon in your area and have decided to take up the challenge, *Marathon Training For Dummies* can help you get the right gear, figure out how far and how fast you need to train, do speed workouts to improve your fitness, prepare yourself to race, and cross the line successfully.

About This Book

Although you can find plenty of books on running, this one is specific to marathon training. Whether your goal is to finish a marathon (26.2 miles) or some other long distance that's anywhere between 13.1 and 26.2 miles, or you want to qualify for the Boston Marathon, every page is geared specifically to your marathon training. Every bit of information in this book helps you move closer to not only finishing a marathon but also racing it. In this book, you find chapters on finding the best running shoes, going on your first run, increasing your mileage, eating right, dealing with injuries, preparing for races, and so much more. You also find training plans that you can customize to your own background and marathon goals. And in case you're new to running, all the jargon you hear marathoners use is demystified.

What makes this book especially unique, though, is that, as your author, I'm experiencing marathon training right along with you. Although I've been running and racing for 27 years (since I was 9 years old) and have had the good fortune to earn running awards, titles, and scholarships, I've spent the last 18 months training specifically for my first marathon. I'll race my first marathon just a few weeks before the final chapters of this book are due to my editor. After that first attempt, I'll run three more marathons over the following 18 months, trying to qualify for the U.S. Olympic marathon trials.

Conventions Used in This Book

This book uses only a few strange conventions, but I listed them as follows:

- ✔ **Runner:** You're a *runner,* not a *jogger.* Jogging, by definition, means *to wiggle,* and I don't think running has anything to do with wiggling. So I call you a *runner* throughout this book and dispense with that word about wiggling.

- ✔ **Mileage:** This is the amount that you're running per week. Whether you measure that mileage in minutes or in actual miles (see Chapter 4), the idea is the same: It refers to the amount that you're running each week.

- ✔ **Speedwork** and **strides:** These terms refer to workouts that you do that are faster than your training pace. Chapter 7 describes these in detail, but the bottom line is: Speedwork and strides make you a faster, stronger runner, so even though they're more difficult than going on a training run, they'll help your marathon more than you can imagine.

- ✔ **Marathon:** This means the 26.2-mile distance that you're training for. However, because not all areas of the world have marathons that you can train for, you can use the information in this book to train for a *half-marathon* (13.1 miles) or any distance in between the two.

Foolish Assumptions

I make only one assumption about you, dear reader: You want to run a marathon, and you want to run it well. You may be training for your 20th marathon, or you may be scared as heck about having just decided to do your first, but either way, this book is going to help you reach your goals.

How This Book Is Organized

The information in this book is organized logically into parts, each of which contains several chapters. You can find the following parts in this book.

Part I: Getting Started with Your Marathon Training

This part helps you get up off the sofa, get out the door, and take your first run. You find chapters on buying equipment, knowing where to run, stretching, and more.

Part II: Taking Your Running a Stride Farther

In this part, you go from your first run to your first successful marathon. This part tells you how to increase your mileage, work on your running technique, do speedwork and strides, and eat like a marathoner.

Part III: Dealing with Running Injuries

Injuries are the bane of every marathoner's existence. This part not only tells you how to treat injuries — everything from blisters to stress fractures — but also reminds you that by following the advice throughout the rest of this book, you can avoid injuries in the first place.

Part IV: Planning Racing Strategies

This part is all about the reason you train — race day! From choosing your marathon to deciding what to eat the day of the race to settling those pre-race butterflies in your stomach, this part makes your marathon a day to remember.

Part V: The Part of Tens

Every Dummies book has a delightful part that includes lists of ten whatevers. In this book, the Part of Tens chapters include information on keeping running fun, finding the best marathons, getting a list of tune-up races, and logging on to great running Web sites.

Icons Used in This Book

Icons are the little pictures that you'll find in the margins of this book. They're like highway roadside signs that tell you when construction is nearing, when traffic is heavy, or the road is smooth sailing. In this book, the following icons alert you to certain kinds of information:

After nearly 30 years of running, I've heard and experienced stories about running that are just too much fun not to pass along. Some stories are about my own experiences, and other tales are the experiences of Olympians and world champions. And some are good stories from beginning runners who discovered truths about running the hard way — by experiencing them!

This icon highlights running jargon and its translation into English. Use these terms at the next meeting of your running group, and they'll think you're a running guru.

These are tidbits of information that you'll want to tattoo on your brain — or just stick on the refrigerator — as constant reminders.

This icon gives you tips, tricks, and shortcuts that save you time, energy, and money.

Do as these icons suggest, and you'll avoid injuries, dehydration, and other painful mistakes.

Where to Go from Here

Want to know how to buy a great pair of running shoes? Start with Chapter 2. Are you already running and want to increase your mileage? Flip to Chapter 6. Confused about all the conflicting information you've heard about the best way to eat? Check out Chapter 9.

The beauty of a *For Dummies* book is that you don't have to start at the beginning and slowly work your way through the book. Instead, each chapter is self-contained, so you can start with whatever chapters interest you most.

If you have no idea where to begin, start with Chapter 1. Or skim the Table of Contents or the Index to find what you're looking for. Or just open the book and start reading wherever you land.

Part I
Getting Started with Your Marathon Training

The 5th Wave   By Rich Tennant

"I'm not sure I can live up to my workout clothes."

In this part . . .

In this part, you find out how marathon training changes your life — in many good ways and a few not-so-great ones. You select your basic gear, such as running shoes, shorts, and pants. You also find out when and where to train effectively and get a plethora of pointers for your first training run.

This part even offers you a sample training plan for your first month and gives you the bottom line on one of the most hated words in a runner's vocabulary that you're now going to love: stretching.

Chapter 1

Realizing the Risks and Rewards of Running

In This Chapter

▶ Measuring the distance

▶ Finding out how rewarding it can be

▶ Costing you time, energy, and money

▶ Keeping your eye on the target

*F*or some reason, running a marathon appeals to you. Perhaps you spied this year's brochure about a marathon in your town and figured this is finally the year. Maybe a friend or co-worker recently decided to run a marathon, and you've been drafted into training, too. Maybe you enjoy a great challenge or want to see how fit you can get. Or perhaps a dear friend or relative is ill, and you can help raise money to fight the disease by finishing a marathon.

Whatever your reasons for running a marathon, this chapter helps you understand marathon basics: what a marathon is (and isn't), what training for a marathon can do for you, what training for a marathon may cost you in terms of time and money, and how to begin thinking about your goals for your first marathon.

Focusing on the Fundamentals

Okay, consider the most basic marathon fact: A marathon is 26.2 miles long. Although that may not seem extraordinarily far when you're commuting to work or heading out for a weekend getaway, when your only means of covering that distance are your legs, feet, and a pair of shoes, 26.2 miles is looooong! Still, that's the distance of a marathon, so if you want to complete one, you have to train to run that distance. That's what this book is all about.

Knowing what a marathon isn't

An *Ironman triathlon* is a marathon that's preceded by a long swim in the ocean and just over 100 miles on a bicycle. Non-Ironman triathlons, often just called *triathlons,* include shorter swims, bikes, and runs — often with a 10K (6.2 miles) run instead of a marathon at the end — but they're considered wimpy as compared to the Ironman.

An *ultramarathon* is 50, 100 or more miles — often through a desert when the temperature outside is 110 degrees.

Keep in mind that, while they may sound similar to marathons, Ironman triathlons and ultramarathons are insane events. The marathon, however, at "just" 26.2 miles, is a completely normal, reasonable, sensible event to compete in. Even more sane is a *mini-marathon* (also called a *half-marathon*) which, at exactly half the distance of a marathon, runs 13.1 miles. A half-marathon is a noble event to train for in its own right, and if you can find one that's being held about two months before the marathon you plan to run (see Chapter 18), a half-marathon is also a fantastic way to gauge how your training is going.

Finding a marathon to race

Hundreds of 26.2-milers are held throughout the United States and much of the world. In the United States, marathons are usually held in spring (April and May) and fall (September and October). In southern and western states, you may also find winter marathons, and Duluth, Minnesota, hosts a mid-June marathon every year. See Chapter 18 for details on a few dozen major marathons around the world. Almost no one offers a midsummer marathon, simply because of the added risks from the intense summer heat.

Preparing yourself

The modern world doesn't exactly prepare you to run long distances. SUVs, elevators, and remote controls have made exercise an option rather than a necessity, and fast food and pizza don't exactly fuel the human body efficiently. So in order to race 26.2 miles — an event that's really not natural to human beings — you want to train for at least 4 months or for as many as 18 months before the race.

If you haven't run a step in your life (or haven't for many years), flip to Chapter 4 for tips and tricks on managing your first few weeks of training. Then see Chapters 6, 7, and 8 for information on the meat of your training for the next several months. Chapter 13 helps you picture what your marathon experience may be like and helps you get ready for the big day.

 If you just heard about a marathon that's coming to your town next month and you're thinking of reading this book, doing a little running, and entering the race, I beg you to reconsider. Running 26.2 miles wreaks havoc on your body, and if you enter a marathon that you're not prepared for, you can do serious damage. You could end up injured (see Part III for the lowdown on dealing with injuries), dehydrated (which may require a trip to and stay in a hospital), or even — how do I say this delicately? — dead. Marathons haven't killed many people (see "The first marathon" sidebar), but for the undertrained, the risk is always present. Give those 26.2 miles the respect they deserve: Running a marathon is extremely difficult, and only serious training before the event can keep you from hurting yourself.

The first marathon

Do you wonder why a marathon is 26.2 miles, instead of a nice round number like 20 or 30 miles? For the answer, you need to flash back to ancient Greece in roughly 500 B.C.

Legend has it that Pheidippides, a soldier, ran with news of a battle from the plains of Marathon to the city of Athens, which was just under 25 miles away. He finished the distance, got out the word *niki* ("victory"), collapsed, and died. (That's gotta make you feel good about your decision to run a marathon, huh?)

At the first games of the modern Olympics in 1896, officials held a marathon to commemorate Pheidippides' run. The distance was 24.85 miles (40 kilometers), and Spiridon Louis, who was also Greek, won it in just under three hours (2:58:50 to be precise).

The modern unround distance of 26.2 miles arrived in 1908, when the Olympics were held in London. The Brits wanted to start the race at Windsor Castle and end it at the stadium 26 miles away. They then added .2 miles so that the race could finish right in front of the royal family. After many international disputes, the official distance of the marathon was changed from 24.85 to 26.2 miles.

So as you're suffering through the last 1.35 miles of your marathon, you can thank the British royal family for your agony.

Discovering the Rewards of a Marathon

Given that a marathon is long and difficult, you may wonder why anyone would have any interest whatsoever in running one. You train so much for months (or even years) that you sacrifice most of your free time, you spend gobs of money on equipment and races, and you endure bloody feet and soreness in muscles that you didn't even know existed — all to get a medal for finishing a race that takes hours and makes you suffer through excruciating pain. That sounds like a great idea, doesn't it? Still not convinced? This section helps you understand what all the fuss is about.

It's incredibly challenging

This is it — the number one reason most people run a marathon: It's difficult. Because a marathon is so challenging, after you've done one, you know you've completed something that's so hard that only a handful of people in the world (well, closer to a million, but only a handful in your neighborhood or office) have ever accomplished it.

Think of a marathon like a *quest* in Arthurian times. A knight would be given a challenge — rescue a fair maiden, kill a dragon, or find a worthy treasure — then go and do it. If he came back alive, he was celebrated as a part of select group of daring knights who had completed similar feats. A marathon is a modern-day quest. The challenge is laid before you when you see the brochure, newspaper ad, or Web site for a marathon somewhere near your hometown. You then spend several months training to hone your skills, and then you go and do the difficult task — running 26.2 miles. When you come back, you're a hero, even if just to the person who works in the cubicle next to you, who has never dared do anything so challenging.

The training gets you into fantastic shape

One of the best byproducts of training for a marathon is that, if you train hard enough and long enough (following one of the plans in Chapter 6), you can get into absolutely fantastic shape. You can reduce your body fat and define many muscles in your body. Your cardiovascular system benefits, too; you slow your resting heart rate and reduce your blood pressure.

Yes, you'll likely lose weight provided that you don't start eating more and, therefore, make up for the calories you're burning. However, if you've ever seen someone who has trained for a marathon, you know that the training is more than just about losing weight. As you begin to get into better shape, you just feel better — stronger, energized, and confident.

Running relieves stress

You know how people like to work out their problems by taking a drive in the country? Well, taking a run in the country (or in the city, on the treadmill, or in a park) is even better. Training for a marathon gives you plenty of time to think, work out problems in your head, practice presentations or conversations before they happen, or just unwind. Because of all this quiet time while running, marathoners are a naturally mellow bunch.

For people who don't train enough for a marathon, the impending doom they feel as the race day approaches actually creates more stress than it relieves because they know they aren't doing enough to prepare their bodies for the physical punishment of a marathon. But when you do train correctly (see Chapters 6 through 8) and eat right (take a look at Chapter 9), you know that your marathon is going to be a rewarding — albeit difficult — event.

You can raise money for charity

A little-known fact of marathons is that they're often run in conjunction with one or more charities, such as the Leukemia and Lymphoma Society (Team in Training), Habitat for Humanity, American Diabetes Association (Team Diabetes), Arthritis Foundation (Joints in Motion), and many others. Generally, the process works like this:

1. **You make a commitment to run the marathon (or a half-marathon) in order to raise money for the charity.**

   You may even be paired with a person who suffers from the illness and for whom you're raising funds. Seeing a person living with a life-threatening illness can be quite motivating to your own training. A little soreness or a blister seems minor by comparison.

2. **The charity offers you support and often excellent training advice (and in some cases, race clothing, the race entry fee, and travel expenses) in exchange for your commitment.**

Most charities meet regularly to train, talk about training, or offer motivation.

3. **You agree to raise a certain amount of money for the charity. In some cases, you may agree to pay the charity out of your own bank account if you're unable to raise the funds.**

4. **You send out letters to every person you ever met throughout your lifetime, asking for contributions.**

   Some people will sponsor you for a set amount of money (say, $100), and others may pledge a certain number of dollars per mile. All, however, are usually asked to pay in advance.

5. **After you successfully complete your marathon, you send letters to or call everyone who donated money and brag about your accomplishment.**

Besides being able to help a good cause, the most exciting aspect of running for a charity is that you may be able to run your marathon in a race that you'd otherwise have little chance of competing in: one that requires evidence of a qualifying time at a previous marathon, such as the Boston Marathon does (see the "Qualifying for Boston" sidebar in Chapter 16), one that has a lottery for getting in like New York City does, or one that's in an exotic location like any of the marathons in Alaska and Hawaii. (See Chapter 18 for more specifics on big marathons around the world.) Running for a charity in one of these marathons is like being allowed to play in the Super Bowl or driving at Daytona because you agreed to raise money for charity.

People think you're a little nuts

Okay, so maybe having your spouse, co-workers, kids, and friends think you're crazy isn't your typical benefit. But have you ever noticed how, when you think someone's a little nutty or eccentric, you give them a little more latitude, a little more space? That could be a good thing in your life.

I heard a story about a woman who was the living definition of *eccentric*. She lived in a beautiful house decorated with fish in every possible way. Her doorknobs and front-door knocker were in the shape of fish. Her rugs, pictures on her walls, shower curtains, and tableware all had fish motifs. And in her living room was an enormous fish tank that took up an entire wall. People who came over, of course, commented on how beautiful the fish motif was. As soon as they said this, however, she would cover her ears with her hands, yell, "I hate fish!" and storm out of the room, not to return until they left. If you knew this woman, you'd think she was a little loopy, right? Keep in mind that this is how people are going to think of you when they find out that you're training for a marathon.

Investing Yourself, Your Time, and Your Money

You probably already know that training for and running in a marathon isn't all rosy. The event is a difficult one both to train for and race, and this section spells out how your life can change after you commit to running a marathon.

Training time and energy

To train for a marathon, you want to run a *minimum* of 40 miles per week (see Chapter 6). That takes both time and energy. Plan on spending 10 to 12 hours per week training, stretching, planning your mileage, and so on.

If you currently have plenty of free time, you won't feel much of a pinch in your schedule. But if your days, like those of most people, are already jampacked, you may have a hard time fitting in that much training every day. In order to successfully train for your marathon, something has to go. Some ideas for carving out running time follow:

- ✔ If you watch much TV, you can record your must-see shows and watch as you stretch (see Chapter 5) or massage your legs (see Chapter 11).

- ✔ If you want to spend time with your spouse or boyfriend/ girlfriend, you can ask him or her to ride a bike while you run and spend a little time together that way.

- ✔ If you do some of your running on a treadmill (see Chapter 3), you may be able to watch a news program or video while you run.

- ✔ If you're allowed to eat at your desk at work, do part of your training at lunchtime and eat lunch after you run and stretch. (Just make sure that you have time to stretch after you run, or you'll be ridiculously sore at the end of your workday.)

Don't plan to run at lunchtime if you live in a hot climate!
Instead, run in the early morning or late evening to escape
the heat.

Extra sleep

You may come across an interesting conundrum: The fitter you
get, the more energy you'll have. You'll take the stairs instead of
the elevators and go on walks and hikes. However, the training
requirements for a marathon can also zap your energy if you're
not sleeping enough, so if you try to survive on 6 hours of sleep,
you may struggle to even stay awake.

If you can manage it, try to get between 8 and 10 hours of sleep per
night. You'll feel better on every run, you'll race faster, and you'll
have energy for other activities in your life. (See Chapter 10 for
more on the benefits of sleep.)

Of course, sleeping an extra 10 or 12 hours per week *and* training
for another 10 to 12 hours per week probably requires a pretty radical shift in the way you organize your life. Keep in mind, though,
that unless you get hooked on marathoning, this is a temporary
shift. For a set amount of time, you may be able to shift some of
your responsibilities to your kids or spouse, hire someone to mow
the lawn and clean the house, and cut down on your work hours.

Extra calories

Marathoners need to eat more than people who aren't training at
your level of intensity. You may find that you need to add at least
1,000 calories per day to maintain your current weight. This may
seem like plenty of fun, but you want to make sure that the food
you're eating is the best fuel for your body (see Chapter 9). Sorry,
you don't just get to stuff yourself with candy bars and the like. In
addition, these extra calories cost money, so be prepared for an
increase in your grocery bill.

If weight loss is one of your reasons for running a marathon, don't
increase your calories until you reach your target weight.

Equipment costs

Marathoners have one core piece of equipment: running shoes
(which are discussed in excruciating detail in Chapter 2). Although
the $85 you may spend on that pair of shoes may not seem like a

tremendous investment, keep in mind that you need to replace your shoes every 400 to 500 miles (depending on the shoe and how you wear it). So, if you're running 70 miles per week, you need to replace your shoes every 6 to 7 weeks — that's a new pair of shoes every month and a half.

If you don't replace your shoes every 400 to 500 miles, chances are, you'll develop joint pain (knees, ankles, and hips), shin pain, foot pain and/or bruises, and so on. See Chapter 10 for details on running injuries.

When non-marathoners ask me how often I replace my shoes (and, surprisingly, this comes up often) and I tell them every 4 to 5 weeks, I always get a look of utter astonishment. Among non-marathoners, they generally reply, "I only buy new running shoes every year." This, I suspect, is a throwback to the old back-to-school shopping days, when you got a new pair of gym shoes every fall, and by golly, they had to last until the following fall.

Running gear other than shoes is largely optional, although you do want a few good pair of running shorts (ones that won't chafe you) and an ample supply of *singlets* (a fancy word for lightweight tank tops — see Chapter 2) or T-shirts. (If you're a woman, you'll want a few exceptionally comfortable running bras, too.) You can definitely get by on just a few shorts and Ts, but unless you like to do laundry pretty frequently or enjoy wearing stinky clothes, you may want to purchase more.

At last count, I had 15 pair of running shorts in my closet. This isn't part of some crazed obsession to collect running clothing; instead, it makes my life easier. I run nine or ten times per week, and I don't like to wear stinky clothes, so by owning enough pairs of shorts, shirts, running pants, and other clothing, I have to do laundry just once a week or less.

Race entry fees and travel expenses

Race entry fees and travel expenses can add up fast. If you're used to running in local 5K or 10K races, you've probably paid entry fees that vary from as little as $8 to as much as $20, and they may have seemed pretty reasonable because you walked away with a new T-shirt, a full belly from all the post-race food, a medal or some other age-group award, your final race time, and perhaps, your times for each mile (called mile *splits*) along the way.

A marathon, however, requires quite a bit more coordination on the part of the race director, so it may cost quite a bit more. Entry fees range from $40 if you register early (3 months before) up to $100 if you register a few weeks before the marathon.

In addition, unless you're lucky enough to run in a marathon that's in your hometown, chances are, you're going to have to travel out of your area. And because marathons often start early in the morning (at 7 or 8 a.m.), you probably won't have the opportunity to drive to the race the morning of. This means you'll have to pay for at least one night in a hotel on top of gas or a plane, train, or bus ticket.

If you're going to stay in a hotel, check for one located a couple blocks (or less) from the starting line: It may be the official hotel of the marathon. Even if the rooms cost $20 or $30 more there than at other hotels in the city, the added convenience is well worth the cost if you can afford it. You get to walk down from your hotel room and be right at the starting line, which means that you can get a little drink of water right before the race, take off your warm-up clothes and not have to worry about where to put them, or go to the bathroom one last time without having to wait in line to use a portable toilet at the race site.

Examining Your Marathon Goals

Before you begin outlining your training plan (see Chapters 4 and 6), you want to establish a goal for your first marathon. (If you've already run one or more, set a goal for your next marathon.) Having a goal helps you determine what sort of weekly mileage you need to run, what your training pace needs to be, what sort of workouts you want to do, and so on.

But if you've never run a marathon, how do you know what your goals should be? Well, your goal for your first marathon doesn't have to be that specific. See the following examples:

- ✔ **Your goal is to finish with a combination of walking and running.**

    This is a fine goal, and your training should reflect it: You'll do a combination of running and walking, with your mileage on the low end (40 miles per week), and you can focus on building your endurance and not worry too much about how fast you're training.

Many marathon courses close after 5 to 7 hours, so if you're planning to walk or walk/run a marathon, make sure you can do it in the allotted amount of time. When the course closes — even if you're still out there — traffic resumes (which can be dangerous for you), water stops disappear (which can also be dangerous in hot weather), and no one will greet you when you finish, give you a medal, or record your time.

Root, root, root for your runner

If you know someone who is training for a marathon — your spouse, child, parent, sibling, best friend, or co-worker — keep the following tips in mind:

- ✔ **Don't pressure!** Everyone has a different commitment to training, and no one is under any pressure to do more than she wants to.

- ✔ **Understand that consistency is critical.** Don't ask your marathoner to take time off so that you can do other activities together. You'll just make the marathon that much more difficult when race day comes.

- ✔ **Remember that marathoners train during vacations and weekends.** Just because your boss gave you a week off for vacation doesn't mean that your runner gets a break from training.

- ✔ **Know your runner's route on long runs.** If the weather makes a sharp turn for the worse or your marathoner isn't back in the allotted time, jump in the car and see whether he needs help.

- ✔ **Put up with sweaty hugs.** Marathoners are often sweaty because they have to run plenty. Put up with this: It, too, shall pass.

- ✔ **Acknowledge small improvements.** Marathoners reach many milestones: The first 10-mile run, the first 20-miler, the first tune-up race, and so on. Congratulate your runner when she reaches each landmark.

- ✔ **Go along on racing trips.** At least you get to spend time together.

- ✔ **Stay quiet at the start of a race.** Races are serious business. Wish good luck well before your marathoner is on the starting line.

- ✔ **Get to as many spots on the course as you can.** After the race starts, cheer like crazy in as many spots as possible. Yell out your marathoner's name and say, "Great job!" or "Way to go!" Don't be critical during the race.

- ✔ **Stay until the end of the race.** Okay, watching a marathon is a little boring but don't go home at 16 miles. Your marathoner needs your support. Be in the finish area (sometimes called *Friends and Family Area*) when your runner finishes.

- ✔ **Remember that there's always the next race.** Even if this one was a disappointment, your marathoner can always try again.

✔ **You want to run the entire marathon.** This is actually a much different goal than simply finishing. Although your time is still not of critical importance, you want to make sure that you have enough of a mileage base (discussed in detail in Chapter 6) to enable you to sustain your pace for 26.2 miles.

✔ **You want to complete the marathon in under four hours.** This, too, is a fantastic goal. You have to run around 9 minutes per mile for the entire marathon, and knowing this race pace helps you to determine your daily training pace and the pace at which you'll do your workouts (see Chapter 7). You'll also want to enter some tune-up races (see Chapter 19) before your actual marathon, so you can test how this race pace feels.

✔ **You want to qualify for the Boston Marathon.** For most people, qualifying for Boston is the pinnacle of their running lives, and although you may not accomplish this in your first marathon, it may be a future goal for you. (I know people who qualified for Boston in their first marathons, so it isn't impossible.) See the "Qualifying for Boston" sidebar in Chapter 16 for qualifying times, which are based on sex and age.

Keep in mind that even if you've run a qualifying time, you still may not be able to get into the race because they set a limit on how many runners can enter the event each year. Still, Boston is the ultimate marathon goal for most people. If this is what you want to do, you'll want to take advantage of the workouts discussed in Chapter 7.

Chapter 2

Choosing Your Running Gear

- -

In This Chapter

▶ Getting to know your local running store

▶ Finding the best shoes for you

▶ Investing in a sports watch

▶ Sorting through all your clothing options

- -

*R*unning gear is big business: If you go for the best, most up-to-date shoes and clothing and replace them often, you can easily spend $1,000 per year on running shoes and apparel. Thankfully, except for running shoes, most of what you buy lasts for years before you have to replace it. Even though you may make a heavy investment upfront, you won't have to replace shorts, shirts, running bras, running pants, your watch, and so on very often. I still wear clothing I bought 10 years ago that has been worn and laundered hundreds of times.

If you're new to running and can't afford to invest much right now, spread the word to friends and family that you'd like certain running products for your birthday or the holidays. Or better yet, ask for a gift certificate to your favorite running store or catalog: After the holidays, you may be able to find some special deals *and* use your gift card.

Finding Running Gear

If you live in the United States or Canada, odds are that a running store is located within a 1-hour (driving distance) radius. Wherever you live, to find a running store in your area, look in your phone book or search the Internet for "running store" and the name of your area.

Running stores specialize in outfitting runners, and many of the employees are average to very good (maybe even elite) runners. Because they know so much about running, the store's employees usually offer quality service. A running store is always your best bet for buying running gear, especially shoes.

Choosing Shoes to Match Your (Running) Style

Do you really need $125 shoes? That's kind of a loaded question, but it's one I get asked plenty. I need to answer it in a sort of roundabout way. The fact is, you really do need *running* shoes (not basketball shoes or tennis shoes), but you need the ones that fit your foot the best. Just because your friend, coach, running partner, or whoever else likes a particular shoe doesn't mean the same shoes can work for you.

The perfect running shoe should feel terrific on your feet and shouldn't cause blisters, blacken your toenails, make your feet go numb, cause pain in your arch or heel, slip off your heel, or make your knees ache. These ailments are a sign that you're wearing the wrong shoes or a worn-out shoe. See the "Knowing How Often to Change Your Shoes" section, later in this chapter, for details. So if the right shoe for you costs $125, then yeah, you really need $125 shoes. But perhaps you'll be lucky and find that your perfect shoe costs just $65.

Buying running shoes is like getting your car repaired. If you trust the person who tells you that you really need something expensive, you go along with it, because you know that, in the long run, this is a good investment. But if you don't trust the person telling you to spend, say, $125 on a pair of running shoes, you may always feel that you were ripped off, whether you really were ripped off.

Few people need the most expensive shoes on the market. If the person helping you to find a pair of running shoes doesn't ask any questions and/or watch you run or walk and then recommends the highest-price pair of running shoes in the store, you're working with a shyster. Go elsewhere for your running shoes.

TIP

Saving on shoes

Running stores rarely discount their new models of shoes unless you're affiliated with a team, running club, or marathon training class (see Chapter 4), or you buy in volume. Get on the store's mailing list so that you're notified of any sales or promotions, and if a running store sponsors a road race that you're running in and gives out discount coupons in conjunction with that race, choose that time to stock up on shoes or running clothing. And if you don't mind wearing last year's color, you may be able to get discontinued models at a deep discount.

Another way to save money is to shop through catalogs and the Internet, such as Road Runner Sports (www.roadrunnersports.com) or Eastbay (www.eastbay.com). I'm a bit hesitant to recommend these online stores, because you never get the service from a catalog or online store that you do from a real person at a running store, and I'd hate to see local running store owners — who pay a pretty penny for their store space and experienced employees — go under and have to close up shop because of competition from online running stores and catalogs.

One benefit to buying running gear online through Road Runner Sports is their Run America Club (RAC). This club costs $20 per year in dues, but with your membership, you get 2-day shipping for the cost of standard shipping and are allowed to return any shoes, whether you've worn them or not, within 60 days. Few running stores can offer this sort of return policy, and if you're having trouble finding a shoe that's comfortable for you, joining the RAC may serve you well. Another lower-cost option is to visit a sporting goods store, especially a discount store. Although you generally won't find any experienced runners working there, if you know exactly what you need and can do without professional advice, you may find a good deal.

A good running shoe salesperson looks at three major factors when deciding which shoe is best for you:

- How your foot strikes the ground when you run (See the "Making a happy landing" section, later in this chapter.)

- How hard you strike the ground (See the "Listening to the pitter patter of your feet" section, later in this chapter.)

- What happens after your foot strikes the ground but before it leaves the ground again to take another step (See the "Rolling to your toes: Pronating, supinating, or staying neutral" section, later in this chapter.)

Making a happy landing

One of the most crucial aspects of your running style — and, therefore, your shoe needs — is how you land. You need to pay attention to how you strike the ground. Figure 2-1 shows the three ways your foot may strike the ground.

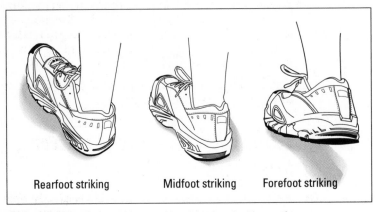

Rearfoot striking   Midfoot striking   Forefoot striking

Figure 2-1: Figuring out how you strike the ground with your feet.

The best way to figure out which category you fall into is to have someone watch you run from behind — how you strike will be pretty obvious to the observer. (Most good running store employees do this as a rule.) However, you can also place pieces of construction paper all along your kitchen floor, wet your bare feet, and *run* across the paper. If you clearly see the outline of your heel, you're a rearfoot striker. If you don't see any heel at all, you're a forefoot striker. If you see only a bit of the top of your heel, you're a midfoot striker. More information on each type follows:

✔ **Rearfoot striking:** The most common way to land, you land first on your heel before rolling up through the rest of the foot. Rearfoot strikers tend to have slower *turnover* (the time between when your foot hits the ground and when it leaves the ground), and slow turnover usually means slower per-mile times.

   When looking for a pair of running shoes, look for extra cushioning, gel, or air on the rear of your running shoe to act as a shock absorber for your heel.

✔ **Midfoot striking:** A midfoot striker lands near the midsection of the foot so that the back of the heel never actually strikes the ground. Midfoot strikers have established a happy medium between not striking the ground so far back on the foot that they have slow turnover but also not striking so far forward that they have a tendency to get injured. In other words, midfoot striking is a good thing.

Look for cushioning, gel, or air in both the heel and forefoot. (Ideally, you'd want it in the middle, but few shoes are made this way.)

✓ **Forefoot striking:** Forefoot strikers land on the forefoot (the ball of the foot) so that the heel and midsection never touch the ground. Although most elite athletes are forefoot strikers to greater or lesser degrees, the truth is that forefoot strikers get injured far more often than midfoot strikers.

Find a running shoe with extra cushioning, gel, or air on the forefoot if you're a forefoot striker.

Listening to the pitter patter of your feet

The heaviness or softness of your landing is exactly what it sounds like: A hard lander comes down hard on the ground, generating a noisy clunk, but a soft lander just barely touches the ground before pushing back off again. Heavier runners and rearfoot strikers tend to be hard landers, but forefoot strikers and lightweight runners tend to be soft landers. Middleweight, midfoot strikers tend to be what I call Goldilocks landers — not too hard and not too soft.

Not all forefoot-striking, lightweight runners are soft landers: Some runners simply get in the habit of seeing how much of a commotion they can make with each step. To get rid of this clunky habit, think of yourself running along the tops of glassware or fine china without breaking it. You don't want to tippy-toe, but you also don't want to break the imaginary glassware below you.

When looking for a running shoe, you want to determine what sort of *outsole* (that's the rubbery or hard plastic portion of the outside sole of your shoe) it has. A carbon-rubber outsole is shock absorbent but heavy and rather inflexible. A blown-rubber outsole is flexible and light but doesn't provide much cushioning. Some shoes have one type of material on the heel and another on the forefoot. See the preceding section, "Making a happy landing," to determine whether you need more cushioning in the heel or forefoot.

✓ **Hard landers:** Look for heavy, durable cushioning with a full carbon-rubber outsole. (You probably won't be able to recognize this type of sole on sight — just ask for it or look for a shoe online that fits this description.)

✔ **Medium (Goldilocks) landers:** Look for a combination blown-rubber and carbon-rubber outsole.

✔ **Soft landers:** Look for a blown-rubber outsole.

Rolling to your toes: Pronating, supinating, or staying neutral

After you strike the ground, you roll to your toes as you prepare to leave the ground again. Runners generally roll from the backs of their feet to their toes in one of three ways — *pronation,* the *neutral position,* or *supination* — all of which are shown in Figure 2-2.

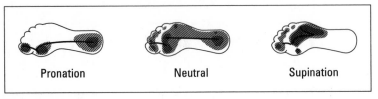

Pronation   Neutral   Supination

Figure 2-2: Do you pronate, do you supinate, or are you in neutral position?

To determine which category you fall into, place several dark-colored pieces of paper (construction paper works great) in a line on the floor of your bathroom or kitchen. Take off your shoes and socks and lightly wet the bottoms of both feet. Now walk naturally over the construction paper. You'll see an outline of your foot that will look like one of the outlines in Figure 2-2.

When shopping for shoes, look for certain buzzwords mentioned in the three following sections. Keep in mind, too, that that word *last* refers to the shape of the base of a shoe and to how that base is constructed. The last may be made of a variety of materials and may be shaped one of several different ways.

✔ To determine the *shape last (curved, semi-curved, or straight)* flip the bottom of the right shoe over and look at where your big toe would go. If the area for the big toe shoots straight up from the heel, you have a *straight last.* (Note that straight lasts, because they can feel pretty inflexible, aren't used in many shoes anymore.) If the area for the big toe curves a bit to the right from the heel, you have a *semi-curved last;* if it curves a lot, you have a *curved last.* Figure 2-3 shows various types of lasts.

✔ To determine the *construction last (board, slip, or combination),* hold a shoe in your hand, top-side up, and remove the insert that sits inside the shoe. Look at how the shoe is constructed: If you see a glued-in piece that runs the length of the shoe, you have a *board-lasted* shoe. (Board lasts can feel like bricks on the bottoms of your feet, though, so they aren't used very often.) If all you see is stitching, you have a *slip last*. A *combination last* has a board over the heel and midfoot and stitching from the midfoot to the toes.

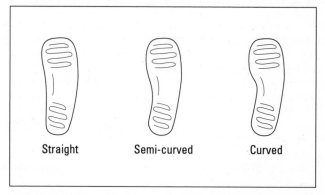

Straight   Semi-curved   Curved

Figure 2-3: Looking at the bottom of straight, semi-curved, and curved lasts.

Turning inward: Pronation

Pronation means that as you roll onto the ball of your foot (your *forefoot*), you roll inward and off of your big toe. If you're a pronator, look for shoes that say they offer *motion control* when you go out shopping. Shoes for pronators usually have a *straight* or *semi-curved last*. This shape keeps the foot from rolling inward. Also look for shoes meant for *flexible arches* or *flat feet*. If you have low arches, look for a *board* or *combination last*.

Note that a *flexible arch* doesn't necessarily mean a *low arch*. Some people who overpronate have a high arch, but because their arches are so flexible, their arches cave in with each step. If you're one of these runners, look for a *semi-curved last* that's *slip* or *combination lasted,* but do talk to a running shoe professional about your situation before buying shoes. Also consider making a trip to a podiatrist for a pair of *orthotics* (rigid inserts that are molded to your foot and fit into your running shoes). You may benefit from having your high, flexible arch supported by graphite or other sturdy materials. This type of runner can easily be confused with a supinator. (See the "Rolling to the outside: Supination" section, later in this chapter.)

Staying in the neutral position

If your feet tend toward *neutral position,* you roll from the heel through the middle of your forefoot and off your second toe.

Neutral shoes don't control the motion of the foot, allowing it instead to move naturally. Look for shoes with a *semi-curved last.* Other buzzwords are *neutral shoes, medium arch,* or *stability shoes.* (Your arch may actually be high or low, but it doesn't flatten out much when you walk.) Look also for a *combination* or *slip last.*

Rolling to the outside: Supination

If your feet *supinate,* then you roll from your heel (or may land on your midfoot or forefoot and never touch the heel — see the "Making a happy landing" section, earlier in this chapter) onto the outside of your forefoot, and then roll back toward (but not all the way to) the neutral position and off your middle toe.

If you're a *supinator,* find shoes with a *curved last.* Look also for shoes meant for people with *high, rigid arches* and a *slip last.*

Knowing How Often to Change Your Shoes

Change your shoes at least every 400 to 500 miles. This means that if you're running 50 miles per week, you need to change your shoes every 8 to 10 weeks; at 80 miles per week, you need new shoes every 5 to 6 weeks.

Does that sound insane to you? I wish I could tell you that it's all a joke, but it's true: Running shoes were meant to last 500 miles at most. If you run 15 miles per week (as many fitness runners do), your running shoes can easily last 20 to 33 weeks — more than 6 months — and that's assuming you run that mileage week in and week out. But as soon as you begin training for a marathon, your timelines change because you're putting so many more miles per week on your shoes.

Don't think in terms of weeks; think in terms of miles. Make a notation in your running log (that's discussed in Chapter 4) of when you start a new pair of shoes. Every week or so, add up how many miles are on those shoes and toss them when they've reached 400 to 500 miles. Replace them even if they don't look worn out. Running shoes break down inside long before they look worn outside, and after 400 or 500 miles (that 100-mile difference depends on how substantial the shoe you select is to begin with), they just don't support your feet and legs anymore.

Another option is to buy a second pair of running shoes when you reach about 150 to 200 miles, and then begin alternating shoes for every run. This makes keeping track of the miles on each shoe a little trickier, but some runners like having a newer pair to wear every other day.

If you don't replace your shoes every 400 to 500 miles, you risk a myriad of injuries: joint pain (knees, ankles, hips), shin pain, foot pain and/or bruises, and so on. Chapter 10 discusses the need for consistent shoe replacement in detail.

Sporting a Sports Watch

In my mind, the right sports watch is nearly as important as the right running shoes. You can find sports watches in nearly every discount, department, and sporting goods store, but the key is not just finding one —finding the *right* one for your needs is what matters.

If you already have a watch and like using it, keep it until it wears out. But if you're in the market for a new watch, I suggest looking for one with the following options:

- ✔ **Stopwatch:** You probably figured you'd use this feature. You simply press a button when you start your run and another (or the same one) when you finish to get a total time.

- ✔ **Interval (lap) timer:** When you're trying to figure out your distance-run pace (see Chapters 4 and 6) or are running a speed workout (discussed in Chapter 7), hitting the Split button gives you the time since you last hit the button. This means that, instead of having to calculate your mile times in your head, the watch does it for you.

- ✔ **Countdown timer:** This is a cool feature. You set the timer to whatever length of time you want (say, 2 minutes), and the watch beeps when it reaches that time.

  Some watches allow you to count down and stop or count down and start again. The latter is useful when doing circuits or fartleks (see more on both in Chapter 7); the countdown/ stop feature is useful when you're timing a pie in the oven.

> ✔ **Alarm:** I use the alarm for nearly everything from waking me up in the morning as a backup to my alarm clock (especially on race mornings) to reminding me of upcoming meetings to telling me to take my inhaler 20 minutes before leaving for a run. Look for an alarm that's easy to set and use.

The more you get into running, the more likely you are to use your running watch as your everyday watch. I used to wear a fancy leather watch to work and a Timex to run in, but after I started running 90 miles a week, changing watches became a luxury that I could live without.

You don't need to spend a fortune on a watch. While you can find some that sell for over $100, you can probably find one with all the features you need for about $35 — even less on sale.

The battery on most watches lasts about two years. If the display goes dead, take your watch to any discount or department store and get a new battery for about $5.

Dressing for Fitness and Fashion

Sure, running clothing can be about fashion, especially if you buy "outfits" of running bras or shirts that match perfectly with running shorts or jackets that match running pants. If that's your thing (and it's mine), match to your heart's content.

Don't, however, choose running clothes on the basis of looks only. Color, matchability, and how well running clothes show off your fit caboose must always play second fiddle to comfort and utility. Always buy clothes based on how well they fit you, looking especially for the following:

> ✔ **Size:** Don't buy anything that feels too tight or too short. You're always better off with slightly loose clothes than tight ones. Loose clothes also allow a little room for shrinkage in the dryer.

> Don't put running shorts or bras in the dryer. Instead, use a clothesline or get a wooden drying rack to air-dry your delicate running clothes. If you dry delicate running clothes in the dryer, they may shrink or melt. Spare the dryer (using a drying rack, instead) for any fabric that feels silky to the touch or is waterproof (such as Gore-Tex).

> ✔ **Chafing points:** While standing in front of the mirror in your dressing room, run in place to see where shorts or shirts may

rub *(chafe)* your skin. After a marathon (26.2 miles), an area that rubs a little in the dressing room will be a gaping wound, so bypass anything that rubs you the wrong way.

Always try out the clothes that you plan to race in before your marathon. You don't want to find out at 15 miles that your favorite *singlet* (tank top), shorts, or running bra rubs your skin raw.

✔ **Fabric:** Although buying polyester running clothes may seem like a silly decision (after all, polyester is a form of plastic and used to be a fabric that didn't breathe at all), the truth is, the most comfortable running clothes have at least a percentage of polyester. Although cotton is a comfortable fabric, it's also heavy, which is why most running clothes manufacturers have switched to high-tech versions of polyester, such as CoolMax. In summer, you want fabrics that breathe, allowing air to flow through the fabric to your body. In winter, you want clothes that *wick moisture* (that is, they take moisture away from your skin) to keep you from getting too cold.

Layering your upper body for comfort

When dressing the top part of your body, think in terms of layers that you can peel off as needed, as the temperature (and you) heat up.

Even if you don't plan to remove any clothes as you run, use layers as you dress. Layers trap air between them, and this air warms your body.

Supporting running bras

A *sports bra* (often called a *running bra* because runners were among the first to wear them) is essential for women: Even small-busted women can make their breasts quite sore by training in an unsupportive bra or in no bra at all. Even if you're able to comfort-ably wear a traditional bra, running bras tend not to cut into your skin (as bras with narrow straps can do after miles of running), and they last through years of wearing and washing.

Most running bras are made of polyester and spandex, with a nylon/spandex lining. (Spandex makes products give a little but hold their shape.) You can wear a running bra alone or under other shirts. In races and in some areas where you may train, wearing a running bra alone doesn't turn heads. But in some parts of the country — from big cities to rural areas — you may want to wear a lightweight tank top over your running bra to avoid causing a ruckus.

 Buy the biggest size you can find that still gives you support. A tight running bra interferes with your breathing and blood circulation. Never buy a running bra that makes you gasp for breath when you try it on. You may find yourself gasping at the price, though: Most cost between $25 and $40.

Stocking up on singlets

 A *singlet* is a fancy name for a tank top, but it's lightweight and breathable, while tank tops can be made from hot, heavy fabrics. You won't go wrong asking for either at a running store, although people usually think you're going to wear a singlet to race in and a tank top for training. Go figure.

 Singlets and other lightweight tank tops are usually made from breathable polyester and cost from $18 to $30. Like shorts, the price seems outrageous for what you get. Heavier cotton tank tops cost less, usually around $15.

Topping off with T-shirts

T-shirts, especially those you get for free from races, are an inexpensive way to outfit your marathon training during spring and fall. If you have to buy them, look for lightweight cotton Ts that are long enough to tuck into your shorts but not so long that they bunch up and feel uncomfortable. And buy them larger than you need unless the tag says they're made of preshrunk cotton; cotton shrinks the first few times it's dried in the dryer.

Long-sleeved Ts are the product of choice for warming up before fair-weather races, because they're warm, but not too warm. Getting a free long-sleeve T-shirt from a race is a rare bonus, so look for races that offer these.

 My favorite cold-weather layer under a jacket is a Lands' End 100% cotton turtleneck ($15 online from www.landsend.com). I can't explain why they're so comfortable — after all, cotton should get hot, wet, and heavy after a few miles under a Gore-Tex or nylon jacket or vest — but, these turtlenecks are, far and away, the most comfortable I've ever worn in cold weather. Buy these in your normal size — they run large and shrink the first time you launder them. The disadvantage of wearing cotton is that, when you get back to your home or office, you'll be wet to the skin. Change out of any cotton underlayer right away to avoid catching a chill.

Several other cold-weather fabrics, including Thermostat, Micro-fleece, Dry line, silk, and others can keep you warm on brutally cold days. If you can't find these at your local running store, try an outdoor or hunting store.

On cold days, always tuck the layer of clothing that rests against your skin into your running pants or tights. This way, wind can't get up under your shirt and give you a bad chill. If you're going to wear many layers (as opposed to one layer and a jacket), you want your *base layer* or *underlayer* (the layer closest to your skin) to be able to wick moisture away from your body. Otherwise, each layer acts as a sauna, keeping you wet — and potentially miserable — during your run.

Investing in jackets and vests

If you live in an area that experiences moderate cold and occasional rain, a nylon jacket or vest may be all you need. (A vest is simply a sleeveless version of a jacket.) Buy an unhooded, lightweight jacket and wear it over a long-sleeved T-shirt. (Wearing nylon over a short-sleeved T-shirt — or on any bare skin — can be uncomfortably sweaty.)

If you live in an excessively rainy or cold area, you can't beat a Gore-Tex jacket. Gore-Tex is a waterproof, windproof, and extremely breathable fabric that makes all but the most severe weather comfortable for running. (On those really bad weather days, you can switch to treadmill running.) Gore-Tex is the granddaddy of waterproof, breathable fabrics, but it's no longer the only player. Gelanot, for example, is waterproof and breathable and is much like Gore-Tex. Microfiber jackets actually breathe better than Gore-Tex, although they aren't as water resistant.

Don't wear Gore-Tex when the weather is over 45 degrees Fahrenheit or 50 degrees. You'll burn up. Although Gore-Tex does protect beautifully against rain, it isn't warm-weather rain gear.

I bought my first Gore-Tex jacket about 5 years ago, and it changed my winter running forever. I used to dread winter and often took entire weeks off of training, just so I wouldn't have to face the cold. Ever since getting that first jacket, however, I rarely miss a winter running day. When combined with a lightweight silk turtleneck under the cotton turtleneck, running pants with an underlayer of running tights, mittens, a face mask, and hat (all discussed in the two following sections, "Draping your million-dollar gams" and "Covering your head and hands"), I can run comfortably on the coldest, windiest days of the year.

Gore-Tex is really expensive. Your best time for deals is in late January or February, when running stores put them on sale. Also look for percentage-off sales from running catalogs (see the "Finding Running Gear" section, earlier in this chapter), in which all merchandise — including Gore-Tex — is 10 or 15 percent off. A $100 Gore-Tex jacket is a great bargain; I found my first for $59 and wish now that I had bought ten of them to last the rest of my life. Regular prices start at about $150 and go up to about $250, although Gore-Tex competitors may cost a little less. Jackets should fit well: large enough to fit over a cotton or polyester turtleneck but not large enough to fit over a bulky sweatshirt.

Draping your million-dollar gams

Even in the coldest weather, you generally don't have to layer the clothes that cover your legs, because your legs rarely get overly cold on distance runs. Do, however, choose shorts, tights, or pants, as appropriate for the season.

Shimmying into shorts

From about 50 degrees to 55 degrees Fahrenheit up to the hottest weather you can think of, running shorts are your best bet. Running shorts are different from soccer shorts or basketball shorts, which are usually heavier, longer, and baggier than shorts made for

---

You gotta wear shades

Depending on where you live and how you feel about getting wrinkles around your eyes, sunglasses may or may not be optional gear. In fact, some sunny southern college cross-country teams are sponsored by Oakley, the major manufacturer of sunglasses for runners, cyclers, and other sports types.

If you plan to wear sunglasses while running or racing, buy ones designed for runners. When you try them on (they're available from sporting goods stores, some running stores, specialty stores, and special kiosks located in the center aisles of some shopping malls), shake your head back and forth and up and down to make sure they don't slide around on your face. If they slide — even a little — when you're not sweaty, imagine what they'll do when you've been running for 15 miles. Plan to spend from $90 to $150.

For $5 or $10, a baseball cap can provide some of the same protection as fancy sunglasses. When running into the sun, run with the hat's brim forward. When you're away from the sun (and you find the brim annoying), turn the cap around backward on your head.

running. Wearing anything other than running shorts in hot weather can likely chafe the tender skin on your legs near your groin.

Running shorts range from short shorts that with a 2-inch inseam (often called *V-notch shorts* because of the large upside-down "V" cutout on the outside of each leg) to baggy shorts that have a 5- or 6-inch inseam and hit just above the knee. Most coaches prefer shorter shorts, simply because they're lighter and don't get in the way of your swinging legs, but runners train in all types.

Some people like to wear fitness shorts with Lycra/Spandex/Tactel (one or all those names may appear on the label). These are long, tight-fitting shorts that some people layer with traditional running shorts. I personally think they're hot, sweaty, and uncomfortable, but that doesn't mean they won't work for you.

Most running shorts are made of thin, silky polyester (often called *microfiber*), although some are a little bulkier. Look for the thinnest material you can find, because they'll drape best on your legs as you run. Plan to spend from $20 to $35 per pair, which is going to feel like highway robbery when you see how little fabric and workmanship goes into each pair. Check for end-of-summer sales at your favorite running store.

 Look for shorts with built-in underwear that's usually made of CoolMax, a product from DuPont that pulls moisture away from your skin and helps keeps your backside cool and dry. Also make sure that any shorts you buy have a *key pocket* — a place to store your car or house key and maybe a buck or two for a bottle of your favorite noncarbonated sports drink after your run.

Zipping into tights

Running tights are silky, lightweight and made of tight-fitting Lycra/ spandex. Think of Olympic speed-skating outfits, but just the pants instead of a full-body suit with a hood. Running tights fit snugly around your butt and legs, enough so that you may draw stares or whistles if you're around people who aren't used to seeing runners in tights.

Running tights are most useful on cold, rainy days, during which running pants (described in the following "Running in the right pants" section) get soggy with rain, and on ultra-cold days underneath running pants. Plan to spend from $30 to $60. Look for ones with zippers on the lower backs or sides of the legs, for ease in putting them on and taking them off.

If you like the material but not the tight fit, Hind has recently introduced a baggier version that's styled like their Munich running pants (see the following "Running in the right pants" section) but in the lighter-weight Lycra/spandex material.

Running in the right pants

Running pants, a wonderful product that was invented nearly 20 years ago, have only begun to catch on in the last few years. They're like running tights (see the preceding "Zipping into tights" section) but are usually much thicker, so they're perfect for cold-weather running, and baggier, which makes them ideal for warming up before a race or workout because you can easily wear shorts underneath them.

Hind makes the most popular running pant called the *Munich pant,* which costs (gulp!) about $65. Sporthill running pants are another good choice, although they tend to not be quite as baggy as the Hind pants.

Another kind of running pant is the kind that makes up the bottom half of a winter running suit; the top half of the suit is a jacket. These are also called *wind pants* and are usually made of nylon (which can make an annoying swishing sound when you run and may get hot against your bare legs) or Gore-Tex. They range in price from $40 for nylon to $150 for Gore-Tex.

Covering your head and hands

If you live in an area that experiences even moderate winters, get yourself a lightweight hat and a pair of running gloves. As with other types of running clothes, you're better off buying a hat and gloves geared specifically for running than using a thick winter hat and gardening gloves from your favorite discount store. Running hats and gloves are super-lightweight (those made by Wigwam are my favorite), but they keep you warm on all but the coldest days. Expect to pay about $10 each for a basic running hat and well-fitting running gloves.

Always wear a hat in cold weather. You lose about 50 percent of your body heat through the top of your head.

For colder winter weather, you may need two additional pieces of gear: a running face mask and a pair of running mittens. A *face mask* covers your entire face except your eyes, nostrils, and mouth, and you put it on by slipping it down over your head. I own about a dozen running face masks that are miserable failures and two that I wouldn't be without. Hind makes one of the two great face masks;

it's lightweight (made of nylon, polyester, and spandex) and covers the entire head with a large hole for the eyes, nose, and small pin-point holes for breathing through the mouth. It's not too tight, which can restrict breathing. The other, made by Nike, is a half mask that comes up to just above the nose, leaving the eyes and head open for a hat and sunglasses. Your breathing area — your mouth and nose — is covered with a baggy, breathable material, but the bulk of the face mask is made of Polartec, so it's warm. Face masks run from $15 to $25.

Severe winter weather is also too cold for running gloves. Because gloves separate your fingers, each finger loses warmth quickly, and your hands can soon become numb. On those cold days, wear Hind's WindJammer Mitt running mittens, made mostly of water-proof nylon with a thin cotton strip that keeps moisture from build-ing up inside the mitten, which could (if allowed to build up) frost-bite your fingers. (I personally think the cotton is a snot strip because if you wiped your nose on the rest of the mitten's nylon material, it wouldn't absorb anything. The snot strip allows you to wipe your dripping nose — a must in cold weather. Just don't tell your mother that you're using the mittens this way.) These mittens cost about $20.

Socking it to 'em

Socks seem like a pretty basic accessory, right? One that, perhaps, you wouldn't expect would receive an entire section of its own. But after your shoes, socks may well be your most important piece of gear, because they're all that comes between the ground and your tender tootsies.

Because sock companies have designed socks especially for run-ning, I recommend that you buy five or six pairs of honest-to-gosh running socks at your nearest running store and wear them instead of the socks you may find at your local discount or department store. Look for the following features when shopping for running socks:

- ✔ **Weight:** You want your socks to be lightweight (read that as "thin") every place but the sole. The entire bottom portion of the sock should be cushioned.

- ✔ **Fabric:** Look for a percentage of the fabric to be made of CoolMax, a product from DuPont that wicks moisture away from your body and keeps your feet cool and dry. If you train in cold-weather areas, you may also consider getting socks that have a wool component, although wool socks can heat up quickly, even in cold weather. The remainder of the fabric should be a blend of cotton (which absorbs moisture) and stretchy nylon or lycra (which help socks retain their shape).

- ✔ **Style:** Most runners prefer a high footie or low crew sock, so that the top of the sock hits a bit above your ankle. You may have other preferences, however, and can go with whatever style appeals to you.

- ✔ **Size:** Buy socks according to your shoe size, keeping in mind that men's and women's shoe sizes are on two different scales.

I've tried a kazillion socks. I like a very thin sock but also want some cushioning on the bottom of my foot, and Wigwam's C-T series fills the bill. The socks are quite thin on the tops but are nicely cushioned on the bottoms. The C-T Marathon sock, which is their most heavily cushioned variety, is a bit too thick for me and results in hot feet, but it may work well for you. The C-T Distance sock, which is a little less cushioned on the bottom, is my personal favorite. Another brand to try is the Thorlo's Lite Running sock, which is also thin everywhere but the bottom. Finally, check out SmartWool socks, which contain wool, a natural fabric that wicks moisture away from your skin. Most running stores carry all three brands.

SmartWool sometimes operates a booth at road races, offering race participants a free pair of socks. When I saw the booth at a race, I ventured over, eager to get my free pair. The guy manning the booth asked me to take off my shoes and then proceeded to take off my socks and throw them in a bin. My lucky racing socks tossed into a trash bin! I had to go in after them, but eventually gathered them back up and then gave up the idea of getting a free pair of socks. Want some advice? Always bring an extra pair of your least favorite socks to races — if you see a SmartWool truck or booth, you'll be all set!

Expect to pay $4 to $11 per pair for good running socks. Seems like highway robbery, doesn't it?

Chapter 3

Figuring Out Where and When to Run

- -

In This Chapter

▶ Finding the best places to run

▶ Getting the lowdown on trails, tracks, and treadmills

▶ Braving the elements

▶ Running when it's dark out

- -

This chapter offers you basic information on where and when to train. Whether you live in a large city or the smallest hamlet, and whether it's the dog days of summer or the middle of a harsh winter, you can find a place and time to run that's safe, interesting, and — most of all — fun.

Blazing the Best Trail

Figuring out where to run may seem like a simple proposition: Turn left out of the driveway and start running, right? Many people train on city streets and sidewalks, but urban thoroughfares aren't the most interesting — nor the safest — places to train.

Sidewalks are very *hard* — literally — and this isn't good for the health of your legs. Concrete surfaces don't provide any cushion for your legs the way that asphalt does. (*Asphalt* is the black pavement that surfaces many driveways and bike trails.) Like dirt and grass, asphalt offers some *give* so that your feet and legs aren't receiving a shock every time you hit the ground. Running every day on concrete surfaces dramatically increases your chances of injury (see Chapter 10). You probably won't be able to escape running on concrete entirely, but as a general rule, try to run at least one-third to one-half of your mileage on dirt or grass.

So what are your alternatives?

- ✔ **Suburban streets:** Streets in the 'burbs sometimes offer a wide, gravel shoulder, which may be just the relief your legs need from time to time. The scenery usually isn't great (just developments and neighborhoods), so you may have to put up with some boredom while running these routes!

- ✔ **Bike paths:** These routes offer a level, car-free surface that may be convenient to your home or work. Because they often aren't very long, these paths are especially good for shorter runs.

- ✔ **Country roads:** Especially if they're dirt, country runs may allow you to run without having to stop for traffic lights or for cars crossing in front of you.

Rural routes may have some disadvantages, too, such as big, unconfined dogs and fast-moving cars or trucks driven by people who aren't expecting to see a runner.

- ✔ **Dirt trails:** Unless you have a propensity to get lost or the trail area you're thinking of running is quite short and you won't be able to run for long without getting bored, dirt trails are usually a great place to train.

- ✔ **Golf courses:** If you can get access to them, golf courses provide an interesting, soft-surfaced alternative to roads. Parks with grassy areas are also possibilities, although they usually don't offer much acreage for your longer runs.

- ✔ **Cemeteries:** Larger cemeteries are sometimes open to the public and may provide several miles worth of well-maintained paths or roads. Do be sensitive to families who are burying (or visiting) loved-ones. Change your route to avoid interfering with a gathering of people.

- ✔ **Tracks and treadmills:** Although boring, these are better than concrete.

All these surfaces, including city streets, are discussed in detail in this section.

Charging through city streets

If you live in a city, especially a big city, you may tend to think that running on city streets is your only option, because getting out to country roads or to a park with trails is a long drive from your home. Although driving or taking a train or bus each day to an area with a dirt or grass surface may not be practical, perhaps you can make the trip one or two days per week to give your legs a much-needed break from concrete.

If you live in a city, one alternative to running on city streets and sidewalks is to join a health club and run on its treadmills or buy your own treadmill. The "Pacing treadmills" section, later in this chapter, gives you the lowdown on these machines.

Big-city running presents some challenges, but you can deal with them in the following ways:

- ✔ **Traffic:** Cars, especially those turning onto a street that you're running across, can present a safety hazard. But every city has some streets that are quieter and less heavily traveled than the rest. Aim for those quiet streets whenever you can.

  Whenever you come to an intersection, glance at the driver to make sure that he sees you. If he stops, you can keep going. If he doesn't see you and/or keeps turning the corner, run back and forth the way you came to keep yourself warmed up and ready to go after the driver makes the turn.

- ✔ **Frequent stops and starts:** The purpose of long runs is to run for a sustained amount of time without stopping or starting. Every time you slow down or stop for a stoplight, traffic, or pedestrians, you essentially chop a long run into a series of short runs. If a marathon was 26 one-mile stretches with 20- or 30-second breaks in between, stopping and starting on your city runs wouldn't be a problem. But a marathon is 26.2 miles, without breaks, and your runs should mimic that.

  Instead of waiting or running in place at stoplights, simply turn right every time you hit a red light. Your run may not go along the route you planned, but you won't have to stop for traffic lights. If you hit four red lights in a row, go ahead and run that big square.

- ✔ **Crowds:** If you run along downtown sidewalks in big cities around lunchtime or when most people are going to or leaving work, you face large, slow-moving crowds. These crowds make you slow down — or worse, stop — or move onto busy streets to get around.

  Plan your run around less-crowded times of the day, such as early morning (5:30 or 6:00). Also, plan your route so that you avoid the entrances to high-rise buildings, subway stops, and bus stops that attract crowds.

✔ **Personal safety:** Cities can be dangerous places (although, so, too, can be parks and country roads). For this reason, never run in a area that makes you feel unsafe, and avoid running at night.

If you live in an area where you ever fear for your safety, take a can of pepper spray with you on each run. These cans are small and light, so they fit comfortably in your hand. You can find pepper spray at most discount stores.

No matter what time of day you run, make sure that someone knows your route and what time to expect you back. If you fall and twist an ankle (or encounter something even more serious), it's reassuring to know that eventually someone will come looking for you.

Sailing through the 'burbs

Suburban streets usually have a bit of city street and country road in them. They have a steady stream of traffic but offer ample room to run on the shoulders, which are often unpaved. The shoulders of the road often extend for a half-mile or mile between stoplights, and they're probably convenient to your home. (See the preceding "Charging through city streets" section and the "Winding along country roads" section, later in this chapter.)

The two biggest drawbacks of suburban streets are

✔ **They're boring.** Suburban streets don't have the heart-stopping, life-and-death excitement of city streets nor the unbroken silence and beauty of country roads. You're running past housing developments and business parks, and that's not very interesting.

Don't combat boredom by wearing a portable radio or CD player! These devices disconnect you from traffic. You're more likely to get into an accident because you're not paying attention to drivers. Running to the rhythm of your favorite rapper or listening to the morning's news through the radio's earphones makes you a prime target for a personal attack, because you won't hear someone coming up behind you.

✔ **Traffic turns in and out of subdivisions and business parks.** Although suburban stoplights may be spaced less regularly than in cities, you may frequently find yourself crossing entrances to subdivisions and businesses. Keep a watchful eye out for traffic as you run on these streets and avoid running on these roads during the peak commuting times: morning, lunchtime, and early evening.

Bounding down bike paths

Bike paths are usually paved with asphalt, which is far softer than concrete, so they're a good alternative to sidewalks. (You still want to spend some time on dirt or grass, however, because although asphalt is softer than concrete, it's still hard on your legs.)

Bike paths often don't go far, but if you loop around and double back, you may be able to get in a long run that goes entirely on the trail. If you live in a populated area, you may find that walkers and people pushing strollers crowd the path. If this is the case, avoid using the trail in early evening, which is a popular time for families to walk together. Also watch out for bicyclists and rollerbladers, who may be flying down the path and not see you.

Also, you may find that the paths aren't lined with many trees, making them blazing hot in summer (keep your sunscreen handy) and windswept and icy in winter. Some towns do, however, plow the paths, so they may be your best bet for winter training.

Winding along country roads

Country roads — especially those that are aren't paved — are ideal for marathon training. Many country roads go on for miles and miles without a stoplight or traffic to interrupt your run. The right rural route may suit your training to a "T" and may even present you with some hills, which help build strength (see Chapter 7). If you live out in the country or otherwise have access to less-traveled roads, take advantage of them.

Country roads aren't all good, though, and they can present you with some challenges:

- **Dogs:** Perhaps the biggest challenge on country roads is that you run into dogs, some of which are friendly, but some not. A dog bite on your leg can sideline you for months, putting your marathon out of reach. See the "Keeping canines at bay" side-bar for tips on dealing with dogs.

- **Fast-moving (though infrequent) traffic:** Although you won't see much traffic on country roads, when you do see a car or truck, chances are, it'll be flying. Country roads aren't often policed, so drivers make up their own speed limits. In addition, these fast-moving drivers — often driving right down the center of the road — aren't expecting to see you. Keep well to the side, facing oncoming traffic, unless the road is steeply graded. (See the information on "Steep grading" that follows.)

Keeping canines at bay

If you come upon a dog, do two things first: Cross the road to get as far away as possible and look for rocks or large stones within your reach. Many dogs won't leave their yards (that is, they won't cross the road), and many others are friendly.

If the dog comes at you and bares its teeth, though, yell loudly and deeply (something like, "Go home!") and bend to pick up the rock, but keep your eyes on the dog so that you can try to jump away if it attacks. (Keep in mind that some dogs see staring as an act of agression, so watch the dog without staring it down.) Chances are, you won't have to throw the rock at the dog; the mere act of bending down for it, combined with a loud, forceful yell, scares most dogs away. Do everything possible before hurling a rock at any dog — throwing anything at a dog is a form of attack, and it may strike back.

If you're running in an area with many loose dogs (or just one vicious one), carry a can of pepper spray with you. You can find these small, lightweight canisters at most discount stores.

And after you figure out which routes have mean dogs, take a different route.

- ✔ **Steep grading:** In areas that get plenty of snow, country roads are *graded,* which means that they angle down from the center line of the road. Sometimes, the grading on country roads is quite steep, which means that, with each step, one of your legs has to reach farther than the other. This may not seem like a big deal, but running 10 miles with your hips cocked at a ten-degree angle to accommodate the grading on the road can quickly lead to a hip or leg injury.

  On steeply graded roads, always try to run in the middle of the road, but watch for cars. And if you come to a hill that blocks your view of oncoming traffic (or blocks the oncoming traffic's view of you), move to one side of the road until you're back on flat ground. Don't run on the other side of the road to try to "even out" the impact on your legs, because you'll have your back to oncoming cars. Always face the cars coming toward you so that you can jump out of the way if they don't see you.

- ✔ **Isolation:** Although country roads are usually peaceful and quiet, if you do meet some unwelcome company and call for help, chances are no one will hear you.

  For this reason, many distance runners now carry cellphones, putting help just a quick phone call away. Be aware of the names of the roads you're running on, as well as any landmarks that may make you easier to find in an emergency. Also, test your cellphone occasionally to be sure the phone works in the area in which you're running. And try to purchase or lease a small, lightweight phone so that you're not lugging around a half-pounder for miles on end.

Digging dirt trails

Getting a chance to spend time on dirt trails is, in my opinion, the best perk of running. Trails are interesting, challenging, good for your legs, and offer beautiful scenery. Whether you're running on a hot summer day, when it's raining, or during the middle of winter, trails offer a peaceful setting that few other running routes can match. You may see other people, but you may also see only squirrels, deer, and birds.

Whatever you do, don't wear a portable radio or CD player when you're running in the woods — the whole point is to listen to the sounds of nature and be a part of it. More important, wearing headphones makes you prone to a personal attack because you can't hear someone coming up behind you.

To find dirt trails in your area, call or visit your local running store and ask which trails they recommend. You can also search the Internet using the name of your town or area and the word "trails." Some of those trails may be paved, but you're likely to find some in your area that aren't. In addition, check the Internet site of the park system in your state (and, perhaps, your city) to see what dirt trails it offers.

I had the good fortune of spending time on the Appalachian Trail (AT) in Roanoke, Virginia. The AT runs over 2,000 miles — unbroken — from New Hampshire to Georgia. Although parts of the AT aren't suited to running because the grade is too steep or the trail is lined with slippery stones, the particular area I ran on was, in my experience, the best darned running trail I ever saw. Most parts of the AT are quite hilly, which is good for your training, and because its location isn't advertised with signs or billboards, the trail is quiet and peaceful. (Search *Appalachian Trail* on the Internet or peruse AT books at your local bookstore or library to find out how to pick up the trail.) You may have to climb up makeshift ladders that go over barbed wire that's meant to keep out horses and bicycles, but those ladders are a small price to pay for never, ever running out of trail — even on your longest runs.

Although dirt trails are a wonderful resource, they have three potential disadvantages that you want to keep in mind:

✔ **Trails are often short.** Dirt trails, which are often located in state and local parks, may seem plenty long enough to a walker or to someone running for 20 or 30 minutes. But most trails aren't meant for marathon training, and you may find yourself at the end of a trail with only 15 minutes on your watch. By combining many different trail loops, you may be able to run for an hour or more: Look for parks that offer several trails that intersect or one long trail that's 4 or more miles long.

✔ **Trails can be confusing.** If you tend to get lost, carry a trail map in your hand. Sure, the map can get soft in your sweaty palm, but you'll have it if you get turned around and can't find your way back. Maps are often available at the *trailhead* (the entrance to the main trail).

✔ **Be prepared to fall.** Most trails are rooty. If you don't lift your feet high enough with each step, you can trip over tree roots and crash. If you do fall, take your time getting up to make sure that you haven't broken anything and clean out your wounds when you get back. An antibacterial cream can speed healing, too.

I've fallen dozens of times on trails, and although I haven't yet broken anything from those falls (knock on wood), I have been bloodied and bruised. I now accept falling as a part of trail running, and although I'm careful, I still expect to fall once in a while.

Galloping through golf courses, cemeteries, and parks

Most golf course supervisors wouldn't dream of allowing runners on a golf course for fear of tearing it up, but you may get lucky and live near a golf course that encourages runners to train there. Golf courses have wonderfully soft grass and take up several hundred acres, giving you ample room for mileage. Stay off the greens (the shortest, softest grass right near each hole), though, if you ever want a chance to come back.

An alternative to a golf course is a grassy park maintained by your city, county, or state. If the grass is well mowed and the park is large enough, you may be able to do your shorter runs in parks. Most grassy parks, though, are meant only as playgrounds or for short strolls. To cover any significant distance, you have to run many, many loops around the perimeter.

Avoiding indoor tracks

Some recreation buildings and health clubs offer an indoor track that's usually about 150-meters around. Unlike outdoor tracks, which are boring but not unhealthy, indoor tracks have tight turns that aren't natural to your legs and can cause injury. (If you find yourself training on an indoor track, change directions frequently, although some well-visited tracks force you to run a certain direction so as to improve traffic flow.) Plus, at 12 laps per mile, you'll be bored out of your skull.

Some cemeteries may also offer grassy areas to run for short distances, although most offer only paved paths for walking and running.

Trotting around tracks

If you're thinking of training for a marathon entirely on the high-school track near your home or office, forget it: Within a week, you may be so bored that you'll give up on your marathon goals. Tracks are b-o-r-i-n-g: I don't recommend them for anything but strides and drills and, perhaps, the occasional workout (see Chapter 7). Instead, hit the roads, bike paths, and trails.

Pacing treadmills

A treadmill is almost as boring as a track (see the preceding "Trotting around tracks" section), but by placing a TV — and even a VCR or DVD player — near the treadmill and turning the volume way up to overcome the treadmill noise, you can kill two birds with one stone. You can watch your favorite TV show, business report, or movie while getting in a few runs per week. You can also play with the incline and speed at given times (say, every 10 minutes) to break up the monotony. (See Chapter 7 for more on training on hills and playing with speed.) Because you're on a treadmill, you also know exactly how fast you're going, which is one benefit that most other running surfaces can't offer.

If you think you're going to do the majority of your training on a treadmill (as did Alaskan Dr. Christy Clark, winner of the 2000 U.S. Olympic marathon trials), buy one. The treadmill at your local health club probably doesn't have a TV that you can hear well or that you can tune to your favorite show. Long lines for the treadmill may prohibit you, and it may not go fast enough to accommodate your training. You can get a high-quality treadmill for around

$1,000. Sure, that's plenty of dough, and you still have to find a place in your home to put it. Having a treadmill in your home, however, is convenient in several ways because you

✔ Never have to wait in line

✔ Can set up whatever media center you want

✔ May actually do some of the workouts discussed in Chapter 7 on the machine

Table 3-1 gives you some features to look for when you decide to buy.

Table 3-1	Treadmill Buying Guide
Feature	*What to Look For*
Sturdiness	Test every treadmill you're considering. Jump on and begin running. Look for one that doesn't jiggle or move excessively, even at high speeds.
Speed	The treadmill should go at least 10 miles per hour but preferably faster, so you can do strides on it (see Chapter 8).
Incline	The incline feature mimics hill training, so be sure your treadmill has it. Also look for a separate motor for the incline (or make sure your treadmill has the largest motor available), or the treadmill may slow down whenever it inclines.
Hand-rail controls	Some treadmills feature small, convenient switches on the hand rails that control speed and incline.
Size	If space is at a premium in your home, look for a treadmill that can fold up when not in use.

If you live in an area that experiences severe winter weather and you plan to train on a treadmill only during that time, consider training on a treadmill one day a week during the rest of the year, too. While treadmill belts move forward, you don't. Going cold turkey during the winter months and giving up stable surfaces (you move forward and the ground doesn't) without having used a treadmill the rest of the year isn't the best means of conditioning your body to run a marathon. Your body may have trouble suddenly switching to your treadmill — that is, you may sustain an injury. On the hottest day of the week during the summer, place your treadmill in an air-conditioned area or have a fan blowing on you while you run, so you can keep up your once-a-week treadmill training.

Deciding When to Run (and When to Stay Indoors)

If you only run on beautiful days, you won't run very often. In order to train for a marathon, you have to get used to the idea that you train regardless of the weather or darkness of night. Using a treadmill (see the preceding "Pacing treadmills" section), you may be able to avoid bad weather and training in the dark, but you can't race a marathon on a treadmill. So sooner or later, you have to face the weather.

Handling hot, humid weather

In hot, humid weather, run early in the morning — as soon as day breaks or even earlier. The closer to midday you run, the greater your chances are of experiencing *dehydration* — not taking in enough water, sometimes leading to organ malfunction —or *sunstroke* — serious overexposure to the sun. This means that if you live in a hot climate, don't run at lunchtime. Instead, run before or after work.

One of the early signs of dehydration is excessive thirst. If you're drinking enough, you should never feel thirsty. By the time you feel thirsty, you're already down a few ounces of fluids. Signs of more serious dehydration include dizziness, seeing stars, diarrhea, and chills.

Sunstroke is equally dangerous. Symptoms include fever, excessive sweating (or worse, completely dry skin), and collapse, sometimes followed by a complete loss of control or even a coma. One of the first signs of sunstroke is a very red face after running, although people with sensitive skin often develop a red face with just a little exercise — if that's the case with you, it's nothing to worry about.

The most important step that you can take toward ensuring safe runs during hot weather is to *rehydrate*, which simply means drinking plenty of fluids. Some people take water with them on hot runs; others drink up and replenish their body's fluids when they get finished. However you decide to do it, drink both water and a noncarbonated sports drink.

Don't let recent news about hyponatremia keep you from hydrating enough. *Hyponatremia* is over-hydration caused by drinking too much water, and a woman running the Boston Marathon died from the condition. To avoid this situation, make sure about 40 percent of your fluid intake comes from a noncarbonated sports drink.

I used to think water was the best fluid I could drink. In fact, I thought Gatorade and other drinks like it were all hype and no substance. Then during my first summer of running 70+ miles per week, I couldn't seem to rehydrate. I was always thirsty, even though I was drinking about 100 ounces of water per day. I soon began experiencing diarrhea and then began getting chills, even though these were the hot days of summer. Not knowing what else to do, I began replacing 32 ounces of water with Gatorade. Within two days, all my symptoms were gone, and I felt better out running than I had in weeks. Now, I make sure that I drink at least 32 ounces of Gatorade directly after each run and drink water throughout the rest of the day.

The powdered version of Gatorade costs about one-tenth of the price of bottled Gatorade. Simply add water and stir.

If you want to make yourself sick, walk directly into an air-conditioned room after finishing a run on a hot day. If you want to stay healthy, walk around a bit outside (to stop sweating), change out of your sweaty clothes, and stretch before heading into an air-conditioned environment.

Cruising through cold, icy weather

Although most marathons aren't run in the winter, if you're training for a spring marathon, you're likely to run in cold and icy conditions.

Guarding against cold and snow isn't difficult. By wearing running pants, a Gore-Tex or similar type of jacket, running mittens, and a face mask (see Chapter 2 for details on special clothing), you'll hardly notice the difference between a harsh winter day and a sunny day in April. Yes, you have to buy these products — and they aren't cheap — but they last a long time and can serve you well. Be sure, however, that when you step out the door, you feel a little cold. If you're warm before you begin your run, you'll be way too hot by the middle of it.

Ice, on the other hand, can be a real problem for runners. One slip on a patch of ice can, in an instant, cause a serious injury to your hamstring, groin, back, or other areas. Your best bet in icy conditions, assuming you can't move to Florida for the winter, is to run on a treadmill (see the "Pacing treadmills" section, earlier in this chapter).

If you must run outside in icy conditions, slow down and when you get to a patch of ice, shuffle your feet instead of running. Don't run in the dark when the ground is icy, because you won't see the ice. Watch for *black ice* that forms on asphalt and looks so clear that you can't distinguish it from the asphalt.

Singing in the rain

Rain has never hurt a runner (although lightning can), but what you wear and how you take care of yourself after a run does make a difference:

- ✔ If the temperature is under 45 degrees Fahrenheit or so, wear a Gore-Tex or similar type of jacket (see Chapter 2) on rainy days. Gore-Tex doesn't allow rain to penetrate the jacket and get through to your skin, but it can also get hot, so I don't recommend it for warmer rainy days.

- ✔ If the weather is hot and rainy, wear as few clothes as possible so that you aren't lugging heavy, wet clothes throughout your run.

- ✔ Wear a baseball cap to keep your head dry for as long as possible.

- ✔ Whether you're soaked to the skin or just a little damp when you get back from your run, change into dry clothes immediately, before you stretch. If you're still cold, take a warm shower as soon as you're done stretching.

- ✔ If you see lightning before you start running, put off your run until later in the day or run inside on a treadmill. If you see lightning while on your run, seek shelter immediately. Stay away from trees, too, which may be hit by lightning.

Keep in mind that wooden bridges and other surfaces may be quite slick after a rainstorm — almost like a patch of ice.

Doing your distance in the dark

Whether you're planning your training runs around your work schedule, beating the heat of the day, or attempting to run when streets are less crowded, you may find yourself running in the dark. The streets are peaceful, and the weather is mild at night or in early morning, but running in the dark can also be dangerous: You may never see a pothole that twists (or even breaks) your ankle, and if you're running in the dark in cold weather, you may hit a patch of ice that you didn't even know was there. And if you run in an unsafe city area or desolate country road, you may put yourself at risk of a mugging or other crime.

If you can avoid running in the dark, do so. If not, consider these two suggestions to keep you safe:

✔ **Bringing your own light.** You can buy a small, lightweight flashlight that you can hold in your hand and use to light the road in front of you.

You can also purchase a light that you can wear around your head, kind of like a miner's hat. Okay, these look completely dorky, and they haven't caught on yet in the running community, so you probably won't find them at many running stores. However, you can find them at a home repair/remodeling places, and they really do work. The idea is that a strong flashlight beam comes from your forehead and down on the ground, freeing up your arms to swing as usual. Nike also makes a hat that comes with an attached light that may be strong enough to light your path.

✔ **Wearing a reflective vest.** Although a vest won't protect you from potholes, it can protect you from drivers who can't see you. Most reflective vests are lightweight, so you can wear one even in summer. And they're pretty cheap: $15 to $20 at most.

Chapter 4

Taking Your First Run

. . . .

In This Chapter

▶ Getting started with a training regimen

▶ Beginning at a slower pace

▶ Minimizing the inevitable aches and pains

▶ Figuring out how fast and far

▶ Training in good company with a class, club, or coach

. . . .

*I*f you've been training pretty consistently, you probably don't need to read this chapter — see Chapter 6, instead. This chapter is all about your *first* run. If you never ran a step in your life, you haven't run since you were in school, or you've been sidelined while recovering from an injury, this chapter can help you get into a training regimen and begin building your mileage.

In this chapter, you also find several tips to consider before you actually lace up your running shoes. You discover how to approach your first run and find out how fast and how far that run should be, as well as the speed and distance of the runs to follow in the first five weeks of your training. You also discover how to find training partners, if you're looking for running companions. Then, as an added bonus, this chapter tells you how to deal with the unavoidable soreness that you'll begin to feel just 12 short hours after your first run.

Pointing Yourself in the Right Direction

Before you go out on your first run (or your first one in 10 years), you want to keep a few pointers in mind to make your first runs more comfortable, safe, and productive.

Dressing appropriately

As Chapter 2 tells you, the most important piece of gear you wear is a pair of running shoes. Before you step foot outside to run, make sure not only that you're wearing running shoes (as opposed to basketball or tennis shoes or your favorite loafer) but also that you're wearing the best running shoes *for you*.

Running shoes are a personal choice. Just because your best friend loves a particular shoe doesn't mean those shoes will work for you. Running shoes aren't supposed to cause blisters, blacken your toenails, make your feet go numb, cause pain in your arch or heel, or make your knees ache. If any of these conditions happen to you, you're wearing the wrong shoe — or a shoe that's worn out. Shoes are meant to last for only 400 to 500 miles, which at 50 miles per week, is just 8 to 10 weeks. If you're used to buying a new pair of running shoes every year or two, get ready to spend substantially more as you train for a marathon. (See Chapter 1 for other expenses you may incur as you train for a marathon.)

Although a local running store is always the best place to shop for running shoes, make sure that they have a return or exchange policy if your shoes are causing any problems. If they don't, consider buying your shoes from Road Runner Sports (www.road runnersports.com or 800-551-5558), which, after joining the Run American Club for $20 per year, allows you to return any shoe — worn or not — after trying it out.

The second most important piece of gear you can wear is a running watch; that is, any watch that includes an accurate stopwatch. It doesn't have to be fancy as long as the watch accurately records the time you spend running.

Chapter 2 has more information on the gear that you need, the gear that you may want, and where to get it. The bottom line, though, is that you want to dress appropriately for the weather: cool and lightweight clothing for summer, warm layers for winter, rain gear for storms, and so on.

Avoiding blisters

Blisters plague new runners, and even some experienced runners suffer from them. The primary ways to avoid getting blisters are

> ✔ Wearing shoes that aren't too tight and that have an ample *toe box* (the area of the shoe that encloses your toes and forefoot — see Chapter 2).

> ✔ Always wearing socks, preferably thin ones (also discussed in Chapter 2).

If you're wearing the proper shoes and socks and still fear you'll suffer from blisters, rub petroleum jelly (a low-tech solution) or products like Skin Lube or Body Glide (higher-tech, less squishy products) on sensitive areas of your feet before you run. Yes, it feels squishy and a little disgusting, but applying a coat of petroleum jelly is an effective way to prevent blisters. For advice on how to treat blisters if they do occur, see Chapter 11.

Being sure not to eat and run

Remember what your parents told you over and over again about swimming and eating: Don't swim less than an hour after you eat a meal, right? Well, the same concept applies to running, except that instead of an hour, you want to wait two to five hours before running. You have to figure out for yourself how much time you need, but I never met anyone who ran less than 2 hours after eating without developing a painful stomach cramp. And such a cramp can last hours — even days — after you first develop it. So a stomach cramp is a gift that keeps on giving — and one you can't return. Better to avoid stomach cramps all together by waiting to run after you eat.

Plan your meals around your run: If you plan to run in the late afternoon, don't eat a late lunch. Instead, drink a bucket load of water and if you must eat something, snack on a piece of fruit; avoiding anything heavy.

One of the reasons so many runners like to train in the morning, right after waking up, is that they don't have to worry about getting cramps from their previous meals. Sure, it's crazy to set an alarm for 5:00 a.m. just so you don't have to worry about getting a cramp on your run, but training for and racing in a marathon is pretty nutty, too. Besides, finishing your run at 6:00 or 7:00 a.m. and watching your neighbors wake up and turn on their lights is fun. Like the old Armed Forces slogan, you'll do more by 7:00 a.m. than most people do all day!

I know a guy — an Olympian, no less — who occasionally eats a big meal, and then within a half hour or so, goes out for a long run. He does this, no kidding, to *practice* getting cramps. His logic is that if he's used to getting cramps, when a cramp comes up in the middle of a race, he'll be better equipped to deal with it. Here's my take: This is a little crazy. Cramps aren't inevitable; instead, they're directly related to how much and how soon you eat before a train-ing run or race. So you don't have to train for them — you can avoid them completely. And don't forget that running is supposed to be fun. Creating a painful situation when you can easily avoid that pain is simply not fun.

Running a good route

Before you tackle your first run, think about the running routes that are available to you — the types of surfaces (soft or hard) that you can run on, the way you run the route (straight out and straight back or a loop around town), and the number of variations of routes you can come up with. This section gives you some tips and ideas for finding a good route. See Chapter 3 for even more detail on choosing great places to train.

Scanning the surface

Because Chapter 3 dissects the advantages and disadvantages of training on city streets, country roads, trails, golf courses, tracks, and treadmills, this section contains only one reminder: You want from a third to one half of your weekly miles to be on dirt or grass; more if you're prone to injuries.

Concrete is the hardest surface you can run on, and if you spend every day running on concrete, you risk a number of injuries from bruises on the bottoms of your feet to stress fractures in your legs (see Chapter 10). Asphalt (that's the black stuff people use on driveways and on most bike trails) is softer than concrete, but asphalt is still hard on your legs.

Plan now to find a dirt road or trail that you can run on several days per week, even if you have to take the time to drive there. Spending the time and energy that it takes to drive to a dirt road or trail is much better than spending time and energy time with a physical therapist, rehabbing after a stress fracture. If you don't know of any good dirt running routes in your area, go to an Internet search engine (such as www.google.com or www.yahoo.com) and type in the name of your city and the words *running trail*. Chances are, someone in your area has written about one or two dirt trails or roads in your area. If this doesn't work, go to your local book-store and ask for a book that describes the trails in your state. Any trail that's meant for walking can also be run on, but look for ones that are described as "easy" or "moderate" and aren't too hilly or full of roots.

Keep in mind that most runners have to slow down on grass and trails in order to maneuver through the mushiness, undulations, roots, and rocks. Because your marathon finish time is directly related to your training pace, you don't want all your runs to be on these slower surfaces. Except for a few trail marathons offered around the country, marathons are always run on hard surfaces, and in your training, you want to mimic your marathon (time of day, weather conditions, hilliness, windiness, *and* hardness of the running surface) as much as possible.

Choosing between loops and out-and-backs

Runs generally come in three forms: loops, out-and-backs, or a combination of the two, all of which are shown in Figure 4-1:

✔ **Loop:** A loop has the same starting and ending point (at your house, car, or workplace), and you run down various streets or paths that eventually bring you back to your starting point without running the same path twice. If you know your route well or are flexible about exactly how far you want to go on a particular run, a loop is the most interesting way to run.

Be sure that you know where you're going when you run a loop, especially if you're running trails or other unpopulated routes. A few years ago, I decided to run for an hour on some hilly trails in Arizona. Fifty minutes later, nothing looked familiar, and I was starting to panic. I ended up approaching two men who were just getting into their car and asking them how I might get back to mine. They told me I was a good 8 miles away and offered me a ride. I was petrified, because I had been taught not to take rides from strangers, but I didn't have many other options. They deposited me safely back at my car (for which I'm still grateful) and taught me an important lesson about choosing my running routes carefully.

✔ **Out-and-back:** An *out-and-back* run is one in which you run for a certain distance or time, and then turn around and come back along the same route you just ran. This type of run, while less interesting than a loop (because you see the same scenery twice), is the easiest way to run for a predetermined distance. Simply run the "out" portion for half the time or distance you want to run, and the "back" portion will be approximately the same length. (I say "approximately" because the going could be uphill, for example, and of course, the coming back will be downhill — or vice versa.) Out-and-backs are particularly useful when running in a new area or on a trail that you don't know very well, because as long as you keep track of where and what direction you turned, it's almost impossible to get lost on this type of run.

Elite runners often try to run the "back" portion of the run a little faster than the "out" portion. This is a good way to train your body to *negative split* during your marathon (that is, to run the second half of your marathon faster than the first half). By the way, runners who set world records at every distance from 800 meters to the marathon ran negative splits.

✔ **Combination:** A combination loop and out-and-back involves an out-and-back with one or several loops run along the way. Combination loops and out-and-backs allow you to lengthen your run, as needed.

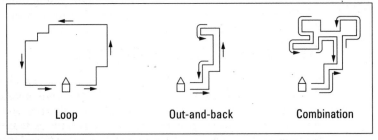

| Loop | Out-and-back | Combination |

Figure 4-1: Choose your route based on your propensity for getting lost.

Varying your route

Don't run the same route every day. The first reason is simple: Running the same route every day is boring, and training for a marathon, while not a barrel of laughs all the time, is supposed to be fun. If you run the same route every day, you'll probably begin to experience running as a chore instead of an adventure. Instead, try to figure out at least six different runs in your area. An easy way to establish four routes is to have one that heads north out from your house, one that heads south, one that goes east, and one west. The other two routes can overlap with those four a little, but they should be different enough that you don't feel, after a few weeks of running, that if you see that house, the same tree, or the same guy on his bike one more time, you'll scream.

The second reason to vary your route is for your own safety, especially for women: If you run the same route every day at the same time, someone could lay in wait and try to hurt you. Don't allow others to set their clocks by you and your routine.

Taking identification with you

Unless you live in a really small town where everyone knows you by sight, be sure to take some sort of identification with you on every training run. If you should fall or suffer from dehydration, someone driving by can assist you and notify a friend or relative. Most running shorts (see Chapter 2) come with an inside pocket that's just large enough for a credit card or hotel key. Consider putting your driver's license or some other form of ID in that pocket. Some people also put personal information in their shoes, but you may be in the hospital before someone notices that.

You may also want to carry a cellphone on all your runs. Get the lightest-weight, smallest phone you can afford, though, because you don't want the burden of carrying something heavy on your longer runs.

Avoiding antiperspirants

No, really. Never apply antiperspirant before heading out for a run. Think about the word: *Anti* combined with *perspire* means *against perspiration.* The purpose of antiperspirant is to keep you from sweating under your armpits, and that can be dangerous if you're running on a hot day. Your body needs to sweat in order to cool itself down, so you don't want to block even a small portion of your body from being able to do that. You'll smell bad — that's for sure — but you'll be much healthier.

If you're concerned about how you smell during and after your run (and, after you spend weeks or months training for your marathon, you probably won't be), purchase a product that calls itself "deodorant" only. Most underarm applications are both deodorants and antiperspirants, but you can find a few varieties that are only deodorants. This means that they don't stop you from sweating, but you'll smell nicer than sweat.

Recording your mileage

Even before your first run, plan to keep track of your mileage in a *running log.* A log is a terrific tool for tracking how effectively your training is preparing you for tune-up races (see Chapters 13 and 19), so that you can make adjustments in your training in the weeks or months before your marathon.

Running the gamut of details

Depending on how much detail you want to record about your running, consider putting the following information into your running log:

✔ **Observations:** Develop a simple notation for how you felt — from "ran fast!" to "feel a cold coming on" to "darned hills."

✔ **Conditions:** You don't have to be descriptive, but write down whether the weather was hot, cold, rainy, and so on.

✔ **Food:** Although you need to have a fairly large writing space to record your daily meals, keeping track of food can help you trace food allergies and determine whether you're getting the best balance of carbohydrates, protein, and fat. (See Chapter 9 for more on nutrition.)

✔ **Heart rate:** Elite runners sometimes measure their resting heart rate before they get up in the morning (or after going to the bathroom and lying back down again for a few minutes). Any elevation warns them that they may be developing an illness or overtraining (see Chapter 16). In order for this method to be effective, however, don't check your rate just after waking to an alarm. The ringing alarm temporarily elevates your heart rate.

✔ **Weight:** Some runners weigh themselves every day or week and log their weight. If you do this, be sure you don't go overboard and begin obsessing over your weight — you'll always have fluctuations depending on how well you're hydrating, whether you're ovulating, and so on. A fine line is drawn between being fit and being underweight, so just be careful. (See Chapter 9 for more information on nutrition.)

✔ **Complementary training:** Write down whether you did strides and drills (see Chapter 8), circuits or a speed workout (see Chapter 7), or sit-ups.

✔ **Other activities:** If you shopped (and were on your feet) for 6 hours, write that down. That may help you figure out why you're tired the next day.

Whether you use logs as sophisticated as *The Runner's Training Diary For Dummies* and *Runner's World Training Diary For Dummies*, both authored by Allen St. John (Wiley) or use a plain, spiral-bound notebook, find some sort of a log in which to record your daily mileage and other information. (See the "Running the gamut of details" sidebar for additional information to record in your running log.)

Marathoners have, traditionally, measured how far they run in miles. So when you ask a marathoner how long he runs per week, the answer will be something like, "45 miles" or "100 miles." This seems like a logical way to record your training, right? Well, not really, because you have to figure out how many miles each of your training runs adds up to. Whether you're running on city streets, country roads, or trails (see Chapter 3 for information on how to choose your running surfaces), you have to measure miles in one of the following ways:

- ✔ **Mileage wheel:** A *wheel* looks like a small unicycle with a handle, and it costs around $125. You walk, pushing this contraption in front of you, and it records the number of feet or meters that you travel. You then need to divide the number on the display by 5,280 (for feet) or 1,609 (for meters), and you know how many miles you ran. The disadvantage, besides the prices, is that a wheel is cumbersome to run with, so you have to run your route as you normally would and then walk that same route with the wheel to find out how far you ran. Of course, you can do this one time with each of ten or twelve different routes, and you never have to do it again. Unless you move.

- ✔ **Pedometer:** A *pedometer* (ped-*ahm*-mitter) is a small device that attaches to your shoe and records the number of times your feet hit the ground. (It costs anywhere from $25 to $200, depending on the quality.) If you set a pedometer to your exact stride length, it multiplies the number of times your feet hit the ground by your stride length and calculates the mileage you ran.

  It seems nifty, but pedometers present a problem in that your stride length is difficult to measure accurately, and even if you're able to get an accurate measure (see the instructions that come with the pedometer) your stride length changes throughout your run, depending on whether you're going up or down hills, tiptoeing through ruts on a trail, or running faster or slower than your normally do. As your stride length changes, the mileage measurement on the pedometer becomes inaccurate, so you're likely running longer or shorter than the pedometer measures.

  New pedometers are emerging that use GPS/satellite technology to determine how far you ran. Yes, this technology could be about the coolest thing ever invented for runners, but wait for prices to drop and for manufacturers to work the kinks out of the systems before buying.

- ✔ **Odometer:** You can also use the odometer in your car to measure how far you ran by driving your route after you finish running. Of course, this method doesn't really work with trails and golf courses. In addition, odometers tend not to be extremely exact, so you'll likely be off by a quarter mile every few miles. This may not be that big of a deal, but it can add up to plus or minus a few miles per week.

You may wonder why you can't just run on a track or treadmill every day. They both give you accurate mileage measurements, sure, but truth be told, they are two of the most boring ways to spend your time training. If you were training for the mile, which means you'd train for far fewer but much faster miles each day, using a track or treadmill may be doable. But marathon training requires quite a few miles per day, so just imagine running 9 miles on a track: That's 36 laps! And if you always train on a treadmill, you may never get to train under an open sky, and that's just not a normal part of running. You get far more enjoyment out of your training if you take in the beauty of the woods or the excitement of a town or city during your runs.

So what's the solution? A growing preference among marathoners is to measure not weekly *miles* but weekly *minutes*. You may decide that you're going to go on a 50-minute run, and you do that, going on whatever route you please. You know you're done with your run that day when 50 minutes is up. The biggest advantage of running for minutes instead of miles is that it's extremely convenient. You're just not going to find an easier way to keep track of your weekly training than just starting your running watch (any watch with an accurate stopwatch built into it) at the beginning of the run and stopping it at the end.

Keeping track of minutes does have a couple disadvantages, however:

✔ One is that you have to get a watch, but you pretty much have to do that anyway, because even if you measured your training in miles, before long, you'd want to find out how fast you were running those miles.

✔ Which brings me to the second disadvantage: You really don't know how fast you're running anything and in order to know that, you still have to measure the distance you ran.

What I recommend is that you measure just one or two routes — preferably fairly flat concrete or hard-packed dirt road routes that simulate the surface you'll run your marathon on. Once or twice a week, run one of your routes and use your stopwatch to see how fast you're running per mile. You'll have a good sense of how fast you're running (see Chapter 7 to improve on this time), but without the hassle of having to measure everything you run. On your other runs that aren't measured, note in your log whether you think you're running slower or faster than you did on the measured day.

Calculating minutes per mile

To calculate minutes per mile when you're running one of your measured road routes, use a calculator and do the following:

1. **Round your seconds to minutes. For example, 36 minutes and 33 seconds becomes 37 minutes. Change hours to minutes. (One hour, 10 minutes and 24 seconds becomes 70 minutes.)**

2. **Divide the minutes by the number of miles.**

3. **Subtract the minutes, so that you're left with just a decimal (that represents the number of seconds), and then multiply that decimal by 60.**

   For example, if after you divide your minutes by miles, you're left with 9.27, subtract 9 and multiply .27 by 60 to get 16.2, rounded down to 16.

4. **Put the number of seconds back with the minutes, and you have your pace.**

   Using the previous example, you end up with 9 minutes + 16 seconds = 9:16 minutes per mile

If you run on a treadmill, you may need another formula to convert miles per hour to minutes per mile. Here's how:

1. **Divide 60 by whatever miles per hour the treadmill displays.**

   For example, if the treadmill says you're running 7.1 miles per hour, divide 60 by 7.1, and you get 8.45.

2. **Subtract the minutes, so that you're left with just the decimal that represents the number of seconds and then multiply that decimal amount by 60.**

   Subtract 8 and multiply .45 by 60 to get 27.

3. **Add that number back to the minutes, and you have your pace.**

   8 minutes + 27 seconds = 8:27 minutes per mile

One important benefit of recording minutes instead of miles is that you don't know exactly how fast you run every day. Runners — especially marathoners — tend to have a compulsive streak, and if you're always keeping track of your daily running pace, you may never give yourself days to recover from your harder runs. See Chapters 6 and 7 for the particulars on balancing hard and easy training runs.

To snot or not to snot

If you train during the winter, in the rain, or during allergy season, chances are, you need to blow your nose during your run. Runners can be divided into two general categories: those who carry a tissue, which they pull out, as needed, and delicately blow their noses into, and those who don't. The non-tissue-carriers simply cover one nostril and blow, letting the wind carry their nasal mucus where it may. They then repeat with the other nostril.

You get to choose which type you'll be: The tissue carriers tend to think that their more Neanderthal counterparts are vile and disgusting, especially if they've ever been pegged by flying snot while running in a group. Let-it-fly runners think of tissue-carriers as uptight namby-pambies. Keep in mind that if you choose to carry a tissue, you have to figure out what to do with it after it's . . . er . . . used. But if you choose the nontissue approach, be sure to always check out who's downwind of you.

Starting Slowly but Surely

Whether you're taking the first run of your life, returning to the sport after a long layoff, or coming back from an injury, a great way to get into running and quickly build your mileage is to start with a combination _run/walk_. The idea is fairly simple: After you put on your running clothes, shoes, hat, watch, sunscreen, or whatever else you may need (see Chapter 2), head out the door and do the following:

1. **Run at a comfortable pace until you begin to feel fatigued.**

   The amount of time this takes varies greatly from person to person, but just run until you're pretty tired but not exhausted. That may be 5 minutes or 15 or even more, depending on your current fitness level.

   Keep in mind that, eventually, you want your training runs to consist of all running (and no walking), so the farther you can run each of your first few weeks (instead of walking), the more quickly you'll get into the meat of your training.

   For now, don't focus too much on how good — or how poor — your running technique is. Chapter 8 shows you how to improve your running technique, but getting out the door and starting to run is what's most important.

2. Slow down and start walking — briskly.

Don't stop and take a breather between the running phase and the walking phase. In order to build your endurance, you have to keep your heart rate up during the entire run/walk.

The amount of time you walk — like the time that you run — varies, based on your fitness and ability. You may need to walk only a minute or two, or you may walk just as long (or even longer) than you run.

3. When you feel like you can begin running again, start running.

Again, don't rest between the walk and the run. Simply speed up your walk and begin running.

4. Repeat as needed.

Don't worry about the ratio of running to walking; instead, think about the total time you're out there training. I recommend starting with a total of 15 to 30 minutes per day for 4 days of the first week, taking 3 days off but not 3 days in a row. (You may decide never to start back up again!) If 30 minutes seems long now, keep in mind that a marathon is 26.2 miles and will likely take you from 3 to 5 *hours* to complete!

Be sure that, while running, you keep your pace consistent. Don't start off each running phase running much faster than you can maintain and then slowing down as you begin to get tired. Keep in mind that your training prepares you for your racing, and the key to success in marathon racing is running a consistent, even pace, regardless of how good or how tired you feel. See Chapter 6 for more on running pace.

The beauty of a run/walk is that it allows your first few runs to be fairly long — say, 20 to 30 minutes — without putting excess stress on your body the first time out. If you started out with just a run (no walking allowed), you probably wouldn't be able to last more than about 10 minutes, unless you have amazing natural ability.

People with natural ability are easy to hate. I'm talking about the guy who bowls 200 his first time out or the woman who can hit 50 free throws in a row. Well, marathoning is no different. Some people can run at a good clip for 5 miles their first time out, without needing to build up their mileage with run/walks. American Jeanne Hennessey, as a newcomer to elite distance running, had been racing for only 6 months and was already running step for step with the Kenyan women, who are among the best in the world.

Although other elite runners have trained literally for decades in order to qualify for the Boston Marathon or Olympic Trials, some runners run those qualifying times in their first attempts.

Your first week of training is your honeymoon. Just get out there and do what you can. In the next few weeks, work on gradually increasing the percentage of time you spend running instead of walking and your speed.

Taking Care of Aches and Soreness

I wish that I could give you a formula for avoiding soreness completely, but if you haven't been running for a while, chances are good (100 percent good) that you'll spend your first week feeling pretty sore. The best I can do is help you manage the soreness:

- ✔ **Warm up and cool down.** Always warm up and cool down to ease into your runs or run/walks (see Chapter 5).

- ✔ **Stretch.** Using the Active Isolated Stretching method found in Chapter 5, stretch directly after each run. In addition, if you begin to feel sore in the hours after you run, stretch the sore areas again.

- ✔ **Take a cold — not a hot or even a warm — bath.** When you run, your muscles are both stretched beyond their normal limits and slightly torn. Cold water heals these small tears, while hot water (or a heating pad) doesn't because it encourages blood to flow into and pool in the sore tissues. While you may have heard that heat is better (and I agree that a warm bath is a nicer thought than an ice bath), ice or very cold water is exactly what you need to repair minor muscle tears. (Chapter 11 tells you more.)

Cold baths can be painful. Keep something warm (even a sweatshirt) over your upper body as you sit in the tub and stay in for no more than 10 minutes. Dry off completely when you're finished and put on sweatpants or running pants (see Chapter 2).

Figuring How Far and How Fast to Go the Next Month

After your first week of training, as your soreness begins to wear off, develop and stick to a running plan, both in terms of how much you run and how fast you run it.

Pacing your run

Many people, when they start training for a marathon, they figure that how *far* they run is much more important than how *fast* they run. Although this idea has some truth to it, keep the following in mind:

> How fast you race your marathon (that is, your marathon finish time) is directly related to how fast you train.

So if your goal is to *race* a marathon — that is, you want to see how fast that you can run 26.2 miles — think about how fast you train. If your goal is to *finish* a marathon, your pace is less important, but don't write off pace altogether: Most marathons establish a cutoff time, generally 5 to 7 hours, after which they close the course. If you're willing to dodge traffic after that time, you may still be able to finish, but the water stations along the course will be long gone, as will the crowds, the DJ spinning inspirational music, and your medal for finishing.

 Chapter 7 helps you figure out how to train and race faster, but give yourself 5 weeks of running before you tackle the intensive workouts. For now, if you feel as though you're running slower than you want to (and you may feel this way if a more experienced marathoner passes you on a road or trail), try this technique:

1. **Run for 10 minutes at your usual pace.**

   Don't stop after this amount of time. Keep running, but in Step 2, change the pace at which you run.

2. **After the first 10 minutes (the *warm-up* phase), look around for a tree, lightpost, fire hydrant, or other object that's down the road, but still within sight.**

3. **Increase your speed and run faster until you reach that object.**

   As soon as you get to the object you chose, slow down again to your normal training pace — or even to a pace that's a little slower than what you were running.

4. **Continue running for another couple of minutes and then choose another object and repeat Step 3.**

5. **Repeat three to ten more times.**

   Try to choose objects that are shorter and farther away, so that, for example, one is 10 seconds away while another is 25 seconds away.

6. Run 5 or 10 minutes (the *cool-down* phase) at your normal training pace.

This type of running is called a *fartlek* and has nothing to do with passing gas. It's Swedish for *speed play,* which is exactly what you're doing: playing with speed. Chapter 7 dishes the dirt on fartleks and other ways to change your training pace.

The majority of training runs aren't of this type. Instead, for all but one of your training runs each week, you want to run a steady, consistent pace, neither speeding up nor slowing down during the course of your run.

Planning your weekly mileage

In weeks two through five of your training, concentrate on gradually increasing your weekly minutes and on turning your run/walks into 100 percent runs. Table 4-1 gives you a sample 5-week training chart.

Table 4-1 Sample Training: Your First 5 Weeks in Miles

Days of the Week	Week 1	Week 2	Week 3	Week 4	Week 5
Monday	3 run/ walk	2 run	4 run/ walk	3 run	5 run/ walk
Tuesday	2 run/ walk	3 run/ walk	2 run	4.5 run/ walk	3 run
Wednesday	Rest	Rest	Rest	Rest	Rest
Thursday	2 run/ walk	2.5 run/ walk	3 run	3 run/ walk	3 run
Friday	Rest	1.5 run	2 run	2 run	4 run/ walk
Saturday	3 run/ walk	3 run	3 run/ walk	3.5 run	3 run
Sunday	Rest	Rest	Rest	Rest	Rest

Table 4-1 assumes that you've never run before or haven't run for a while and are allowing yourself 6 months to train for a marathon. If you have substantially less time than that before the big race, see

Chapter 6 for alternative training plans that increase your mileage more aggressively.

Getting a Little Help from Your (Running) Friends

If you think you'll have trouble staying motivated to run the mileage required to race a successful marathon — or if you simply find yourself getting bored on your runs — consider finding a training companion or two, even if you join up with them only 1 or 2 days per week. This section helps you figure out some ways to get in touch with other people of similar ability who are also training for a marathon.

Signing up for a marathon-training class

A *marathon-training class* is a weekly or twice-weekly meeting, led by one or more experienced runners, who help you train for a particular marathon — usually one in your geographic area. A training class usually starts meeting from 4 to 6 months before the targeted marathon, starts off with an assessment of your current fitness level and your marathon goals, and sets you up with a training plan for the marathon. Most classes meet for an hour or two to listen to experts on equipment, nutrition, racing strategy, stretching, injuries, and so on. Prices range from $25 to $100 for the entire 4- or 6-month class.

Before or after the speaker(s), the class will likely head out for a training run, often grouping people according to their per-mile training pace (a 7-minute-mile group, a 9-minute-mile group, and so on).

In order to find a marathon-training class, you first need to find a running store in your area. Now, I'm talking about a running store that sells shoes and apparel for running, and possibly for walking, too, not a general athletic store, which sells basketballs, soccer equipment, football cleats, and so on. If you have this sort of running store in your area, I'd give odds that the store offers a marathon-training class.

Not every area has a running store, but most do. Where I live, in a remote area of northern Michigan, the nearest running store is about an hour away, but it does offer marathon-training classes. Although an hour may seem like a long way to drive for a run and some marathoning advice, most classes meet just once per week, and you may actually look forward to seeing some different scenery and running with people from a different area.

Flocking together with birds of the same feather: Running clubs

Many areas of the United States, Europe, and Africa — particularly in larger cities — have *running clubs* that are made up of runners who want others to train with. Clubs vary greatly in the number of times per week the group meets, the intensity of the training, the talent of the club's members, and whether this is a training-only club or one that races together as a team.

The benefits of running clubs are twofold:

- ✔ **You get people to train with.** Motivationally, having a group of people to train with, even just 1 or 2 days per week, can really help you stay on track with your marathon training.

- ✔ **You can save money.** If your club is one that travels to races, splitting travel expenses among several people can save you money on gas and hotel expenses.

The major disadvantage of running clubs is that they often combine runners of such varying talent and experience that you may end up training alone anyway (which, obviously, diminishes the value of the club) or you may end up training more slowly than you could be, which only serves to make you a slower runner. In addition, the club members may have a variety of goals, some of which may conflict. All members may want to run the same marathon that you're planning to run. On the other hand, quite possibly no one in the club is planning to run that marathon and everyone else is focusing on 5K and 10K races. A final potential disadvantage of running clubs is that running enthusiasts who are looking for running companions but may or may not have a great deal of knowledge about the sport often start a running club. So even though the club founder is often looked to as a mentor, coach, or captain, the club founder may know squat about training for a marathon.

Be careful when deciding to join a running club. Before joining one, consider the following:

- ✔ Make sure other club members are training at or near your goal training pace (see Chapter 6). Don't just assume they are. Ask specific questions about the training pace, mileage, and workouts of the club's members.

- ✔ Find out whether others in the club are training for the same marathon you're training for.

- ✔ If the club is going to be doing certain workouts — say, mile repeats — make sure they're the right workouts for you. Check out Chapter 7 and then compare what's there to the club's expectations in terms of speedwork.

- ✔ Find out what the fee is to join the club. If the club provides you with a racing uniform or brings in speakers from time to time, you have to pay for that in your club fee, of course, but you don't want to be funding anyone's salary unless you're getting expert coaching, with an emphasis on the word *expert*.

- ✔ Make sure that if you win any sort of award or prize money at a race, you don't have to split that with the club. If that fine day comes your way, the money should be yours to keep!

Drumming up your own band

If you aren't able to find a running club in your area or if you don't find one that's right for you, you can always start your own running group with people from work, family, friends, neighbors, and so on. Like a running club, make sure this group has someone in it who is training at your pace so that you aren't running too slowly or if everyone trains faster than you, doesn't leave you training all by your lonesome self.

Your group can be official — with a name and special racing uniforms — or a low-key group that simply meets periodically and encourages one another.

Hiring a coach or trainer

If you want one-on-one advice for your training, consider hiring a coach or trainer. Doing so is expensive, but you get individual attention that you just can't get anywhere else.

To find out who may be qualified and willing to coach you, ask first at your local running store. You want someone who has coached marathoners or run in marathons and who has been successful in one or the other. If this lead turns up nothing, consider asking a collegiate coach to train you. While the marathon isn't a college running event, the training is close enough to that of 10,000-meter runners that a college coach may be able to help.

Be aware that coaches at all college divisions — but especially those in Division III — don't always know what they're doing. Sometimes, college coaches are hired just to fill a slot with no expectation of ever succeeding.

The mark of a good coach is that she always discusses and takes into account your background, experience, current fitness level, and goals before issuing a training plan. Steer clear of anyone who asks you to pay for a training plan that isn't individualized — except for this book, of course. If I could find out your background, by gosh, by golly, I'd customize the training plans in Chapters 6 and 7!

Chapter 5

Stretching, Warming Up, and Cooling Down

● ●

In This Chapter

▶ Discovering when and how you should stretch

▶ Finding a new way to stretch: Active Isolated Stretching

▶ Understanding the many benefits of being a flexible runner

▶ Knowing how to warm up and cool down during your runs

● ●

*S*tretching — the dirtiest word in running. Even runners who do everything right (from eating right to doing sit-ups every day) usually detest stretching.

But this chapter gives you something completely different: a new way of stretching that makes your body feel fantastic, even after an especially hard or long day of training. You get step-by-step instructions for stretching all the major running muscles, plus some other tips on how to gently warm up your body for running and cool it down afterwards.

The Great Stretching Debate (s)

For a long time, runners understood some unchallenged rules about stretching and flexibility:

   ✔ All runners are inflexible, and nothing can change that.

   ✔ Stretch before you run to avoid injury.

   ✔ Hold all your stretches for at least 30 seconds.

Well, not so fast. While some runners have succeeded with these rules, others have suffered chronic injuries or have never felt quite "stretched enough."

So perhaps it's time for some new rules about stretching and flexibility — rules that elite runners around the world are beginning to embrace. If you're satisfied with the way that you've been stretching for years, keep it up — traditional (or *static*) stretching definitely works for some people. But if you're dissatisfied with your stretching options, consider these new stretching principles:

- ✔ **Although many runners start out inflexible, with some simple coaching in how to stretch properly, they can soon become extremely flexible.** Maybe you won't be the next Nadia Comaneci, but you can become far more flexible than you are. (For more stretching information, see the following "Understanding Active Isolated Stretching" section.)

- ✔ **Stretch after you run — not before — to avoid injury.** Do, however, warm up during the first few minutes of your run. (See the "Warming Up to Your Run" section, later in this chapter.) In addition, before you do any sort of speedwork (see Chapter 7), warm up for 10 to 20 minutes, stretch, and then begin the workout.

- ✔ **Hold your stretches for 2 seconds.** Two seconds? Yes — 2 seconds! See the following section for the lowdown on Active Isolated Stretching, the greatest advancement in stretching since . . . well, the invention of stretching.

Understanding Active Isolated Stretching

Active Isolated Stretching (AIS), a method of stretching developed by Aaron L. Mattes, a *kinesiologist* (a person who studies human muscular movements), is a pretty radical shift from the stretching you were probably taught in a physical education class. Instead of stretching to a general area — maybe bringing your forehead somewhere close to your knee when seated on the ground — and holding for 30 seconds, Active Isolated Stretching requires two important components, which I cover in the next sections.

You can find out more about Mattes' stretching methods and books at www.stretchingusa.com. Another great book by Jim and Phil Wharton, aptly named *The Whartons' Stretch Book* (Random House), takes you step-by-step through an Active Isolated Stretching routine. In addition, the SportsStretch program (www.sportsstretch.com) offers a complete package of a stretching rope, book, and other accessories.

If you want to see this method in action, take a look at any of the best Division-I cross-country and track teams in the nation. More than half of them have begun using this method just in the last year or two.

Active stretching

With AIS, the stretch is held for 2 seconds and then released. The stretch is then repeated for a total of eight or ten repetitions, and each entire set can be repeated, as well.

What Mattes discovered was that, after 2 seconds of stretching, the *opposing muscle* — that is, the muscle that's on the other side of the muscle you're stretching, assists the muscle you're trying to stretch. For example, when you're stretching your *hamstrings* (the muscles on the back of your upper leg), after 2 seconds, the *quadriceps* (the muscles on the front of your upper leg) begin to "help" the hamstrings with the stretch. What this means is that the hamstring stops being stretched very well after 2 seconds.

AIS makes you much more flexible than traditional stretching because you stretch only until the opposing muscles begin to "help out," and then you repeat the same, 2-second stretch several times. Suppose you stretch your hamstrings the old-fashioned way for 30 seconds. You're getting 2 good seconds of stretching out of that, and if you repeat the stretch several times, you get a great stretch. More people, however, move on to another stretch, say the calves, after holding the hamstring stretch for 30 seconds. With AIS, you stretch the hamstrings for 2 seconds, release the stretch and relax your leg for a few seconds, stretch again for 2 seconds, release again, and so on. So, if you do two sets of eight repetitions, you stretch the hamstring muscles for 32 total seconds — far longer than the 2-second stretch you'd get from the old 30-second stretch, which really had only about 2 seconds of effective stretching.

Isolating the stretch

With AIS, you isolate a specific muscle and stretch it. You don't just get close — you follow specific instructions. Don't worry. In this chapter, I show you — through the use of photos and instructions — how to get to those exact positions.

Flexing the benefits

The result of using AIS on a daily basis is astonishing:

- ✔ When beginning each day's run, your body experiences almost no stiffness.

- ✔ Your recovery from races, workouts, and long runs is faster than without AIS.

- ✔ You radically reduce your chances of injury.

- ✔ Your racing times improve much faster than they would without AIS.

- ✔ You'll be able to compete much later in life than you would otherwise.

Setting up for the stretch

Have you ever been warned against "bouncing" when you stretch? It's a good warning. AIS isn't about bouncing; instead, you get into position, pull on your *stretching rope* (a half-inch-thick nylon rope that you can get from any hardware store) to get the required stretch, hold for 2 full seconds (count "Elephant one, elephant two") and release so that your leg can relax for a few seconds.

With AIS, you never hold for less than 2 seconds, and you always allow your leg to fully relax after each 2-second hold.

To get your own stretching rope, head on down to your local hardware store and order 10 feet of nylon braided rope that's ½ to ¾ of an inch thick. (Don't get rope any smaller in diameter, or the rope will cut your feet.)

Don't be afraid to stretch each side of your body in different amounts. If your left hamstring is tight, put it through an extra set of hamstring stretches. So, although you want to do a predetermined number of repetitions on each leg (such as one set of 10 or two sets of 8), you can add a few more repetitions to tight muscles, as needed.

Mapping out your bod

Before you begin stretching, you need to know where your muscles are located. Use Figure 5-1 as a guide to help you identify the various muscles that you use when you run.

Becoming a believer

I spent nearly all of my collegiate and post-collegiate years injured, suffering various muscle tears, ligament and tendon strains, and stress fractures in the bones of my lower legs. When I was in my late 20s, a specialist told me that I should give up running and take up some other sport — I'd never be healed enough to compete again. By age 35, I was running only as a fitness runner (not racing or doing any sort of speed work); I hobbled out of bed every morning and never gave a moment's thought to competing. I suffered a new injury every 3 or 4 months, without fail.

Finally, I had a nagging hip pain that became so severe that I couldn't run anymore. A friend suggested that I call Steve Kramer, an Indianapolis-based massage therapist and Active Isolated Stretching (AIS) specialist, who spent the initial visit teaching me AIS. I immediately bought a rope and began stretching after every run. Within a week, I no longer hobbled in the morning. Whereas before, I needed 20 minutes to warm up when I ran, after beginning AIS, I felt great throughout the run — even the first few minutes. Within about 6 weeks, the hip injury was completely gone, and all my other aches and pains cleared up. I found ways to stretch my calves and shin muscles such that stress fractures weren't even a possibility.

Within 3 months of beginning AIS, I started thinking about competing again. I began to gradually raise my mileage to between 70 and 90 miles per week, which I've held for 18 months with only a few days off, without suffering a single injury. Even if all the scientific tests in the world didn't convince me of the power of AIS, my own experience with this stretching routine have made me a diehard believer. It's worth a shot for your own training, isn't it?

Extending Yourself

No more talk: This section gives you step-by-step instructions for trying out (and eventually mastering) AIS. You can approach this material in two ways:

- ✔ Peruse the entire section — carefully reading all the instructions and looking at the photos — before trying the stretches.

- ✔ Read the instructions and look at the photos for one stretch and then put the book down and try that stretch. Repeat for all the stretches.

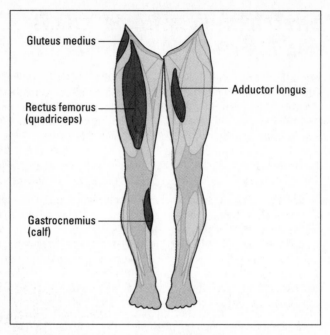

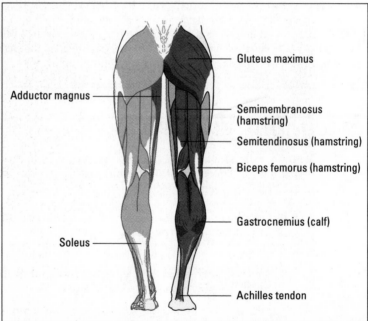

Figure 5-1: Front and rear views of your major running muscles.

Stretching your hams, quads, and hips

Arguably, *hamstrings* (the muscles on the back of your upper legs) and *quadriceps* (your thigh muscles; also called *quads*) are the most important muscles to a marathoner. Those two sets of muscles bear the brunt of your training and must always be relaxed and flexible if you're going to reach your potential.

In addition, hip injuries are on the rise among distance runners, but stretching your *hip rotators* (the muscles that serve to twist the hips) every day keeps you from getting hurt.

Hamstring stretches (straight knee)

Using Figure 5-2 as your guide, stretch your hamstring as follows:

Figure 5-2: Hamstring stretch (straight knee).

1. **Wrap your rope around your left foot and lie on your back, keeping your right leg straight.**

   You can also bend your right knee, if that's more comfortable. Within a few days or weeks of doing this stretch, you'll be able to straighten it comfortably.

2. **Straighten your left leg, lock your left knee, and using your rope, pull your left leg up toward your chest.**

   Don't bend your left knee — keep it locked.

3. **Hold for 2 seconds, and then release, allowing your left leg to relax for a few seconds.**

4. **Repeat Steps 2 and 3 for a total of eight to ten repetitions.**

   If necessary, do an additional set of eight to ten reps.

With your foot position straight (see Figure 5-3a and 5-4a), this stretches your central hamstring muscle. To get additional stretch in your hamstrings, add the following variations:

✔ **Inner hamstring:** Turn your left foot in and follow the steps just given. See Figure 5-3b.

✔ **Outer hamstring:** Turn your left foot out and follow the steps just given. See Figure 5-4b.

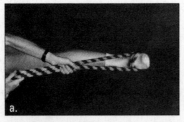 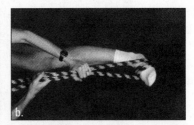

Figure 5-3: Hamstring stretch variations (Figure 5-3a stretches the central hamstring, 5-3b stretches the inner hamstring).

Figure 5-4: Hamstring stretch variations (Figure 5-4a stretches the central hamstring, 5-4b stretches the outer hamstring).

Quadriceps stretch

Your quads carry much of the burden of running long distances. If they tighten up — or worse, become injured — you may have a tough time ever getting to that marathon finish line. Work through the following steps to see how you can get a fantastic — albeit funny looking — stretch in your quads (see Figure 5-5):

Figure 5-5: Quadriceps stretch.

1. **Wrap your rope around your right foot and lie on your left side.**

2. **Bend your left leg and pull it up toward your chest and chin.**

   The quadriceps of your left leg should be parallel to the top of your head.

3. **Bend your right leg and pull your right foot toward your butt.**

4. **Pull the rope over your head and hold for 2 seconds.**

5. **Release, allowing your right leg to relax for a few seconds.**

6. **Repeat Steps 2 through 5 for a total of eight to ten reps.**

   If necessary, do an additional set of eight to ten reps.

Hip rotator stretch (internal)

Even if your hips aren't causing you problems, loosening your hip rotators (using the method shown in Figure 5-6) can make you a faster, more powerful runner.

Figure 5-6: Hip rotator stretch (internal).

1. **Wrap your rope around your right foot and lie on your back.**

2. **Keeping your left leg straight, cross your left leg so that it's right in line or just across the midline of your body.**

   Your *midline* is an imaginary line running from smack between your eyes all the way down your body.

3. **Bend your right leg 90 degrees and pull your right leg toward the opposite shoulder.**

4. **Hold for 2 seconds, and then release, allowing your right leg to relax for a few seconds.**

5. **Repeat Steps 2 through 4 for a total of eight to ten reps.**

   If necessary, do an additional set of eight to ten reps.

To get an additional stretch move your right quad so that it crosses the midline and is at a 45-degree angle (see Figure 5-7).

Hip rotator stretch (external)

This stretch is a mirror image of the internal hip rotator stretch. Be sure to stretch both your external *and* internal hip rotators to avoid an imbalance in your hips. Use Figure 5-8 to guide you as you try this stretch:

Figure 5-7: Hip rotator stretch (internal) with angle.

Figure 5-8: Hip rotator stretch (external).

1. **Wrap your rope around your left foot and lie on your back.**

2. **Position your right leg so that it's straight and away from the midline of your body.**

3. **Bend your left leg 90 degrees and pull your left leg toward the same shoulder.**

4. **Hold for 2 seconds, and then release, allowing your left leg to relax for a few seconds.**

5. **Repeat Steps 2 through 4 for a total of eight to ten reps.**

   If necessary, do an additional set of eight to ten reps.

Like the internal stretch, you can add a second stretch that moves your left quad farther away from your midline and puts it at a 45-degree angle (see Figure 5-9).

Figure 5-9: Hip rotator stretch (internal) with angle.

Hip adductor (groin) stretch

Distance runners often pull their *groin muscles* (that's the tender area where your thigh meets your abdomen), especially on icy winter days or on wet ground after a rainstorm. By stretching your groin daily, you're less likely to sustain an injury, even if you do slip on ice.

1. **Wrap your rope around your right foot and around the back of your leg, lie on your back, and straighten your right leg.**

2. **Position your left leg so that it's straight and away from the midline of your body.**

3. **Pull your right leg away from the midline of your body.**

   Keep your right leg straight and knee locked as you pull your leg outward. You know you've reached the right position when you feel a distinct pull on your groin. This position varies greatly from person to person, so do it by feel instead of by photo (which is why you don't see a photo here).

4. **Hold for 2 seconds, and then release, allowing your right leg to relax for a few seconds.**

5. **Repeat Steps 2 through 4 for a total of eight to ten reps.**

   If necessary, do an additional set of eight to ten reps.

Gaining flexibility in your calves, shins, and feet

Many runners — those who aren't stretching the way AIS advises — have trouble with their calves, shins, and feet. Your feet and lower legs get plenty of pounding as you train for a marathon, so you need to treat them well.

Calf stretches

To keep your calves (also called the *gastrocnemius muscles*) loose and supple, do these stretches (see Figure 5-10):

1. **Sit up and wrap your rope around your left foot.**

2. **Keep your right leg bent or straight — it doesn't matter.**

3. **Lock your left knee and pull your left foot straight back toward your chest.**

4. **Lean your upper body forward (toward your calf) about 10 degrees and hold for 2 seconds.**

5. **Release, allowing your left leg to relax for a few seconds.**

6. **Repeat Steps 2 through 5 for a total of eight to ten reps.**

   If necessary, do an additional set of eight to ten reps.

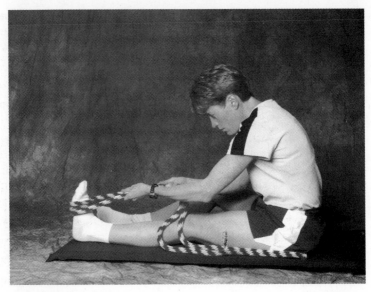

Figure 5-10: Calf stretch.

You also want to include the two following variations in your stretching routine:

✔ **Evertor:** Rotate (as opposed to angling) your left foot inward and follow the preceding steps. See Figure 5-11. Okay, realistically, you can't see much difference between Figures 5-10 and 5-11. Look closely, though, at the foot and see how the foot is rotated slightly inward (toward the inside of the leg) in Figure 5-11. That's the subtle rotation you're going for.

✔ **Invertor:** Rotate (don't angle) your left foot outward and follow the preceding steps.

Soleus stretch

The stretch for the *soleus* (the muscle that covers your lower calf and attaches to the Achilles tendon, which runs down your heel) is a simple one that doesn't use the rope (see Figure 5-12 for an example):

1. **Sit up with your left leg straight.**

2. **Bending your right knee, bring the foot of your right leg as close as possible to your butt.**

3. **Pull back on the ball of the right foot and hold for 2 seconds.**

Figure 5-11: Everter (calf) stretch.

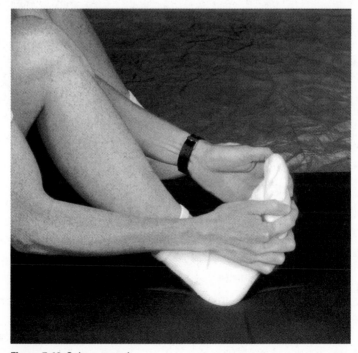

Figure 5-12: Soleus stretch.

   4. **Release, allowing your right leg to relax for a few
seconds.**

   5. **Repeat Steps 2 through 4 for a total of eight to ten reps.**

     If necessary, do an additional set of eight to ten repetitions.

Achilles stretch

This stretch (see Figure 5-13) is nearly identical to the soleus
stretch, but stretches the Achilles tendon (that tender area running up the back of your foot), which is difficult to get to in any
other way:

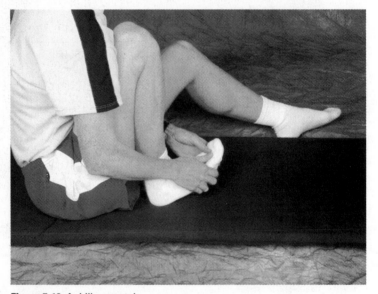

Figure 5-13: Achilles stretch.

   1. **Sit up with your left leg straight.**

   2. **Bend your right leg 90 degrees.**

     You should still be able to reach your toes with your hands.

   3. **Pull back on the ball of the right foot and hold for
2 seconds.**

   4. **Release, allowing your right leg to relax for a few
seconds.**

5. Repeat Steps 2 through 4 for a total of eight to ten reps.

If necessary, do an additional set of eight to ten repetitions.

Ankle stretches

The ankle stretch is like the soleus stretch, but in addition to the foot being stretched backward, it's also stretched forward and is rotated left and right (all held for 2 seconds each). See Figure 5-14.

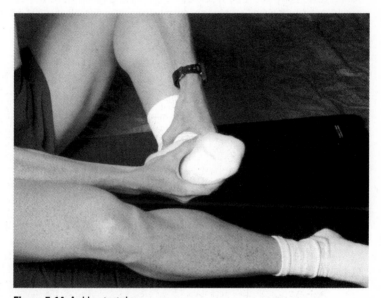

Figure 5-14: Ankle stretches.

Toe stretches

Although you probably wouldn't think to stretch your toes, this stretch makes your feet feel terrific. Because the toe joints are so small, the movement is subtle; however, the idea is to isolate each joint of the toe and stretch it forward, backward, left, and right, all for counts of 2 seconds.

Stretching your butt and lower back

Until AIS was invented, your butt muscles (also called *glutes,* which rhymes with *boots* and is short for *gluteus maximus*) and back muscles were notoriously difficult to stretch. No more! Add the following two stretches to your routine.

The importance of sit-ups for marathoners

Most injuries occur because of an imbalance between opposing muscles. This means that you pull a hamstring muscle if your hamstring is significantly weaker than your quadriceps or vice versa; you'll get shin splints or calf pulls if your shin muscles are significantly weaker than your calves, and so on.

Although running gets nearly all your body very fit, one area that it doesn't help much is the abdomen. You probably see plenty of runners who run plenty but still have a gut. And this is also part of the reason why so many distance runners struggle with back pain: the imbalance between the abdomen and the lower back.

The solution is to add sit-ups to your daily routine. In addition to doing sit-ups during circuits (see Chapter 7), start doing 50, 100, or more after each run. As you strengthen your abdominal muscles, you greatly reduce your risk of back injury.

Butt stretch

If you ever experienced a butt cramp during a run, you know that they're among the most painful cramps that you can experience. A strong, flexible butt helps you run hills and run fast (and has the added bonus of looking good, too!). Use Figure 5-15 to guide you in this non-rope stretch:

1. **Lie on your back with your left leg straight.**

2. **Bend and raise your right leg.**

3. **Place one hand on your right knee and place your other hand behind your right hamstrings.**

4. **Gently push your right leg toward your left shoulder, using your hands to assist.**

5. **Hold for 2 seconds and release, allowing your butt to relax for a few seconds.**

6. **Repeat Steps 2 through 5 for a total of eight to ten reps.**

   If necessary, do an additional set of eight to ten reps.

This stretch also gets your *gluteus medius* (a direct translation is your "middle butt," but it's actually much closer to the hip than the butt. Tightness in the gluteus medius can feel very much like a hip injury.

Lower-back stretch

This stretch, shown in Figure 5-16, gives your lower back (also called the lumbar) a good stretch without using a rope:

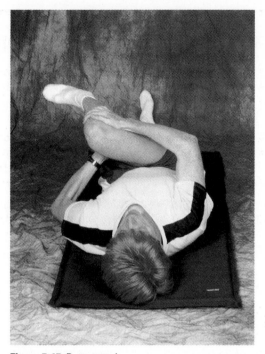

Figure 5-15: Butt stretch.

Figure 5-16: Lower-back stretch.

Working out kinks in your neck

Although stretching your arms and neck isn't as critical to staying injury-free as stretching your legs is, you may still want to work out soreness and kinks in your neck that may come from sleeping poorly, driving, or working in an uncomfortable position at work.

To stretch your neck, use the principles of AIS but without the rope. Simply lay your hand on top of your head and use your hand to move your neck to the right, bringing your ear down to your shoulder (or getting as close as you can). Hold for 2 seconds and release, repeating for a total of eight to ten reps. Repeat on the left side.

Another set of neck stretches is similar, but this time, you're stretching at an angle. Using your hand on top of your head, move your head forward and at a 45-degree angle to your right. Hold for 2 seconds and release, repeating for total of eight to ten reps. Do the same on your left. You can also do the same stretches but move your head *back* and at a 45-degree angle to the right (and then to the left).

1. **Sit up with both knees slightly bent and spread wide.**

2. **Place your hands around your neck.**

3. **Rotate your upper body so that your elbows both face left and then bend from your waist toward the floor.**

   Do not bend and then rotate. Instead, sit upright, rotate, and then bend your upper body toward the floor.

4. **Hold for 2 seconds and release, coming back up to a sitting position to allow your lower back to relax for a few seconds.**

5. **Repeat Steps 2 through 4 for a total of eight to ten reps.**

6. **Repeat the entire stretch on the right side.**

   If necessary, do an additional set of eight to ten repetitions on each side.

Warming Up to Your Run

Although you don't want to stretch before you run, you do want to use the first part of each run to warm your body up. This means that you don't charge out your door at breakneck speed. Instead, spend the first 8 to 10 minutes of your run at an easy pace, allowing your legs, back, and arms to warm up gently. On certain days, especially the day after your longest run, you may feel stiff and sore. (Regular stretching, however, eliminates most of your early-run stiffness.) Use the early part of the run to work out all those kinks.

When the first 8 minutes are up, begin gradually increasing your pace until — at about 10 minutes into the run — you're running as fast as you need to be. (See Chapter 6 to find out exactly how fast that should be.) You then maintain that pace until you have about 5 minutes left to go in your run.

Cooling Down After Your Run or Workout

Middle-school and high-school coaches across the country have been — and still are — teaching kids to sprint for the last minute or more of their distance runs and then stop, walk into the school to get a drink, and go home. My guess is that they're hoping to develop a *kick* (that's a late-race sprint) in their young runners. All they're doing, however, is putting their kids at risk of injury.

If you run — whether it's a standard distance run, a workout, or *strides* (short fast sprints; see Chapter 8) — and then don't cool down (by stretching, walking, or doing some additional running), you finish your running day with tight muscles. These muscles then continue to tighten throughout the evening and night, so that you'll wake up with aching legs. After enough days of this, you may have a full-fledged injury that keeps you from training and racing.

To avoid developing an injury from tight muscles, do the following:

- ✔ **Use the last 5 minutes of your distance runs as a cool down.** Just as you warm up for the first few minutes of your distance runs, cool down in the same way. When you're 5 minutes from finishing your run, pull the throttle back a little and slow down. This helps your body cool down naturally. Follow your run with a full stretch.

- ✔ **Don't sprint the last minute of your run.** Sprinting for one minute at the end of some of your runs doesn't develop your speed. Workouts (see Chapter 7), strides, and drills (see Chapter 8) develop speed and running efficiency. Always run a short cool-down run after a workout and always walk a bit after doing strides and drills. After both, stretch immediately.

- ✔ **Walk around the block after your run.** This is an alternative to using the last 5 minutes of your run as a cool down. Instead of slowing down the pace for the last 5 minutes, take a short, slow walk after you finish running. After you walk, stretch.

✔ *Always* **stretch directly after your run.** Don't get something to eat, run an errand, or watch some TV directly after you run. Instead, walk into your home or office, get your stretching rope out, and go through your stretches. How good you feel on the next day's run and how your running begins to improve overall will amaze you. Make a habit of never running without stretching.

Part II
Taking Your Running a Stride Farther

The 5th Wave   By Rich Tennant

ⒸRICHTENNANT

"She's a great motivator on my speedwork runs."

In this part . . .

This part is the most technical of the book, explaining how to build up your mileage and eventually add speedwork and strengthening workouts to your routine. You also find out how to improve your running technique. (Yes, you can run with good technique or bad technique, just like any other sport!) In Chapter 9, you find out how to tell good carbohydrates from bad ones and good fats from not so good. Chapter 9 also offers you information on energy gels and the lowdown on how much water you really need to drink each day.

Chapter 6

Developing a Mileage Base

In This Chapter

▶ Knowing what mileage means

▶ Finding out whether LSD is good for you

▶ Deciding whether to schedule days off

▶ Customizing training plans

*M*ileage (that is, the number of miles you run each week), along with the length of your longest runs each week, are the two most important parts of your marathon training. Other aspects of your training are important, too, but even if you do all the workouts discussed in Chapter 7, improve your running efficiency exactly as described in Chapter 8, and eat perfectly (see Chapter 9), yet don't run many miles or have a very long weekly run, you won't be able to run a successful marathon. Miles are to marathon training as beer is to bowling.

The bottom line is that you have to run many miles every week to train for a long race like the 26.2-mile marathon. This chapter discusses how mileage fits into your overall training plan, how to add to your current weekly mileage, how long your longest runs should be, what pace to run those miles, and when (or whether) to take days off. As a bonus, you get several sample training plans that you can use and customize for your own marathon training.

Getting More for Your Mileage

Most coaches and distance runners agree about three important phases of training — building your base, strength-speed, and sharpening.

Building your base

Think of a *base* as the bottom of a training pyramid. You build a base by running many miles, and as you progress up the training pyramid, you rely on the fitness that you gained while building your base to run races. If you try to run a marathon without having built a base, your training pyramid collapses, and you won't finish, or you'll get injured.

In this phase, you increase your mileage to the level at which you want to train consistently. (This level depends on how much time you have before your marathon, how much time you're willing to put into your training each week, and how much mileage you think your body can handle.) You build up gradually, adding no more than 10 percent of your previous week's mileage to the next week. That means if you run 30 miles one week, you can increase to 33 the next week.

I suggest totaling your mileage in minutes, not miles. Although the two systems aren't much different, by training in minutes, all you need is a stopwatch: You don't have to measure the distance of every route you run. See Chapter 4 for details.

The base-building phase can last from 6 weeks to 18 months, depending on how much time you have. And while you're in this phase, keep in mind that you experience plenty of muscle soreness as your body becomes used to running at a higher mileage.

Increasing strength and speed

In this phase, you usually continue to run the mileage that you reached in the last week of building your base and add on some basic speed workouts (see Chapter 7). You may also enter some short races (5Ks or 10Ks) or do a tune-up race of 10 miles or a half-marathon (see Chapters 13 and 19). The strength-speed phase is physically demanding because you're teaching your body to train and race faster than it has been used to training. This phase usually lasts from 4 to 12 weeks.

Sharpening before your race

This is the phase in which you cut back a bit on your mileage (a process called *tapering* that's designed to make you feel fresh going into your marathon), do shorter but more intense speed workouts, and generally prepare yourself for the big day. This phase ends with your most important run: your marathon.

This phase usually lasts from 3 to 8 weeks. You may feel better during this phase than during the other two because your mileage and workouts are less demanding.

You can find several dozen different running philosophies. Most stick to this rough outline, but every coach puts a unique slant on it. If the person who's teaching your marathon-training class or coaching you has some different advice, listen to it and choose the method that makes sense to you.

Doing LSD (Long, Slow Distance)

American runners in the 1970s coined the term *LSD* — long, slow distance — that effectively made fun of the drug culture in the United States but emphasized the joys of running. Runners talked about "doing LSD" and then laughed heartily. Funny guys, those '70s runners.

The idea behind LSD was that the bulk of your running focused on distance runs that weren't overly strenuous: They were long, but you ran them at a comfortable pace. And runners who used this technique were able to run well over 100 miles per week because 5 or 6 out of 7 days, they ran 15- to 20-mile, easy-pace runs.

The term lasted for a couple of decades and then fell out of favor in the '90s because of the emphasis on *slow*. Another idea replaced LSD, which is "Your training pace determines your racing pace." Runners began to focus on *quality* (the pace of runs) instead of *quantity* (the number of miles). The term *junk miles* was tossed around: Any mileage that was too slow was considered useless to your training.

So which is right? Ask any group of coaches or distance runners, and you'll probably get a split decision with half supporting each side. But they're *both* right. You absolutely need to run an abundance of miles to run a good marathon, but you also have to watch your pace. Run too slowly on the majority of your runs, and you train your body to run slowly. But, as a marathoner, if you try to run faster, high-quality runs most days of the week, you end up injured or fatigued, or you'll be fast and efficient for the first third or half of a marathon but unable to endure 26.2 miles. What you need is a balance between the two.

Striking a balance

The perfect balance would seem to be long, *fast* distance, right? If you can run 120 miles per week (yeah, right!) and do it at a fast pace, you'll be one of the best marathoners in the world, won't you? In theory, fast distance runs seem like a great idea, and many a would-be-great runner has tried this approach, but most end up injured or just plain worn out.

Long, fast distance every day doesn't work because your body needs rest in order to become stronger. Whenever you do anything that your body perceives as hard (fast running or long runs), you tear your muscles a little bit. This is a good thing because as that tearing heals, your muscles become stronger. So you want to push your body in small doses and then give it plenty of time to heal. How much time? For every day that you push your body hard in a fast, shorter workout (see Chapter 7), in a race, or in a very long run, you need 1 — or better yet, 2 and sometimes 3 — days of recovery. In this context, *recovery* doesn't necessarily mean time off, nor does it have to mean cross-training with other sports. If you chose to take days off or cross-train in order to recover from hard runs, fine. But a *recovery run* is an option, too (and, in my opinion, a better option): This type of training simply means that you allow your body to run at whatever pace it needs to run (that is, slowly) in order to feel good again and get ready for the next hard dose of training.

Every recovery run is sandwiched between harder, faster training days (such as those described in Chapter 7) or very long runs (such as those discussed in the "Planning a weekly long run" section later in this chapter).

Putting yourself through the paces

Your training pace during your distance runs dictates your racing pace. Ideally, you want to keep your training pace during your distance runs from 1–1½ minutes slower than your goal marathon pace. (If you don't already have a race pace in mind, see Chapter 13 for more on establishing your goal marathon pace. Also, Chapter 7 gives you a table that converts total marathon times to training and workout paces.)

To determine your per-mile pace, simply measure out a couple of miles by driving your running route in your car and noting certain landmarks (a sign, an unusual tree, or a house) at the mile markers. On your next run, glance at your watch as you begin and end each mile and see how fast you're running. You don't have to run a measured route every day. One or 2 days per week, run a route on which you've measured a few miles and keep track of your pace on your watch. Before long, you'll begin to *learn pace,* which means that you can tell what per-mile pace you're running without even looking at your watch.

Note that car odometers are notoriously inconsistent and may be off by as much as 10 percent. A better bet is to borrow or buy a mileage wheel. (See Chapter 4 for details.)

Suppose that you want to run 8-minute miles throughout your marathon. Some days, you may train at an 8:50 per-mile pace. Other days, you may be exhausted from a workout or long run the day before (or just from a bad night of sleep or a stressful day at work) and train at a 10:20 pace. Is it preferable for you to speed up your 10:20-pace runs? Well, technically yes, but you also have to listen to your body. Some days, if you're especially tired and sore, you may just need to get out the door and run for 5 or 6 miles at whatever pace you can muster. And on those occasional days, running outside of that 1–1½ minute range is okay. (For more on running times, see the Cheat Sheet at the beginning of this book.)

However, if you find that more of your runs are at a 10:20 per-mile pace than at 8:50 or 9:30, you have to consider whether

- ✔ **You're training too slowly to meet your goal marathon time and have to speed up your distance runs.** This is a tricky proposition, though. Some marathoners do train too slowly and never come close to achieving their potential. However, training too fast during your distance runs can quickly lead to injury because your body wants to go slower in order to recover, and you're not letting it.

- ✔ **You're training too slowly to meet your goal marathon time and have to rethink your goals.** Another way of thinking of this is that your training pace is actually right on target, but your goal race pace is unrealistically fast.

The good news is that, as you gain experience as a runner, your training pace tends to decrease naturally. (Note that _decreasing_ pace means that your per-mile time goes down. _Increasing_ your pace increases your per-mile time, and, thus, means that you're running slower.) Your first year of training, you may run 11-minute miles; after a few years of consistent training and racing, good eating habits, strides and drills, periodic workouts, _circuit training_ (strength training that's specifically meant to build running muscles separated by bursts of fast running — see Chapter 7), and so on, you may find that you run 9-minute miles or faster! This is the main reason that people race more than one marathon and continue to train year after year. They instinctively know that they can do better in the future, given a little more experience and training.

Planning a weekly long run

Each week, you want one training run to be longer than the rest. When you're first starting out, perhaps most of your runs are 30 minutes, and your long run is 45 minutes. That's fine. Before running a marathon, though, you want your long weekly run to be — are you ready for this? — about 20 miles, which at 12-minute miles is 4 hours; at 8-minute miles, it's 2 hours and 40 minutes.

In order to run this long (without the support of a marathon volunteer staff to give you water and stop traffic), you have to do a bit of planning. Somehow, you have to get yourself some water and, if possible, energy gels (see Chapter 9), during the run. You have three options for this:

✔ **Have someone meet you during the run.** This is my favorite option, but it does require a cooperative friend or family member and some advance planning. You simply arrange a time for the person to meet you. Be sure to share your route with the person — and don't change it during the run — so that, if you're running slower or faster than you anticipated, your friend can still find you. He then hands you a water bottle and/or gel pack as you run by and collects the empties in another mile or so.

✔ **Set up your own aid stations in advance.** This option requires both extra time on your part to go around and leave water or gels at certain locations and a trusted community: You don't want your water, sports drink, or energy gels stolen. Some people stock the mailboxes of their friends along the route. This is fine if your long run is on a Sunday, but you don't want to interfere with postal delivery on other days!

✔ **Carry it with you.** I don't like this option for water, although I understand this may be necessary in some situations. Each gallon of water weighs about eight pounds, so even if you carry only a quart (32 ounces), you're still carrying two extra pounds for, potentially, a few hours. Would you carry a 2-pound weight for 10 or 20 miles?

For energy gels, however, carrying them along isn't a bad option. See Chapter 9 for various ways to carry gel packs.

You can certainly run a marathon without having consistently run 20-milers week in and week out for a few months. But don't run a marathon if you haven't attempted at least one long run of 20 miles in the weeks leading up to the marathon because you'll almost surely injure yourself.

Your long run is your chance to mimic race conditions. Try to schedule your long runs at the same time of day as your marathon and experiment with what to wear, what sort of fluids to take (most marathons offer both a noncarbonated sports drink and water), and whether energy gels work for you. If you don't plan to stop running during the marathon to drink water or consume gels, don't stop running during your long run. Try as much as possible to make your long runs exactly like your marathon.

The more long runs you can complete before your marathon, the less likely you'll be to *hit the wall,* a phenomenon in which you feel pretty good before the 20- or 22-mile mark of a marathon but then suddenly feel so terrible that you aren't sure that you can go on. This wall is partly truth and partly urban legend. The "truth" part is that, if you don't run enough long runs and don't run *consistent* weekly mileage (mileage that doesn't vary much from week to week) throughout your marathon training, you'll likely struggle late in the race. The "myth" part is that this terrible phenomenon doesn't have to happen to you. With the right training, you can avoid hitting the wall altogether.

Planning a weekly short run

I highly recommend following your weekly 20-miler with a short day: 3 or 4 miles. Your weekly short run is something to look forward to, both physically and mentally, and allows your body to recover quickly from your long run the day before. You may be sore the day after your long run, so let your short run be as slow and easy as you need it to be.

Always stretch after every run (see Chapter 5), even if it's a short one!

Taking Days Off — or Not!

The question I'm probably asked most often is whether I take a day off every week or so. My answer is "No": I take only 5 to 10 days off per *year.* I don't necessarily advise you to take this approach — keep in mind that part of my living comes from running. But just so you know my rationale, here it is: If taking a day off is an option every day of my life, I figure I'll use that option far more than I should. I don't, for example, make sleeping an option — I make sure I get 9 to 12 hours of sleep per night so that my body can recover from all the stress of training and racing. I also don't make brushing my teeth an option — it's an everyday habit.

If you take a healthy approach to running by scheduling a hard day followed by 1, 2, or 3 recovery days and a long run followed by a short, easy run, I don't believe your body needs days off. In fact, I think the human body responds better when you do an activity regularly than when you do it sporadically. In addition, I always feel sluggish and stiff the day after a day off. On the other hand, I almost always feel great the day after a run that I was thinking of skipping. So if I come across a day when I feel terrible, I start out my morning with a short run at whatever pace I can muster, followed by a good stretch. If I feel better later in the day, I run again. Only once in a great while, when I just need a mental break from training, do I take a day off.

Cross-training with a pool and snow

I can think of only two types of *cross-training* (doing other sports 1 or 2 days per week) that may actually improve your running. One is running in a pool (see a detailed description in Chapter 12), which is an excellent way to stay fit if you're ever injured. It's also a good way to train 1 or 2 days per week if you're not injured but know that you tend to get hurt from running on hard surfaces (see Chapter 10).

The second way, *snowshoe running* or *snowshoeing*, works only if you live in a snowy area during the winter. A fairly new sport, snowshoeing is catching on with runners who live through cold winters: The idea is that you run through snow with snowshoes on. Snowshoes for running are designed so that you can use a normal running motion: You wear running shoes, and the snowshoes attach only to your forefoot, so your foot bends naturally. A good pair of lightweight snowshoes runs from $100 to $400, but they'll last a lifetime. Look for snowshoes that are 8 inches wide by 25 inches long. If your snowshoes are any smaller, you risk not meeting the minimum requirements for snowshoe races. You probably won't find them at your neighborhood sporting goods store, so check out the following Web sites or call these companies:

✓ **Atlas:** www.atlassnowshoe.com; 888-48-ATLAS

✓ **Cresent Moon:** www.crescentmoonsnowshoes.com; 800-587-7655

✓ **Havlick:** www.havlicksnowshoe.com; 800-TOP-SHOE

✓ **Northern Lites:** www.northernlites.com; 800-360-LITE

✓ **Redfeather:** www.redfeather.com; 800-525-0081

✓ **Tubbs:** www.tubbssnowshoes.com; 800-882-2748

✓ **Yuba:** www.yubashoes.com; 800-598-9822

You can also try various models by visiting a local ski lodge that rents snowshoes. If the lodge rents a variety of brands, you can try before you buy.

Consider entering snowshoe races throughout the winter. Many running stores located in snowy areas can give you information about upcoming races. For more information about national snowshoe competitions, contact the U.S. Snowshoe Association at 518-654-7648.

Many marathon training plans suggest that you run 3 or 4 days per week, *cross-train* (train by doing other sports) on 1 or 2 other days and take 1 or 2 days off per week. Frankly, I don't think you can run enough miles on those plans to train effectively for a marathon. And although cross-training can be a fun alternative to running (and a good way to stay fit while you're injured — see Chapter 12), nothing prepares you for running the way that running does. A coach of mine used to say that, if you're a runner and you have time for a bike ride, a weightlifting session, or a swim, along with a run, do both. But if you have time for only one, always run. Swimming, lifting weights, or riding a bike will never make you a better runner.

You may decide that you won't stick to your training plan without some days off or cross-training days, and that's perfectly fine. So, as a balance, the plans in the following section give you one day off with another optional day off that can also be a short-run day.

Have you been using a cold as an excuse not to run? If you get a cold this year, try running through it. Research shows that you can't make a cold worse by exercising through it. And moving around — even for a short, easy run — almost always makes you feel better. If you think you have a more serious condition than a cold (such as a sinus infection, bronchitis, flu, and so on), ask your doctor whether continuing to run is advisable.

Creating a Training Plan

Even if you read this entire chapter, you probably have a burning question: Exactly how many miles should you run every week. I wish I could give you a simple answer, but marathoners run between 40 and 120 miles per week, depending on their goals and experience. To determine how much you need to run each week, consider the following:

> ✔ **The number of weeks or months before your marathon:**
> After you target a marathon (Chapter 13 gives you some ideas on how to choose a marathon, and Chapter 18 lists some of the most popular), get out a calendar and count how much time you have between now and then. You can then choose a plan from the sections that follow that comes closest to the time you have.

> If you have a little more time than the plans listed, always add to the base-building phase.

✔ **How much mileage you're doing now:** If you're currently running 20 miles per week, you can't do 50 next week. (Each week, add no more than 10 percent of your mileage from the week before.) However, if you're currently running 50 miles per week and have 6 months before your next marathon, you can probably get up to 70 or 75 miles per week fairly painlessly.

If your mileage is currently pretty low, you can throw this 10-percent rule out the window. Increasing up to 5 miles per week — even if that amount is more than 10 percent — is probably not going to hurt you.

✔ **How much time each day you can devote to training:** Running miles takes time out of your day: The more miles you run, the more time it takes. If you work 80 hours a week, you aren't going to have time to run 70 miles per week and get the sleep you need.

✔ **What your goals are for this marathon:** If your goal is to finish by using a combination of walking and running, you can get away with running fewer miles than if you're trying to run under 4 hours, qualify for the Boston marathon, or hit some other milestone. The faster your goal marathon time, the more miles you want to run. See Chapter 13 for more on marathon goals.

A 16-week plan for beginners

If you're trying to do a marathon in 16 weeks and haven't run before, flip to Chapter 4 for a 5-week starting plan, which gets you to around 18 miles per week. Then check out Table 6-1.

The plan in Table 6-1 isn't ideal because it places plenty of stress on your body. Ideally, you want to take 6 months, not the 4 months shown here, to train for your first marathon. To make this a 6-month training plan, add in 8 weeks between Weeks 5 and 6 and adjust the mileage so that you increase no more than 10 percent each week, eventually getting both your weekly mileage to 60 miles per week and your long runs consistently at 20 miles every other weekend. Turn to Chapter 4 for a table with a training plan for weeks 1 through 5.

Because training paces differ so much, I used miles in these plans. To get these plans into minutes, simply multiply the miles shown per day and week (such as 60 miles) by your average training pace (such as a 9:30 pace, which is 9.5 minutes per mile), to get your daily and weekly minutes (570 minutes per week).

Table 6-1			**A 16-Week Plan for Beginners**				
Week	Monday	Tuesday	Wednesday	Thursday	Friday	Saturday	Sunday	Total
6	3-5^c	3-4	0	3-5	4	5	0-2	18-25
7	3-5^c	4-5	0	3-5	4	7	0-3	21-29
8	3-5^c	4-5	0	3-5^{s/d}	4	9	0-3	23-31
9	3-5^c	5-7^w	0	4-6	4	9	0-3^c	25-34
10	4-6^c	5-8	0	4-6^{s/d}	4	12	0-3	29-39
11	5-7^c	4-8^w	0	4-7	4	14	0-3^c	31-43
12	4-8^c	6-10	0	5-8^{s/d}	4^{s/d}	10K race	2-3	31-43
13	5-8^c	7-10^w	0	5-8	4-5	8	2-4^c	31-43
14	4-8^c	6-9	0	4-7	4^{s/d}	16	0-3	34-47
15	5-9^c	8-10^w	0	5-8^c	4	10	0-3	32-44
16	3-5^c	4-6	0	4-6	4^{s/d}	marathon	0-3	43-52

C=circuits (see Chapter 7); S/D = strides and drills (see Chapter 8); W = workouts
(see Chapter 7)

A 16-week plan for experienced runners

If you've been running pretty consistently, 16 weeks is plenty of time to train for a successful marathon. This plan starts you off at 30 to 40 miles per week and takes you up to 55 to 75.

The plan in Table 6-2 aims for "perfect" training: 6 to 7 days of running per week, one speed workout per week, one long run per week, 2 days of strides and drills, and 2 days of circuit training. In a perfect world, you'd follow this schedule and run a successful marathon. But life isn't perfect, so you may decide not to do circuits or to do strides and drills only 1 day per week or take 1 or 2 days completely off each week. Or you may decide to change all the days around, doing similar mileage and workouts but on different days. Any or all of that is perfectly fine. No one — not even professional runners — trains perfectly every week, and no one sticks to one particular schedule without adjusting it. You don't want running to rule your life; instead, your marathon training is just one part of your life! Adjust Table 6-2 to fit your needs.

Table 6-2			A 16-Week Plan for Experienced Runners					
Week	*Monday*	*Tuesday*	*Wednesday*	*Thursday*	*Friday*	*Saturday*	*Sunday*	*Total*
1	4-5^c	5-6	5-7	5-6	3	8-10	0-3	30-40
2	5^c	5-7	6-8	5-7	3	9-11	0-3	33-44
3	6^c	6-8	6-8	5-7	3	10-12	0-4	36-48
4	6-7^c	6-8	7-9	6-8	3	11-13	0-4	39-52
5	6-8^c	6-8$^{s/d}$	7-10	6-9^c	4	13	0-5	42-57
6	6-9^c	6-9$^{s/d}$	8-10	6-10^c	4	15	0-6	45-63
7	6-9^c	6-9$^{s/d}$	8-11	7-12^c	4	17	0-6	48-68
8	7-10^c	6-9$^{s/d}$	8-11	8-13^c	4$^{s/d}$	18	0-6	52-71
9	8-12^c	7-11$^{s/d}$	7-9^w	10-13^c	4$^{s/d}$	18-20	0-6	55-75
10	9-12^c	8-11$^{s/d}$	7-10	10-13^c	4-7$^{s/d}$	12-14	0-8	50-75
11	9-12^c	8-11$^{s/d}$	7-10^w	7-13	4$^{s/d}$	Half-mar.	0-4	50-70
12	9-12^c	8-11$^{s/d}$	7-10	10-13^c	4$^{s/d}$	12-14	0-8	50-75
13	9-12^c	7-11$^{s/d}$	7-9^w	7-13^c	4$^{s/d}$	16	0-7	50-75
14	9-10^c	7-11$^{s/d}$	7-9	8-11^c	4$^{s/d}$	20	0-7	55-75
15	9-12^c	8-11$^{s/d}$	7-11^w	8-12^c	4$^{s/d}$	12	0-3	48-65
16	3-8^c	5-9$^{s/d}$	4-7	4-7	4$^{s/d}$	Marathon	0-3	48-65

C=circuits (see Chapter 7); S/D = strides and drills (see Chapter 8); W = workouts
(see Chapter 7)

If you have more than 16 weeks

If you have more than 16 weeks, use Table 6-2, but after the eighth
week, continue with that mileage for however much extra time
you have. So if you have 6 months (about 24 weeks), repeat Week 8
an extra eight times. You don't have to do Week 8 *exactly* the same
or you may get bored to death. But do something similar with
comparable — or slightly higher — mileage.

Be sure to look for the signs of *overtraining* (running too much).
Chapter 16 gives you the lowdown.

Chapter 7
Adding Strength and Speed

● ●

In This Chapter

▶ Getting the lowdown on runs

▶ Building strength with hills and circuits

▶ Outdoing yourself with a plan

● ●

*C*hapter 6 discusses the need for your marathon training to include plenty of mileage and one long weekly run, and that probably makes sense to you: A marathon (26.2 miles) is a long race, so you need to train your body to do long runs.

What may be less instinctive is your need for strength and speed. After all, the marathon isn't a weightlifting competition, nor is it a sprint. So why do you need strength and speed? You need them for two reasons:

✔ **Strength** allows your body to continue after it's exhausted. It increases your stamina. Without having strenghtened your legs, arms, heart, and lungs, you'll simply peter out after 12, 17, or 24 miles. This chapter shares several ways that you can build strength. In fact, many of the activities that build speed also build strength.

✔ **Speed** enables you to race faster than your training pace. I'm not talking about sprinting; rather, I'm talking about doing *speedwork:* workouts in which you run for a certain distance at a specified time with a certain amount of rest before running another (or the same) distance at another specified time. This type of running trains your body to go from its current fitness level to a new fitness level. It doesn't make you a sprinter, though.

If you find that your marathon times have flattened (or *plateaued*), meaning that you've run several marathons and your times don't seem to be improving, add speed to your training regime, and you'll see a big difference.

If you're running your first marathon, I suggest reading the "Doing circuits" section, later in this chapter, and skipping the rest of this chapter. For this marathon, focus on building your mileage and doing your weekly long runs (see Chapter 6), starting strides and drills (see Chapter 8), introducing circuit training, and then running one day per week that's a little shorter and a little faster than the rest. Nothing major — just speeding things up a little bit. That's enough to do for this marathon. For the next one, review the rest of this chapter and add some of the ideas to your training.

Running Rings Around Your Finish Time

Speedwork (also called *speed workouts* or just pain *workouts*) is all about training your body to run a faster pace so that you eventually improve your marathon finish time.

If you look at Table 7-1, you see that if you run most of your distance at 12-minute miles and that's a comfortable pace for you, your pace translates to a 5-hour-15-minute (5:15:00) marathon. (See the Cheat Sheet at the front of this book to figure your pace.) But suppose your goal is to run a 4:30:00 marathon, which means you have to run each mile in 10:19. Sure, you can go out in your marathon at a 10:19 pace and hope you can "hang on" for the next 25 miles, but without having trained your body to run at 10:19s, you probably won't be able to keep up that pace for long. Nor can you suddenly go from running your distance runs at 12-minute miles to running them at 10:19s. That's a huge difference in pace, and unless you approach it wisely (by doing speedwork), you'll probably end up injured.

If you run relatively short distances at faster paces, your body gets used to running faster. Don't get too excited about the thought of running "short" distance, though: For marathoners, the shortest distance for speedwork until the last few weeks of your training is usually a mile, which may not seem that "short" to you. At the very end of your training (as you get closer to your marathon), you get to do some really short, fast distances.

Don't do speedwork until you establish a solid mileage base (running consistently at slowly increasing weekly mileage for at least 6 to 8 weeks). Chapter 6 describes the base-building phase (the time, early in your training, when you steadily increase and then hold your mileage) and also gives you sample training plans that tell you when to do workouts. In general, you want to have trained consistently with long-distance runs for at least 6 to 8 weeks before attempting any speed workouts.

Table 7-1			Pace Chart			
Marathon/ 26.2 Miles	**Half-marathon/ 13.1 Miles**	**10 Miles**	**10K/ 6.2 Miles**	**5K/3.1 Miles**	**Mile**	**400 Meters/ ¼ Mile**
2:10:00	1:05:00	49:37	30:46	15:23	4:58	1:15
2:15:00	1:07:30	51:32	31:57	15:58	5:09	1:17
2:20:00	1:10:00	53.26	33:08	16:34	5:21	1:20
2:25:00	1:12:30	55:21	34:19	17:09	5:32	1:23
2:30:00	1:15:00	57:15	35:30	17:45	5:44	1:26
2:35:00	1:18:30	59:10	36:41	18:20	5:55	1:29
2:40:00	1:20:00	1:01:04	37:52	18:56	6:06	1:31
2:45:00	1:22:30	1:02:59	39:03	19:32	6:18	1:34
2:50:00	1:25:00	1:04:53	40:14	20:07	6:30	1:37
2:55:00	1:27:30	1:06:48	41:25	20:42	6:41	1:40
3:00:00	1:30:00	1:08:42	42:36	21:18	6:52	1:43
3:05:00	1:32:30	1:10:37	43:47	21:53	7:04	1:46
3:10:00	1:35:00	1:12:31	44:58	22:29	7:15	1:49
3:15:00	1:37:30	1:14:26	46:09	23:04	7:27	1:52
3:20:00	1:40:00	1:16:20	47:20	23:40	7:38	1:55
3:25:00	1:42:30	1:18:15	48:31	24:16	7:49	1:57
3:30:00	1:45:00	1:20:09	49:42	24:51	8:01	2:00
3:35:00	1:47:30	1:22:04	50:53	25:26	8:12	2:03
3:40:00	1:50:00	1:23:58	52:04	26:02	8:24	2:06
3:45:00	1:52:30	1:25:53	53:15	26:37	8:35	2:09
3:50:00	1:55:00	1:27:47	54:26	27:13	8:47	2:12
3:55:00	1:57:30	1:29:42	55:37	27:48	8:58	2:15
4:00:00	2:00:00	1:31:36	56:48	28:24	9:10	2:18
4:05:00	2:02:30	1:33:31	57:59	28:59	9:21	2:21
4:10:00	2:05:00	1:35:25	59:10	29:35	9:33	2:23
4:15:00	2:07:30	1:37:20	1:00:21	30:11	9:44	2:26
4:20:00	2:10:00	1:39:14	1:01:32	30:46	9:55	2:29

(continued)

Table 7-1 *(continued)*

Marathon/ 26.2 Miles	Half-marathon/ 13.1 Miles	10 Miles	10K/ 6.2 Miles	5K/3.1 Miles	Mile	400 Meters/ ¼ Mile
4:25:00	2:12:30	1:41:09	1:02:43	31:21	10:07	2:32
4:30:00	2:15:00	1:42:12	1:03:54	31:57	10:19	2:35
4:35:00	2:17:30	1:44:58	1:05:05	32:32	10:30	2:38
4:40:00	2:20:00	1:46:52	1:06:16	33:08	10:41	2:40
4:45:00	2:22:30	1:48:47	1:07:27	33:43	10:53	2:43
4:50:00	2:25:00	1:50:41	1:08:38	34:19	11:04	2:46
4:55:00	2:27:30	1:52:36	1:09:49	34:54	11:16	2:49
5:00:00	2:30:00	1:54:30	1:11:00	35:30	11:27	2:52
5:05:00	2:32:30	1:56:25	1:12:11	36:05	11:39	2:545
5:10:00	2:35:00	1:58:19	1:13:22	36:41	11:50	2:58
5:15:00	2:37:30	2:00:14	1:14:33	37:16	12:01	3:00
5:20:00	2:40:00	2:02:08	1:15:44	37:52	12:13	3:03
5:25:00	2:42:30	2:04:03	1:16:55	38:27	12:24	3:06
5:30:00	2:45:00	2:05:57	1:18:06	39:03	12:36	3:09
5:35:00	2:47:30	2:07:52	1:19:17	39:38	12:47	3:12
5:40:00	2:50:00	2:09:46	1:20:28	40:14	12:59	3:15
5:45:00	2:52:30	2:11:41	1:21:39	40:49	13:10	3:18
5:50:00	2:55:00	2:13:35	1:22:50	41:25	13:22	3:21
5:55:00	2:57:30	2:15:30	1:24:48	42:02	13:33	3:23
6:00:00	3:00:00	2:17:24	1:25:12	42:36	13:44	3:26

Don't confuse speedwork with circuit training, which is discussed in the "Doing circuits" section later in this chapter, or with strides and drills (see Chapter 8). Speedwork consists of specific workouts that should be done only after you've developed a good base. Circuit training and strides and drills are activities that you do after you get back home after a distance run, and you can add them to your routine soon after you start training for a marathon. Speedwork, on the other hand, is not something you do *after* your run, but changes in the way you structure the run itself.

Speedwork generally consists of four different workouts: *tempo runs, fartlek, intervals,* and *repetition.* These sometimes go by other names, but the concepts are pretty universally known in running circles.

Training to the right tempo

Tempo runs, also called *threshold training,* consist of one long, sustained, up-tempo effort at your goal marathon race pace sandwiched between a warm-up and a cool-down pace. (If you aren't sure of your marathon goals, see Chapter 13.) Use Table 7-1 to locate your goal marathon time and then follow that line along until you see the corresponding mile time. That's the per-mile pace at which you want to run the up-tempo portion of the workout.

If you haven't done tempo runs before, this is the first type of workout you should do. Do a tempo run every week or two, making sure you run an easy *recovery run* (a run that you run at whatever pace is comfortable, even if it's terribly slow) the day before and the day after (or even two days after). Stretch well (see Chapter 5) after your workout.

To determine how long your warm-up, up-tempo portion, and cool down should be for your first few tempo runs, use Table 7-2.

Table 7-2	Tempo Run Breakdown		
Weekly Mileage	*Warm Up*	*Up-Tempo Portion*	*Cool Down*
20 miles	1 mile	1 mile	1 mile
25 miles	1 mile	1 mile	1 mile
30 miles	1 mile	1.5 miles	1 mile
35 miles	1 mile	1.5 miles	1 mile
40 miles	1.5 miles	2 miles	1.5 miles
45 miles	1.5 miles	2 miles	1.5 miles
50 miles	2 miles	2.5 miles	2 miles
55 miles	2 miles	2.5 miles	2 miles
60 miles	2.5 miles	3 miles	2.5 miles
65 miles	2.5 miles	3 miles	2.5 miles
70 miles	3 miles	3.5 miles	3 miles

(continued)

Table 7-2 *(continued)*

Weekly Mileage	Warm Up	Up-Tempo Portion	Cool Down
75 miles	3 miles	3.5 miles	3 miles
80 miles	3.5 miles	4 miles	3.5 miles

Go out on a course that you measure in advance with your car's odometer or a mileage wheel (see Chapter 4). You run your warm-up at a comfortable, easy pace, perhaps increasing the pace just a bit for the last minute or two to get you ready for some faster running. Then start your stopwatch, and when you get to the start of your measured course, start the watch and run faster — what feels like your goal race pace.

Don't stop after your warm-up or up-tempo portion. Instead, just move right from the warm-up to the up-tempo portion to the cool down as if it were one, long run.

Your first tempo run will probably feel like a disaster: You may start out too fast and *crater* (suck air; feel like you're dying; have legs of rubber) the rest of the up-tempo portion; you may go out too slowly and not come near your per-mile goal pace. Don't worry too much about this the first time. In the future, try to run the entire mile (or 3 miles or whatever your up-tempo portion is) at a consistent pace, neither slowing down nor speeding up as you progress through it.

Keep in mind that speedwork is all about training your body to run faster, and your body doesn't naturally know what running a mile in 10:19 (or whatever your goal pace) feels like. The more you run tempo runs, the more your body trains to run at your goal marathon race pace.

Each time you run a tempo run, make the warm-up and cool down a minute or two longer and increase the up-tempo portion by a half mile or mile. Eventually, you want to be running 4 or 5 miles each of warm-up and cool down with 4 to 6 up-tempo miles in between.

Recognizing that "fartlek" isn't a dirty word

The word *fartlek* (*fart*-leck) doesn't have anything to do with passing gas; instead, it's Swedish for "speed play." A fartlek is much like a tempo run — in fact, it's run at the same pace as a tempo run (that's your marathon goal pace — see Table 7-1), but it has two major differences:

✔ Instead of doing a warm-up, a sustained fast run, and a cool down as part of a long run, you do a warm-up, a short run, a short recovery, another short run, another short recovery, another short run, and so on, concluding with a cool down. You can apply the warm-up and cool-down information in Table 7-2 for your fartlek workout.

Like a tempo run, a fartlek is a long run without stopping and starting — but unlike a tempo, you adjust (or "play with") your speed throughout the run.

✔ Instead of mapping out exactly how long the up-tempo portion will be as you do with a tempo run, a fartlek can be more freeform or more structured than a tempo. Four examples of fartlek training (not including a warm-up and cool down) are as follows:

- **Pole-to-pole:** Using electrical or telephone poles located along a road, run up-tempo past one pole to the second, run recovery to the third pole, run up-tempo past the fourth pole to the fifth after that, run recovery to the sixth pole, and so on. The idea is to make your recovery runs about half the length of the up-tempo runs. Starting out, you may decide (depending on the distances between poles) to do ten up-tempo portions (that's ten double-pole lengths), gradually increasing by two double-poles every time you do the workout.

You don't have to use poles; you can also use trees, houses, street lamps, and so on. Just be sure to keep your recovery quite a bit shorter than your up-tempo portion.

- **2-1-1-1-1-30-30:** Run 2 minutes up-tempo, run 1 minute recovery, run 1 minute up-tempo, run 1 minute recovery, run 1 minute up-tempo, run 30 seconds recovery, run 30 seconds up-tempo. Starting out, do this one set. The next time, do a 2-minute recovery between sets and do two sets. Then add a third set, until you're up to 5 to 8 miles of the up-tempo portion.

- **Curves and straights:** You do this fartlek on a track. Run the straight portions of the track at up-tempo and recover on the curves. (It's a little boring, but if you can't find other places to train, it's effective.) Run from two to four miles this way your first time out, gradually increasing with time and training.

- **6-2-6-2:** Run up-tempo for 6 minutes, recover for 2 minutes, run up-tempo for 6 minutes, and recover for 2 minutes. The next time, add another 6-2 combination until you get to five or six up-tempo portions.

6-2-6-2 is a tough workout because of the short amount of rest compared to the long up-tempo portion. Don't attempt this one until you do the other three types of fartlek workouts, as well as a tempo run or two, a few times.

Your warm-up and cool down should be the same distance as you use for a tempo run — refer to Table 7-2.

Running intervals

After you add tempo runs and fartlek workouts to your training, you can add one more type of speed workout that falls into the strength-speed phase discussed in Chapter 6. *Intervals* are both similar to and different from tempo runs and fartlek:

✔ Unlike tempo or fartlek, you actually stop running between the up-tempo portions, although you do keep moving, usually by walking.

✔ Unlike tempo or fartlek, you run *faster* than your goal marathon finish time.

To determine your interval goal times, flip to Table 7-1 near the beginning of this chapter and locate your goal marathon finish time. Then count up three marathon times above your goal time and move over to the per-mile time on that line. That's the pace at which you want to do intervals.

✔ Like tempo, the time of the up-tempo portion is heavily controlled.

✔ Like fartlek, the time of the recovery portion is tightly controlled.

Some sample interval workouts are as follows:

✔ **Repeat miles:** To do repeat miles, you measure out a mile in quarter-mile increments on a lonely stretch of road if possible, or you can head to your local track. Warm up using the same warm-up distance listed for tempo runs in Table 7-2 and then begin your first mile. Try to come through the quarter-mile mark at the time listed in Table 7-1, adjusting your speed up or down if you go too fast or too slowly. Your goal when running repeat miles is to hit each quarter-mile and overall mile time as close as possible to the goal time you established. After you finish each mile, walk around for your recovery, which should last about 4 minutes if you're running under 8-minute miles; 5 to 5.5 minutes if you're running from 8-minute to 10-minute miles, and 6 to 6.5 minutes if you're running over 10-minute miles. Because you're running for a longer amount of time if you run 10-minute miles versus 6-minute miles, you need more recovery time.

Start off with three 1-mile repeats. Each week, add an additional mile until you get up to 7 or 8 miles. Always follow the workout with a cool down. See Table 7-2 for the cool-down distance.

✔ **5-5-5s:** This workout is much like repeat miles, but instead of repeating miles, you're repeating 5-minute segments. You still want to run on a mile course, looking at what point in the mile you finish each 5-minute segment. Try to get to the same point (or a little farther) with each succeeding 5-minute segment. Do one set the first few times. Eventually, you want to be able to do two sets of 5-5-5s with a 10-minute recovery break (walking around) between the sets. Be sure to warm up and cool down, too.

✔ **2-1-2:** You're probably hoping that the "2" and "1" refer to minutes, right? Unfortunately, they refer to miles. This is a tough but productive workout. Just like repeat miles, you head to your marked course or track, do your warm-up, and then run 2 miles, rest (by walking around) for the same amount of time you took to run the 2 miles (this is called *equal rest*), run a mile, do equal rest, and run another 2 miles. Follow up with a cool down.

Finding a cinder track or grass course

In addition to marking out miles on a road or using an all-weather track at a local school, you may have two other options that may be a little easier on your legs.

✔ Consider marking out a mile on a grass course, such as a cross country course or at a local park. You'll definitely need a mileage wheel (see Chapter 4) to measure the distance because the park ranger probably won't appreciate your driving over the grass to measure your mile.

✔ Some older schools (and also private schools) still have cinder tracks, which are still usually 4 laps to a mile but are on a packed cinder surface. These tracks are oh-so-soft on your legs.

Generally, running on grass or cinder is slower than running on roads or an all-weather track, so don't be surprised if your times are a bit slow.

Repeating your runs with repetition

Repetition is a type of speed workout, but it's generally used in two ways:

- ✔ Early in your training and continuing throughout your training, usually in the form of strides (discussed in Chapter 8).

- ✔ Late in your training to sharpen your fitness for your marathon.

Repetition workouts are much like intervals with three key differences:

- ✔ The up-tempo distances are much shorter: 100 to 400 meters (one-quarter of a track to one lap around a track).

- ✔ The up-tempo distances are much faster.

  To determine your goal repetition times, go to Table 7-1, count up six times above your goal marathon time, count over to the 400-meter times, and do 400-meters at this pace. (For 200-meter times, divide by two; for 100-meter times, divide by four.)

- ✔ The recovery periods are much longer when compared to the up-tempo portion: Like intervals, you don't run during the recovery period but walk, instead. The recovery should last for two to three times as long as the repetition.

For these reasons, most marathoners adore repetition and want to do it as much as possible. Some sample workouts are as follows:

- ✔ **4 x 400 meters or 8 x 200 meters** (both total 1 mile): Like intervals, you do a warm-up, head to the track, and run fast for 400 or 200 meters. After resting for two to three times as long as it took you to do the repetition, do another 400 or 200 meters and repeat until you do one mile of repetition. Cool down after you're finished. (Use Table 7-2 to determine how long your warm-up and cool down should be.)

- ✔ **100-100-200-200-400-200-200-100-100:** Like the preceding workout, this workout totals 1 mile, but it's done in the form of a *ladder:* You start short, get gradually longer (going up the ladder) and then get gradually shorter again (going down the ladder). Remember to do a warm-up and cool down and to rest for two or three times longer than each repetition you're running. Some people take a 5-minute break at the top of the ladder before heading down again.

Building Strength

Doing speedwork not only helps you run a faster marathon pace, but it also builds strength, which is critical for your late-stage performance in the marathon. However, two other types of workouts can specifically help you build strength.

Running hills: You're not in Kansas anymore

Even if you live in Kansas, try to incorporate hills into your training at least one day per week. The truth is, most marathons aren't that hilly, but nearly all include one hill that's tactically positioned near the end of the race. It's cruel, I know, but that's how race directors entertain themselves.

If you live in a hilly area, don't avoid hills; instead, embrace them and get good at them. I live in a hilly area, and one workout I do is a long run (about 12 miles) during which I run up and down hills hard. On the flats, I relax and run a recovery pace, but I really go every time I get to a hill. This is a terrific way to strengthen your body, improve your performance on hills, and break up the monotony of a long run.

If you live in a flat area, you probably still have access to the one hill in your town or in the next town over. If you have just one hill to work with, consider this workout: You do a repetition workout, but start at the base of the hill, run up, and walk down the hill during your recovery. Do the same number of repetitions that you would do for 4 x 400 or 8 x 200. And don't forget to warm up and cool down!

Remember that, after workouts, you need at least one and maybe as many as three recovery days. So you don't want to do a hill workout the day after a fartlek or any other speed workout.

To run hills effectively, both in workouts and races, remember to swing your arms back hard (as if you're trying to shoot your elbows straight to the moon) and lean your upper body into the hill a little. And most importantly, always keep running *over* the top of the hill. Too many distance runners get near the top and slow down — the result is that marathoners who have trained to always run over the top pass them. You also lose momentum if you slow down before you crest the hill, and that means you slow down. Keep going hard over the top of the hill and hope there's a nice, long downhill on the other side.

Whatever you do, don't walk up hills during your training runs. Your body adapts very quickly to hills if you give it the chance. If you always walk up hills, you never gain the strength that the hill has to offer you.

Doing circuits

A final way to gain strength — *circuit training* or just plain *circuits* — is probably the best-kept secret in distance running. A *circuit* includes a warm-up, a series of strength-building exercises at *stations* (in between which you run fast), and a cool down. Circuits strengthen your body in an incredibly short amount of time. After just five or six circuit workouts, you'll notice a tremendous difference in the strength of your arms, legs, stomach, and buttocks.

If you ask me to choose the one workout in this chapter that can make the most difference in your training, I'd have to say circuits. Unlike cross-training with other sports, circuit training makes you a better runner: The exercise portions are geared specifically to strengthening the muscles that runners use, and the short sprints in between each circuit improves your speed and efficiency (see Chapter 8).

You can set up circuit stations right in your own home. Get yourself the following inexpensive pieces of equipment, and set up stations in your backyard, garage, basement, or some other place, putting them each about ten or twenty yards apart.

- ✔ A sit-up mat or thick towel (for sit-ups, push-ups, crunches)

- ✔ A pair of five-pound or eight-pound weights (for curls, shrugs, upright rows)

- ✔ A sturdy chair (for chair dips)

- ✔ A stairway or step (for step-ups, single-leg squats, toe raises)

- ✔ A pair of two-pound or three-pound weights (for punches and running with weights)

This makes five stations for twelve exercises, so it shouldn't take up too much room. One problem, though, with circuits, is that you can easily forget what exercise you're supposed to do when you get to the station, so I suggest putting a sheet of paper at each station that lists, in order, the one, two, or three exercises that you're doing there.

Don't think for a minute that circuits are easy. In fact, they're so hard that I despise them. I really do. But I do them because I know how much they benefit my training. Go through the following steps to see what I recommend during this workout.

1. **Run for 15 to 40 minutes, depending on how much you're currently running each week.**

2. **When you get back, *immediately* begin doing circuits (described in the following sections).**

   Don't stop for anything but a quick drink of water, if you absolutely need it. Don't walk around or chit-chat with neighbors or anything like that. Run and then go right to the first station.

3. **Set the timer on your watch for 25 to 35 seconds (depending on your current fitness level) and before you begin the first station, start the timer.**

4. **When the watch beeps, run from your station to the next one, set the timer again, and immediately begin doing the next exercise.**

5. **When the watch beeps again, run to the next station, and so on.**

6. **Repeat the entire circuit (all the exercises) at least once.**

7. **When you finish the last circuit, immediately begin your 10- to 20-minute cool down.**

Ready to start? The following sections show you how to do circuit training. Although you don't have to use this exact order, be sure to separate stations that use similar muscles. Try to do an exercise for your abdomen, then arms, then your back, then arms, and so on.

Curls

While standing, put a five- or eight-pound weight in each hand, relax your shoulders, fully extend your arms so that your knuckles are resting on your thighs. Now, without leaning forward, bend one elbow and pull your fist toward your chest (see Figure 7-1). Lower that arm back to its starting position, again without leaning your back forward. As you're lowering your arm, bend the other elbow and pull that fist toward your chest. Repeat until you hear the beeper.

Figure 7-1: Curls strengthen your biceps as well as other muscles.

Sit-ups

You probably already know how to do sit-ups, but just in case, Figure 7-2 gives you an example. Lie on your back, bend your knees, tighten your stomach, keep your back straight, and pull yourself upright, with your hands touching loosely against your head or crossed across your chest as in Figure 7-2. Gently lower yourself back down and start again. Do as many as you can until the beeper beeps.

Figure 7-2: Sit-ups can tighten up a beer belly as well as a mother's postnatal tummy.

Shrugs

Take a 5- or 8-pound weight in each hand, relax your arms by hanging them down at your sides, and relax your shoulders. Now, without actively moving your hands, raise your shoulders, roll them backward, and lower your shoulders (see Figure 7-3). Repeat. When you hit this station again on your second round, roll your shoulders forward instead of backward.

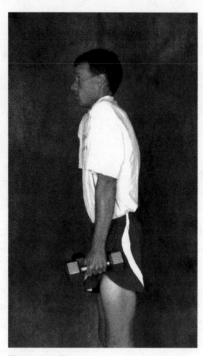

Figure 7-3: Shrugs.

Step-ups

To do this exercise, you need a step — one of the steps on the bottom of a stairway in your home, garage, or on your porch or deck can work just fine. However, it may be more convenient (because it's portable) for you to buy or build a simple one- or two-tiered step. Some have rubber on the top to prevent your feet from slipping.

You simply keep going up and down that one step. You step up on only one step and then bring the other leg up on it, too. Then step back down that one step, following with the other leg. Then up the step again, then back down the step, and so on. See Figure 7-4.

Figure 7-4: Step-ups are like running up stairs.

Chair dips

For this exercise, use a sturdy chair. Extend your legs with your heels on the ground and rest your hands on the outside edge of the chair with your elbows locked. Bending your elbows, lower your butt to the ground and then push yourself back up until your elbows lock again (see Figure 7-5). Repeat until, begging for mercy, you hear the beeper.

Figure 7-5: The dreaded chair dips.

Single-leg squats

To do single-leg squats, stand on your right leg at the edge of the step, so that the instep of your right foot comes right to the edge of the step and your left leg is dangling off the step. Bend your right leg on the step at the knee, until the *heel* of your left leg (lead with your heel, not your toes!), just touches the ground (see Figure 7-6). Straighten the leg on the step and repeat on the other leg.

The heels of both feet should be along the same horizontal line. Also, you may need to hang on to something (perhaps a railing) to keep yourself from falling.

Figure 7-6: Single-leg squats are easier than chair dips.

Punches

Take a two- or three-pound weight in each hand, put each hand in front of its respective shoulder, and stand with your legs wider than shoulder width apart. Take your right hand, cross it over your body, and punch out to the left, as shown in Figure 7-7.

To keep your knees healthy, roll up to your toes on your right leg as you punch out your right arm. Repeat with your left side and vice versa until the dinger dings.

Figure 7-7: Punches are a good way to let out aggression.

Crunches

Start crunches on your back with your legs straight up in the air and your hands resting on your ears. Tightening your stomach, you curl up to your legs, touching your right elbow to your left kneecap (see Figure 7-8). Repeat on the other side until the beeper saves you.

Figure 7-8: Crunches are a form of sit-ups.

Push-ups

Push-ups are a fantastic exercise for runners. Don't do girls' push-ups, however, even if you're female — they're wussy and won't make you any stronger. Instead, rest your body on your hands and tip-toes, keep your back and legs perfectly straight, lower your chest to the ground (see Figure 7-9), and raise your chest back up again until your elbows lock. If you get really tired before you hear the beeper, stay in the elbow-locked position until you think you can lower yourself down again. I guarantee that after about a half-dozen circuit workouts, you'll be able to do many push-ups.

Figure 7-9: No wussy push-ups.

Toe raises

Stand on one leg at the edge of the step, so that your forefoot is on the step and your heel hangs off of it. Lower your heel as far as you can and then rise up on your tippy-toes as far as you can (see Figure 7-10). This feels good at first, but if you get up to 11 or more of these, you start screaming.

You may need to hang on to something (perhaps a railing) to keep yourself upright.

Figure 7-10: Toe raises for the ballerina in you.

Upright rows

While standing, hold five- or eight-pound weights in each hand and put the ends of the two weights together, holding your hands right at your crotch. Keeping the weights together (see Figure 7-11), pull your hands up to your collarbone. Lower and repeat. When you start out, this one can really hurt, which makes that beeper the sweetest sound that you ever heard.

Figure 7-11: When you do upright rows, you look like you're opening and closing a giant zipper.

Sit-ups . . . again

Didn't I already mention this one? Yeah. But create another extra station to do another set of them. Marathoners have notoriously unfit stomachs, which can lead to back problems. Besides, you also get to rest your arms between upright rows and the next station.

Run with weights

Take two- or three-pound weights in each hand and stand with your feet about hip-width apart. Being careful not to hit your hips with the weights, move your arms in your normal running motions. Your thumbs should come right by your hip bones (but not touch them, for fear of the weights hitting your hips), as shown in Figure 7-12. Use the fastest motion you can muster with the weights in your hands.

Figure 7-12: Running with weights in your hands.

Putting Yourself through the Paces on Paper

So when do you do tempo runs, fartlek, intervals, repetition, hills, and circuits? And what about strides and drills (discussed in Chapter 8)? Table 7-3 helps you to schedule all your training exercises in this chapter so that you can add it to the training plans in Chapter 6.

Table 7-3	When to Do Speedwork and Strength-Building	
Type of Workout	*Begin No Earlier Than ...*	*Stop No Later Than ...*
Circuits	As soon as your training begins	The week of your marathon
Strides/drills	4 to 6 weeks into your training	The day before your marathon
Hills	6 weeks into your training	The week before your marathon
Tempo	6 weeks into your training	The week before your marathon
Fartlek	8 weeks into your training	A month before your marathon
Intervals	12 weeks into your training	A month before your marathon
Repetition workout	3 weeks before your marathon	The week of your marathon

Do all these options for speedwork and strength-building just confuse you? Here's a way to simplify your training without complicating the issue:

- ✔ Do circuit training once every 3 or 4 days.

- ✔ Do strides and drills once every 3 or 4 days (see Chapter 8).

- ✔ Every 4 or 5 days, run a harder workout: a tempo run, a fartlek, or repeat miles.

- ✔ Do one long run every 7 days (up to 20 miles).

- ✔ Stretch after every run.

That's pretty much it, in a nutshell. It's not easy, especially if you're running 60 to 70 miles per week, but you'll be amply rewarded when you see the finish time for your next marathon.

Chapter 8

Improving Your Running Technique

In This Chapter

▶ Examining your running posture

▶ Looking at how you swing your arms

▶ Honing your turnover

▶ Developing your breathing while you run

*W*hen I talk to most people about running technique, they look at me as if I just started speaking in tongues — after all, how you run is just a personal quirk that can't be changed, right? Well, no. Just as basketball, soccer, football, and all sorts of other sports have clearly defined techniques that must be taught to all participants in that sport before beginning any serious training, you can run the wrong way or the right way.

This chapter introduces you to proper running techniques, which, when applied to your own training, make you a more efficient, more powerful, and faster marathoner.

Changing your running technique takes time. You'll feel incredibly awkward during the first few runs when you try to change your running technique; however, if you stick with it, your new (and more efficient) technique will soon feel completely natural.

Sizing Up Your Posture

Running posture is similar to the posture that your mother nagged you about when you were growing up: It's how you hold your back, shoulders, and neck. What position is your back in when you run? To find out, have a friend take a video of you (straight on and from the side). If that's not possible, ask someone to take a picture of you, from the side, as you run by. Although not as effective, you can also run in place, sideways, next to a full-length mirror and look at your posture. Either way, evaluate what you see and determine which of the following categories you fall into:

✔ **Your back is perfectly straight up and down.** Running with your back perfectly straight can make for good running posture, as long as it doesn't indicate that your body is as tight as a violin string. Be sure that, in keeping your back straight, your body isn't rigid, such that your neck and arms are tensed instead of relaxed. If running with a perfectly straight back is natural to you and you feel relaxed, don't try to change it. But if you feel tense, try to lean forward just slightly from your waist as you run.

✔ **You lean just slightly forward from your waist.** This is the most common — and most efficient — way to run, with a *slight* lean forward. With just a slight lean, your arms, back, neck, shoulders, and diaphragm relax. See Figure 8-1.

Figure 8-1: Correct running posture inclines ever so slightly forward.

✔ **You lean far forward at the waist.** Although this posture is unusual, some runners do lean so far forward that they look as though they may fall. This posture puts quite a bit of pressure on your lower back and doesn't allow you to keep your eyes up and on the back of the person ahead of you in your marathon. It can also interfere with your breathing. Although changing your posture may seem awkward at first, try pulling yourself back to perfectly straight or a slight lean forward for at least three runs.

✔ **You lean back at your waist.** Leaning too far back makes you unable to fully fill your diaphragm (see the "Breathing Easy" section at the end of this chapter), which means that you can't breathe as well as you would if you leaned a bit forward. Instead, you want to lean forward slightly at the waist. Also think about bringing your chin down, because it's likely tipped back.

The main reason people run with a slight lean back is because they're fatigued in their arms and upper body. If you begin to lean back at the end of workouts or races, consider adding pushups or an entire circuit routine (see Chapter 7) to your training.

When running uphill, lean forward, so that you're leaning into the angle of the hill. Thrust your elbows back hard as you run up the hill. In this position, you run hills powerfully, instead of letting hills conquer you.

Two other common mistakes in running posture are as follows:

✔ **Scrunching your shoulders** so that they're up near your ears. This makes running far more difficult than it needs to be. Instead, relax your shoulders and hold them slightly back — just like your teacher told you to stand when you were a kid. Efficient running is all about relaxation, and you can't relax your body with your shoulders all scrunched.

✔ **Tilting your chin up** so that it points to the sky. Ideally, your neck stays perfectly straight; your chin is neither tilted down toward your chest nor tilted up. Many runners, however, do tilt their chins up, especially as they become fatigued. Practice keeping your neck perfectly straight as you run.

Carrying Your Arms Correctly

Arm carriage refers to how you hold your arms when you run — the most important part of your running technique

The ideal way to hold your arms is so that your thumbs brush by or just barely below your hipbones with each step (see Figure 8-2). If you've been holding your arms too high, you'll think this position is too low, but it's not. You have far more power when you run with your thumbs brushing by your hipbones.

To determine how you're holding your arms, run in place in front of a mirror or ask a friend to take a video or picture of you, from the front, as you run.

Figure 8-2: Good arm carriage means bringing your thumbs past your hipbones.

Your arms should never cross your *midline* (the imaginary line that runs down the middle of your body, from right between your eyes down to your navel). This is called *crossing over.* If you practice actually brushing your thumbs by your hipbones as you run and also keeping your hips still, you won't be able to cross this midline.

Figure 8-3a shows correct arm carriage, as well as carriage that's too high (Figure 8-3b) and crossed-over (Figure 8-3c) carriage. Both are incorrect.

Figure 8-3: Arm positions. (Figure 8-3a is correct, 8-3b is too high, and 8-3c crosses over.)

Some people hold their arms too low, but this is rare. If you fall into this category, use the tips in this section to bring them up to their proper height.

Even if you concentrate diligently on your arm carriage as you start out running, brushing your thumbs by your hipbones and so on, chances are that within 3 or 4 minutes, you'll revert back to your old way of carrying your arms. Set a timer on your watch to go off every 3 or 4 minutes throughout your run. Each time you hear the bell, recommit to carrying your arms correctly.

The more fatigued you get, the more your arms go back to their old ways. Yet, when you're fatigued is when you need efficient arms the most, because your arms follow your legs.

To make your arms as powerful as your legs, start doing circuits, which are described in detail in Chapter 7.

 Keep your hands loose as you run. Don't make them so loose that they flop, but don't clench your fists, either. Unclench your fists and keep your hands loose, almost as though you're carrying an invisible pencil or tube of lip balm in each hand. Rest your thumbs on your fingers — they don't need to stick straight up.

Hitting Your Top Stride

 Strides are short bursts of fast running that help you train your foot to turn over more quickly, which, in turn, makes you a faster runner. Each stride is usually between 100 and 200 meters. (One hundred meters is ¹⁄₁₆ of a mile and is one quarter of the way around a track; 200 meters is ⅛ of a mile and is halfway around a track.) Although most runners do strides on a track, if you don't have access to a track in your area, you can do strides at a park or even up and down your street.

 You do strides *after* your distance run, so that you're fully warmed up before you start.

The process is simple:

1. **Start out by doing 100 meters of fast running.**

   Don't run all out for each 100-meter stride; instead, ease into each stride by running medium-fast (instead of all-out fast) for the first 40 meters. You're running faster than your training pace, but you're still very much in control.

2. **Then accelerate for another 30 meters and accelerate again for the final 30 meters.**

   At no point are you going all out. Even for the last 30 meters, you want to feel like you're running fast but are still in control.

3. **After the stride, walk around (don't stand still) until you feel recovered enough to do another one.**

4. **Repeat three times.**

Eventually, you want to get up to 5 by 200-meter strides or 8 by 100-meter strides (or a combination, such as 4 by 100 meters plus 2 by 200 meters). Do these once or twice per week for several months, and you'll see radical improvements in your training and racing paces.

For some reason, track-team coaches are forever yelling at their young runners to stride out when they want to speed up. That's exactly the opposite of what you want to do. To speed up, you *shorten* your stride. Don't lengthen it. Lengthening your stride increases the time you spend in the air, thereby slowing you down.

Dissecting Drills

Running drills are a series of exercises you do to improve your *turnover* (the time it takes for your foot to hit the ground and leave it) and your technique. Some runners — usually those in college or elites — do a beefed-up version of running drills called *plyometrics* (ply-oh-*meh*-trix) or *plyos,* for short. Plyos involve a lot of hopping and bounding — much more so than the basic drills discussed here — and are geared toward making runners more explosive (such as when they come out of the blocks in a sprint). Explosiveness isn't really very important to marathoners, so the focus here is on making you a more efficient runner.

Drills basically make your feet move more quickly. I recommend doing drills two days per week, just after you do strides. If you struggle with them at first, do half of the repetitions recommended for each.

You do drills after strides, which you do after a distance run, but unlike strides, some drills involve walking, some involve slow running or hopping, and a few involve faster running. Choose an area with level ground for your drills, such as a track or a long driveway. You can also do them on a grassy area, as long as it's stable (not too mushy). You do the first drill and then give yourself a bit of time (from 20 to 90 seconds) to recover before doing the next one.

As you complete your drills, imitate the running motion, even if you're not going as fast as you would while running. When you're moving no faster than a brisk walking pace, still move your arms back and forth as you do when you run. Keep your eyes up, looking straight ahead: Don't look at the ground or at your feet.

Back extensions

To do back extensions, go through the following steps (see Figure 8-4):

Figure 8-4: Back extension.

1. **Begin walking, swinging your arms exactly as you do when you run.**

2. **Rise up onto your right toes and then quickly bring your left knee up so that your upper left leg is parallel with the ground and your lower left leg is perpendicular to the ground.**

   Your right leg, the one you're not lifting, should be fully extended as you rise up on your right toes (the back leg is extended, hence the name of this drill).

3. **Snap your left leg down, landing on your left forefoot (on your toes).**

   The snapping motion is important. You're not taking a slow-motion walk; instead, you're training your feet to hit the ground more quickly.

4. **Repeat on the right side without stopping while you change legs.**

   Do 20 (10 per leg), increasing the speed as you do these more and more.

Back extensions with hop

Back extensions with a hop are just like back extensions, except that instead of rolling up to your right toes (as you do when walking), you hop up onto your toes. At full speed, back extensions with a hop look like skipping — notice the little bit of air between the extended leg and the ground in Figure 8-5. Do 20 (10 per leg).

Figure 8-5: Back extension with hop.

Front extensions

To do front extensions (see Figure 8-6), begin with the same motion as a back extension, but instead of bringing your left foot back down after you lift it, you kick your left leg out forward, making your whole left leg parallel to the ground. (You're extending the front leg, hence the name. You're also extending the back leg, but calling them "front and back extensions" would be too confusing.) Then land on your left toes and immediately roll up onto your right forefoot. Do 20 (10 per leg).

Don't be too worried if you can't extend your leg out perfectly straight. Lift the leg, kick it out as straight as you can, and lower the leg again.

Figure 8-6: Front extensions extend the front leg.

Front extensions with hop

As you probably expect, front extensions with a hop add a hop on the right forefoot as you're bringing your left leg up and out. Do 20 (10 per leg).

High knee

While running on your toes, lift your knees up high toward your chest, so that your thigh is parallel with the ground (see Figure 8-7). Move your arms just like you do when you run. Do 20 (10 per leg).

Figure 8-7: High knees are very simple.

Kick butts

Kick butts are the opposite of high knee: Instead of bringing your knees toward your chest, you bring your heels to your backside as you run, as shown in Figure 8-8. Again, try to get up on your toes, keep your arms swinging, and do 20 (10 per leg).

Figure 8-8: Kick butt when you could just kick yourself.

Quick feet

The quick feet drill is plenty of fun. While running — and remembering to keep your arms swinging just as you do on a distance run — try to take as many tiny steps as possible. Your feet and arms will be moving furiously! See Figure 8-9. (Okay, Figure 8-9 makes it look like I'm not moving at all, but really, I'm taking tiny little steps!) Do 40 tiny steps.

Figure 8-9: Quick feet when you're really in a hurry.

Karaoke

If you ever played organized basketball, you probably did karaoke, which is running sideways and crossing one leg over the other — not singing with a machine in a bar. With your arms out for balance (see Figure 8-10), you run sideways, staying up on your toes the entire time and crossing each leg over while you're in the air. Go 20 steps, and then, while facing the same way, do 20 more in the opposite direction.

Figure 8-10: Karaoke isn't always about singing.

Don't overexert on this drill. Your hips are probably not used to all this motion, so do karaoke gently.

Backward running

Run backward on your toes, swinging your arms hard as you go back and *reaching* back with each foot (see Figure 8-11). You're trying to go fast, so really reach back with each leg.

Figure 8-11: Backward running is just like the name sounds.

Make sure nothing is behind you as you run! You don't want to be looking back. Instead, clear a path before you start this drill and look straight ahead. Do 30 (15 per leg).

Bounding

If you're pretty exhausted from doing the nine drills just listed, don't do bounding. If, however, you're an experienced runner who is used to doing drills, bounding is the ultimate way to improve your turnover (the amount of time that your foot actually touches the ground).

The idea behind bounding (see Figure 8-12) is that you bound off of one foot, float in the air for a split second, and then land on the other foot. Think of bounding as taking exaggerated running steps that involve a lot of time in the air. As you land, however, you're barely spending any time on the ground, because you immediately bound back up again.

Start slowly, so that your bounds are just small skips. Roll up onto your right toes and push off hard. Your arms are in the running position but are exaggerated (see Figure 8-12) because they're trying to keep you aloft. Try to stay in the air for as long as possible. As soon as you land, push off hard again. Ultimately, you want to be able to do 20 of these. For now, even two or four is a good start.

Figure 8-12: Bounding is, by far, the most difficult drill you can do.

After doing drills and strides, walk for a bit to cool down, and then stretch well (see Chapter 5).

Breathing Easy

Of all the different running techniques, the ones for breathing are those that people think are the most bizarre — after all, how often are you asked to train yourself how to breathe?

Good running breathing habits are twofold: how you breathe and how *often* you breathe.

Taking a deep breath

You probably breathe in one of the two following ways when you run:

- ✔ **Chest-breathing:** This is the way that most adults breathe. As you breathe in, you keep your abdomen fairly flat and expand your chest with air. This is the less efficient of two ways to breathe.

> ✔ **Belly-breathing:** Belly-breathing is how most children
> breathe. As you breathe in, your chest stays fairly flat and
> your *diaphragm,* a muscle that sits near the top of your
> abdomen, expands.

To determine whether you're a chest breather or belly breather,
place one hand on your diaphragm (which sits just below where
your sternum or breastbone ends) and the other hand on your chest
as you take a deep breath. If the hand on your chest moves a great
deal as you breathe and other doesn't, you're a chest breather. If
your hand rises off your diaphragm when you breathe in but the
hand on your chest barely moves, you're expanding your diaphragm
as you breathe and can consider yourself a belly breather. This is
the most efficient way to breathe.

Although belly-breathing is more normal to humans than chest-
breathing (which is why children often breathe this way), you may
have to practice belly-breathing, as follows:

1. **Sit upright in a chair and place one hand on your
   diaphragm and one on your chest.**

2. **Slowly take a deep breath in and try to expand your
   diaphragm as much as you can so that you're pushing the
   hand on your diaphragm forward.**

   Think of your diaphragm as a big balloon that you're
   attempting to fill with air.

   Use the hand on your chest to double-check whether
   you're still chest breathing. The hand on your chest should
   move very little as you breathe in.

3. **Breathe out, making your diaphragm as flat and empty as
   possible.**

   The balloon should be emptied of air.

4. **Continue practicing for five or ten breaths.**

   Be careful — you can *hyperventilate* (taking in too much air
   too quickly such that you experience dizziness or fainting)
   if you practice this technique for too long at one sitting.

After you practice for several days or weeks in a sitting position,
begin trying this technique as you run. To check your progress,
periodically place your hand on your diaphragm as you run and
make sure that your diaphragm is filling on each breath in and flat-
tening on each breath out.

Discovering how to breathe differently may take you several
weeks — or even months.

Breathing to the beat of your feet

Your *breathing pattern* refers to how often you breathe in and out as you run. To determine your breathing pattern, go on a run and breathe regularly. Now start counting your steps or counting your arm swings — they're identical to your steps — as you breathe in and then count your steps or arm swings as you breathe out.

✔ **One step per breath in; one step per breath out:** You're probably close to hyperventilating, because you're breathing way too fast. Slow down your breathing and try to take at least two steps for each breath in and two steps for each breath out.

✔ **Two steps to four steps per breath in; two to four per breath out:** This is where you want to be. Most runners take three steps per breath, but that depends on your pace. (During races and workouts, you may find that you breathe differently than during your distance runs.)

✔ **Five steps per breath in; five per breath out:** You're likely breathing too slowly, trying to do too much with one breath. This means that, because your muscles need oxygen to work properly, you're not being as efficient as you can be. Try to get down to three or four steps per breath.

In addition to taking from two to four steps per breath, your steps per breath should be the same whether you're breathing in or breathing out. If you find that you're breathing out in one step but taking three steps to breathe in (or vice versa), you haven't developed a pattern for your breathing, and a pattern is what you're trying to develop here. The idea behind a pattern is that it's fixed — it doesn't change — so if you're breathing in faster or slower than you're breathing out, you're not following a pattern. Get used to counting your breaths as you run and try to get your body used to following a set pattern.

Chapter 9

Eating and Running

● ●

In This Chapter

▶ Drinking and dining before the race

▶ Replenishing your body with the right fluids

▶ Determining whether you have exercise-induced food allergies

● ●

*B*efore you even read this chapter, you hate it, don't you? After all, one of the reasons you're so enthusiastic about training for a marathon is that you heard that you'd be able to eat whatever you want and not gain weight. So why do I have to ruin all your fun by talking about healthy food?

Sorry to be a party pooper. Marathoners tend to worry less about calories than the general public, but you need to be more concerned than others with the quality of your food because you depend on your body more than most people do. This chapter dispels some myths, introduces a few new concepts that you may not have heard before, and reinforces the rules of good eating that you've known for a long time.

Everything in moderation — even moderation! Don't go so overboard on what and how you're eating that you stop enjoying meals. Even in a healthy routine, you can occasionally enjoy a large piece of pie, a bucket of buttered popcorn, or a dinner of ribs. Even Regina Jacobs, a professional who is one of the most successful (and lean) middle distance runners ever to come from the United States, takes Saturday evenings "off" her strict eating regimen. After that one period of eating and drinking whatever she wants, she's ready for another week of healthy eating.

Running to Eat or Eating to Run?

Chances are, one of the reasons you became interested in running or became hooked on it after you started is that you love the idea that you can eat anything you want in any amount you want and not gain weight. When you see elite marathoners on TV or at races, the first thing that you notice is that they're among the leanest people in the world, as are some older marathoners who've been involved in the sport for decades but aren't at the elite level.

But if you look around the next time that you're at a marathon or road race or at a meeting of your running group, you see that the bulk of marathoners really aren't that lean. Marathoners may weigh less than the population at large, but given that 80 percent of Americans are overweight, that simply means that marathoners aren't as overweight as people who don't run.

What gives? Shouldn't all marathoners be rail thin? Not necessarily. How your body responds to marathon training depends on two factors that are inextricably linked:

- ✔ **Your mileage:** Thirty to 40 miles per week of running is enough to get you in pretty good shape if you're careful about what and how much you eat. That mileage, however, is not enough to allow you to eat anything you want and stay thin. In fact, lower-mileage marathoners may actually gain weight throughout their training, because they fool themselves into thinking that they need to radically increase their food intake.

   On the other hand, if you run between 70 and 110 miles per week, you may have trouble eating *enough* food to keep weight on. The majority of marathoners run far fewer than 70 miles a week but believe that they'll end up with the body of elite runners in spite of eating whatever they want.

- ✔ **What you eat:** Believing that elite runners — with their lean, fit bodies — can eat whatever they want and not gain weight is a pleasant thought. Perhaps you imagine elite runners surrounding themselves with high-sugar, high-fat foods three or more times a day, barely able to get enough food in them to keep from losing weight. It's a pleasant dream, but it's just a dream. Most elite marathoners are vigilant about the amount and type of food they eat. Staying thin is incredibly difficult in a society with a fast-food restaurant on every corner and grocery stores stocking their aisles with an abundance of junk food. Elite marathoners are as lean as they are because they choose not to participate in the standard American diet: no fast food (on a regular basis, at least), few simple sugars (except during and after runs, workouts, and races), plenty of complex carbohydrates, lean protein, and only good fats.

This section fills you in on how lean marathoners eat. It may be a bit different than what you had in mind when you first started training for a marathon.

Considering carbohydrates

Carbohydrates make up the bulk of the marathoner's diet, but the category of food called *carbs* includes foods as diverse as broccoli and powdered sugar, carrots and caramel corn, and tortillas and Froot Loops. This section helps you sort out the good carbs from the bad.

Simplifying simple and complex carbs

Simple carbohydrates (also called *simple sugars*) are converted quickly into sugar in your body, which makes them good foods for getting *glucose* (sugar that your muscles and other tissues need) into your body during and shortly after strenuous physical activity. However, if you eat too many sugars, your body may begin to lose its ability to control blood sugar, and this can lead to diabetes, a life-threatening illness that's rampant in the United States right now.

As a result of this increase in diabetes, along with the increase in obesity among Americans, some diet and nutrition gurus have responded by telling people that all carbs are bad, and that they should limit their intake of carbohydrates (that is, eat a low-carb diet). What these people have failed to help you understand is that carbohydrates aren't all the same: *complex carbohydrates* — most vegetables, whole grains, and some less-sweet fruits — convert to sugar in your body much more slowly and are great for your body, but simple carbohydrates generally convert quickly and aren't good for you.

The problem is that people have a hard time telling the difference, so telling people to limit all carbs is easier than being judicious about which carbs to eat. For example, which do you think has more simple sugars in it: a spoonful of sugar or a piece of white bread? Surely, the sugar has more simple sugars, right? Wrong. They're both equal in simple carbs. And a white bagel has even more simple sugars than white bread. White rice cakes have even more than that! What about veggies? Potatoes are just as good for you as carrots or broccoli, right? After all, veggies are veggies. Wrong! Potatoes and sweet corn (but not popcorn) are much higher in simple sugars than are broccoli, asparagus, zucchini, carrots, lettuce, and so on. To discover an easy way to tell complex carbs from simple sugars, see the "Getting the glycemic index" section later in this chapter.

Making your carbs complex to simplify your diet

The bottom line is that, throughout the majority of your day and week, you want to eat complex carbohydrates, not simple sugars. This means that you avoid sugary, processed foods that are white or light in color and, instead, eat dense, whole-grain foods that are brown in color. (One exception to the color rule is popcorn, which is a whole-grain food that's white after it's popped.) Another way is to look for the word "whole" in the first ingredient of your foods. Table 9-1 lists ways to replace simple with complex.

Sixty to 70 percent of your calories need to come from carbohydrates, and the majority of these should be complex. Each gram of carbohydrate has 4 calories, so if you're eating 3,000 calories per day, you need about 450 to 525 grams of carbs per day. If you're eating 2,000 calories, you need 300 to 350 grams per day.

Table 9-1	Carbohydrates
Simple Carbohydrates to Avoid	*Complex Carbohydrates to Eat Instead*
Cookies	Apples, bananas, and other not-so-sweet fruits
Crackers, chips	Air-popped popcorn or popcorn cooked in olive or canola oil, Rye-Krisps
Instant oatmeal	Slow-cooked oatmeal
Potatoes, sweet corn	All green and leafy vegetables, carrots
Sugary, light-colored cereals	Whole-grain cereals without much added sugar
White rice	Brown rice
White tortillas	Whole-wheat tortillas
White and whole-wheat bread and bagels	Dense, heavy whole-grain bread and bagels

Investigating energy gels

Energy gels are about the most basic simple carbohydrate you can find: They're made of sugar and fruit puree and packaged in small containers a little bigger than the catsup packets that you get at fast-food restaurants.

What simple sugars do best is quickly convert food to energy. Although you don't normally want this quick conversion in everyday life, this is exactly what you want while you're running. A piece of broccoli on your run may take a few hours to convert to glucose, which converts to energy, but sugar and fruit puree converts almost instantly.

Pumping up your training with caffeine

Multiple studies link caffeine to better running performance, even in moderate doses. In one study, runners who consumed the amount of caffeine in three cups of coffee were able to maintain their race pace up to 44 percent longer than without the caffeine. In other studies, 2 milligrams (mg) of caffeine for each pound of body weight improved race finish times by 10 to 15 percent. (Brewed coffee contains about 135 mg of caffeine.)

Explanations for this phenomenon abound. Caffeine may cause your body to start burning fat sooner than usual, thus sparing glycogen stores early in a race and making those stores available later than they would be otherwise. The drug may make your nerves and muscles act more efficiently. A third explantion is that caffeine makes you feel as though you're not putting forth as much effort, even when you are.

To use caffeine in your own marathon, take an energy gel with caffeine about an hour before your race and continue taking caffeine gel packs throughout the race. Be sure to test this process in your own training before attempting it in a race.

While caffeine usually doesn't make you urinate more if you take it shortly before or while you're running, it can encourage bowel movements. And it can lead to dehydration in hot and humid conditions. Taking caffeine prior to or during exercise can be dangerous to people with high blood pressure (a condition that often shows no outward signs) because it elevates blood pressure and places a greater workload on your heart. Get your blood pressure and heart rate tested by a nurse of physician. If either is high, don't use caffeine. Also, don't go overboard, thinking that if a little caffeine is good, a lot is better. When you ingest more than the amount of caffeine in two or three cups of coffee per day, you may have trouble sleeping and concentrating, you may shake and develop headaches, and you may develop an addiciton to caffeine. Finally, recognize that caffeine can inhibit your body's ability to absorb iron, can cause heartburn, and can aggravate ulcers.

When I first heard about energy gels, I thought they were a gimmick — just another product to sell to distance runners. Because I wanted to prove they were a gimmick (and be able to tell you that in this book), I bought several packs and took a few with me on a 22-mile out-and-back run. Never, in running this route, have I ever run the second half faster than the first (what's called a *negative split* — see Chapter 4). This time, I took an energy gel at the half-way point. When I went to take my second one (at about 18 miles), I noticed that I had run those 7 miles faster than I ran them going out. By the time I finished the run, I had negative split the second half by almost five minutes! I was astounded and hooked on energy gels.

You can buy energy gels at any running store, through any running catalog, and at some sporting goods and outdoor stores. Table 9-2 compares the most popular brands, but keep in mind that new gel manufacturers may emerge by the time this book is published.

Several gel varieties add caffeine, which is smart, given the benefits that caffeine can add to your training (see the "Pumping up your training with caffeine" sidebar). The gels don't have enough caffeine to show up in a blood or urine test (keep your fingers crossed that you never have to go through that, but elite runners are drug tested pretty regularly). However, if you're not used to consuming any caffeine, you may want to get more used to the substance before you pour it into your mouth on a long run.

Table 9-2	Comparing Energy Gels	
Brand	**Flavors**	**Notes**
Carb Boom	Apple Cinnamon, Banana Peach, Strawberry Kiwi, Vanilla Orange (caffeine)	Great tasting; runnier than Clif Shot, which makes it easy to swallow
Clif Shot	Chocolate (caffeine), Mocha Mocha (caffeine), Sonic Strawberry (caffeine), Razz Sorbet, Viva Vanilla	Made from brown rice syrup instead of corn syrup, and many people are allergic to corn; small, convenient size
GU	Banana Blitz, Chocolate (caffeine), Just Plain (caffeine), Orange Burst (caffeine), Tri-Berry (caffeine), Vanilla (caffeine)	Small, efficient packaging
Power Gel	Chocolate (caffeine), Green Apple, Lemon/Lime, Strawberry Banana (caffeine), Raspberry Cream, Tangerine (double caffeine), Tropical Fruit, Vanilla.	Packaging is larger than the others, making it harder to carry

I recommend energy gels for any long workouts, long races (15K and up), and any run that lasts over 80 minutes. Take one every 40 minutes. Don't use them any more often than this or you won't become efficient at burning fat during long runs; instead, your body will rely on the packaged sugar during your runs, thus making you less efficient.

In addition, eat one or two packs immediately following a long race, especially a marathon. You'll recover so much faster than you would without them.

The biggest challenge with energy gels is how to carry them with you when you run. Yes, you could hold several in your hands, but that's incredibly distracting and uncomfortable. Instead, you need an efficient way to carry gels. Check out the following ideas:

- ✔ **Waist bag:** A waist bag is a very small fanny pack that zips open. You can carry several energy gels inside, although fumbling with the zipper to get to the gel pack can be slow and inefficient. It costs $20 to $30.

- ✔ **Sport pocket:** Each pocket clips onto the waistband of your shorts and carries one or two gel packs. If you put more than one on your waistband, the extra weight may make them fall off. Costs about $15.

- ✔ **Gel carrier:** These rather complex inventions strap around your chest or arm and include small plastic bottles that snap, tie, or zip into a designated area of the carrier. You have to transfer your gel from the packet to the bottle, which weighs more than the packet. And you have to mess with putting the empty bottle back into the carrier, unless you want to toss it and buy new ones each time.

- ✔ **Sewn-in key pocket:** Most running shorts come with a *key pocket,* a small pocket that's sewn into the waistband and is meant for carrying (logically enough) keys. If your pocket is big and that gel pack is small, you can carry one in your key pocket.

To carry more than one, you have to sew in more pockets. This is what I did for my first marathon. Using great care and a good pair of scissors, cut out key pockets from some of your least-favorite running shorts. Then, sew those pockets into your racing shorts, spread out along the front of your waistband. I have a pair of shorts that has four pockets, and although it isn't ideal, it works until something better comes along.

Given the sharply rising popularity of gel packs, new and improved gel holders may appear on the market soon. Keep visiting your local running store or favorite running catalog Web site to see what they offer.

Don't toss your empty gel pack on the road during your long runs or workouts — this is littering! Only throw them on the ground during races, where the race volunteers clean 'em up. During runs and workouts, fold up your empty pack(s) and put it back in whatever carrier you're using.

Sticking with simple carbs right after running

Consume simple carbohydrates within 20 minutes after finishing your runs. Great foods to eat right after running include the following (but remember to stay within the 20-minute window, when your body is trying to recover its glucose stores):

- Cookies
- Dates and some other dried fruits
- Gatorade, apple juice, pineapple juice
- Gummi bears and jellybeans
- Honey
- Kiwi
- Pineapple
- White or cinnamon-sugar bagels

In the two hours following your run, eat a meal consisting of complex carbohydrates and lean proteins in about a 4:1 ratio. See the "Packing in protein" section, later in this chapter, for details. Complex carbs are used more slowly in your body as fuel (and you want this, now that your muscles have soaked up the simple sugars you ate right away), while protein repairs damaged tissues.

Getting the glycemic index

The *glycemic index* assigns ratings to different foods, and the rating tells you how fast those foods are converted to blood sugar over a 2-hour period. A food with a rating of 60 raises your blood sugar 60 percent as high as a food with a rating of 100. For years, diabetics have used the glycemic index to determine how carbohydrates will affect them. Now, however, because of the relative popularity of low-carb diets, the index is the subject of recent books, including *The Glucose Revolution: The Authoritative Guide to the Glycemic Index,* edited by Jennie Brand-Miller, PhD (Marlowe & Company). Online, you can find glycemic index ratings at `www.mendosa.com/gilists.htm`.

The glycemic index is a guide for determining which foods are high in simple sugars and which are low. (Table 9-3 in this chapter gives the glycemic index ratings for various foods.) Foods high in protein, such as peanuts and yogurt, tend to be low on the list, as are foods high in complex carbohydrates. These are the foods that you want to eat most of the time. Foods high in simple sugars usually have a high glycemic index rating. You want to avoid these at all times except during or just after long runs, workouts, and races. The index isn't perfect, though, so use your good judgment when choosing carbs.

Table 9-3	Glycemic Index Ratings of Foods		
Food	*Glycemic Index Rating*	*Food*	*Glycemic Rating*
White rice cakes	110	Doughnut	108
White bagel	103	Dates	103
Pure sugar	100	Croissant	96
Fruity granola bar	90	Pretzels	83
Rice Krispies	82	White potato, boiled	80
Jelly beans	80	Pizza, white dough	80
Pop-Tarts	70	Pineapple	66
Oats, quick cook	65	Sweet corn	60
Bread, sourdough	52	Bread, whole-wheat	52
Oats, old fashioned	49	Chocolate milk	45
Banana, underripe	30	Pasta	32
Black beans	20	Apples	28
Peach	28	Cherries	22
Yogurt, non-fat	14	Peanuts	14

The truth about energy bars

Energy *bars* and energy *gels* aren't the same. You use energy gels during or just after a run, workout, or race to replenish glycogen (carbohydrate stores) in your muscles. Energy bars are meant to be a healthy equivalent to candy bars: handy to carry with you yet dense in calories, high in carbohydrates, and lower in fats than candy bars. They're ideal for cyclists and hikers who need a convenient food that's going to give them many calories, thus eliminating the need to eat much else.

For runners, though, energy bars don't make much sense. Because you don't eat while you run (with the exception of energy gels on certain runs), you would eat an energy bar at other times of the day, when you can just as easily eat a banana, whole-grain bagel, homemade healthy cookie, carrots, or something similar. Energy bars aren't as healthy as other foods, and they're certainly more expensive. I'd steer clear.

Packing in protein

In all the talk from diet experts about low-carb or low-fat eating, protein is sometimes forgotten. The truth is, you need lean protein in your diet to repair the damage you're doing to muscles and other tissues during your long runs, workouts, and races and to speed recovery.

Make sure your protein sources are lean; that is, low in fat (see the "Focusing on fats" section that follows).

Good sources of protein include the following:

- ✔ Eggs, especially egg whites
- ✔ Fish
- ✔ Lean dairy products, such as milk, yogurt, and low-fat cheese
- ✔ Lean meats, including chicken breast, turkey breast, and lean cuts of beef and pork
- ✔ Legumes, such as lentils, split peas, and beans
- ✔ Nuts (almonds are also a good source of fiber)
- ✔ Some dried fruits (compare labels)
- ✔ Soy milk

Ideally, you want to consume about four times as many complex carbohydrates as proteins, so for every four grams of carbs, you want to eat one gram of protein, especially in the 2 hours following your run. (Use the nutrition labels required on foods sold in the United States to determine how many grams of protein foods contain.) Recent research has shown that when you eat complex carbohydrates and proteins together in this 4 to 1 ratio within 2 hours after a run, you replace more glycogen, which your muscles uses during your runs, than if you consume only carbohydrates in the 2 hours following your run.

You don't need protein drinks or protein bars. Too much protein can slow down the time your muscles take to replenish glycogen in your muscles.

You want about 15 to 20 percent of your calories to come from lean protein. Each gram of protein has 4 calories, so if you're eating 3,000 calories per day, you need about 110 to 150 grams of protein per day. If you're eating 2,000 calories, you need 75 to 100 grams per day.

The link between anorexia and marathoners

Many marathoners worry about weight gain and with good reason. After all, you wouldn't want to carry a bowling ball with you for 26.2 miles, and if you weigh five or ten more pounds than you could, that's what you're doing. But this interest in your weight can quickly turn into a preoccupation, along with an inability to stop losing weight and controlling your food intake. You may begin to believe that if being thin is good for your running, being thinner is even better.

When you shift from trying to be as fit as you can be to trying to be as skinny as you can be, even if you're healthy, you may be heading down the slippery slope of *anorexia nervosa,* an eating disorder that sometimes results in death after years of starving yourself. Anorexia doesn't just strike teenage girls; in fact, both male and female marathoners are at risk. In addition to severely compromising your health, anorexia can have the following impact on your training:

✔ **Fatigue:** Although the point of losing more weight is to make you run better, anorexia makes you run slower. Your body converts food to energy, and if it doesn't get the food it needs, it doesn't have the energy to run fast and/or long.

✔ **Stress fractures:** Anorexics are far more likely to develop stress fractures than runners who are at a healthy weight. See Chapter 11 for more information on stress fractures.

Look for the following symptoms of anorexia:

✔ Thinking of yourself as fat when you're already very thin

✔ Thinking constantly about food, especially the food that you're not allowing yourself to eat

✔ Counting calories several times a day

✔ Cooking for others but not eating with them

✔ Running extra to burn off specific calories that you "overindulged" in

✔ Getting pleasure out of denying yourself certain foods

Another symptom among anorexic women is *amenorrhea,* getting so thin that you stop menstruating. If you believe that you have some or all these symptoms, see your physician immediately.

Focusing on fats

Years of conflicting information — "Fat is bad," and then "Fat is good, so eat all you want" — has made *fat* a difficult word to understand. The truth is, some fats are good, and some are bad.

Getting good fats

Good fats are the ones that protect your heart and are found in the following products:

- ✔ Avocados
- ✔ Canola and flaxseed oils
- ✔ Fatty fish, such as salmon, tuna, and mackerel
- ✔ Lean meats from chicken, turkey, beef, and pork
- ✔ Low-fat and no-fat dairy products
- ✔ Nuts
- ✔ Olives and olive oil

Although you want to eat good fats in moderation, you do want to eat them. Make sure that about 20 to 25 percent of your calories come from good fats. Each gram of fat has 9 calories, so if you're eating 3,000 calories per day, you need about 65 to 80 grams of fat per day. If you're eating 2,000 calories, you need about 45 to 55 grams per day.

Busting up bad fats

Bad fats come from the following sources and should be avoided completely:

- ✔ **Animal fat:** Includes hamburger (except 96-percent lean), sausage, lamb, dark meat from chicken and turkey, fatter cuts of beef and pork, pork rinds, jerky, high-fat dairy products, butter, and lard.

- ✔ **Fried foods:** Anything fried contains bad fats.

- ✔ **Trans-fats:** Look for the words "hydrogenated" or "partially hydrogenated" oils on the labels. Chips, crackers, cookies (even low-fat cookies), granola bars, pastries, microwave popcorn, many breads, many cereals, and most peanut butters contain trans-fats. See Table 9-4 for some alternatives.

Table 9-4	Alternatives to Trans-Fat Foods
Trans-Fat Food	**Healthy Alternative**
Breads	Look for breads without hydrogenated oils or make your own with sesame or canola oil instead of lard, shortening, or butter.
Cereals	Look for cereals without hydrogenated oils; granola is a big culprit.

Trans-Fat Food	Healthy Alternative
Chips and crackers	Nuts and pumpkin seeds. (Watch the label though for trans-fats and hydrogenated oils!)
Cookies	Homemade oatmeal cookies made with sesame or canola oil instead of shortening or butter.
Granola bars	Fruit.
Microwave popcorn	Air-popped popcorn or popcorn popped the old-fashioned way (a stir-popper) in olive or canola oils.
Pastries	Pumpkin dessert (pumpkin pie without the crust) or banana bread made with sesame or canola oil instead of shortening or butter.
Peanut butter	Natural peanut butter that's made only of ground peanuts and salt.

Supplementing with vitamins and minerals

Marathoners need more of certain vitamins and minerals, including those listed in Table 9-5, than the general population does. The ranges listed are for all people, but if you're small, take the lowest amounts listed.

Table 9-5	Vitamins and Minerals for Runners	
Vitamin/Mineral	Amount	Food Sources
Calcium	1,200-1,500 mg	Dairy products, seafood, almonds, soy
Magnesium	600-900 mg	Leafy green veggies, legumes, seafood, nuts and seeds
Potassium	435 mg per hour of exercise	Bananas, many dried fruits, avocados
Selenium	200 mg	Legumes, mushrooms, garlic, Brazil nuts
Sodium	100-200 mg per hour of exercise	Gatorade, pickles, olives, table salt
Vitamin E	400-800 IU	Many nuts and seeds
Zinc	30-60 mg	Lean beef, fish, egg yolks, oysters, bran

Battling that bulge

If you decide to lose weight, be careful: Not eating enough while training for a marathon can leave you exhausted, dehydrated, and injured. Don't lose more than one pound every one to two weeks.

Remember that to lose weight, you have to burn more calories than you eat. You burn about 100 calories per mile of running, plus about 1,200 just for getting out of bed, breathing all day, and walking around. Add up your mileage to determine how many calories you're using each day and then eat slightly less than that. The following tips may help you lose weight wisely:

✔ **Load up on vegetables.** Except for potatoes and corn, which are both high on the glycemic index, eat all the veggies you want. If they need to be cooked, grill or steam them instead of frying (which adds lots of oil) or boiling (which washes away many of the vegetable's nutrients) , and don't add any sauces. Most vegetables have a delicious taste of their own — one that people tend to cover up with salt, sauces, and oils.

✔ **Make sure your carbohydrates are high-fiber and complex.** Eat whole-grain pasta, whole-grain breads, whole-grain cereals and oatmeal, brown rice, popcorn, and so on. Avoid foods that have a high glycemic index, such as white rice, potatoes, and white bread.

✔ **Don't drink your calories.** Avoid milkshakes, regular sodas, and fruit juices. If you want something to drink besides water, try tomato juice or V-8, which are naturally low in calories. Limit yourself to one glass or a small bottle of a non-carbonated sports drink after every run. Sports drinks are high in calories but essential for avoiding dehydration.

✔ **Take a daily multivitamin while dieting.** Because you're cutting out and cutting back on certain foods, you may not get the same vitamins from the foods you eat. Although I recommend taking a multivitamin even if you're not trying to lose weight, it's especially important if you are.

 Although you always want to get your vitamins and minerals from the foods you eat, you probably want to take a multivitamin that's formulated for athletes, just to be on the safe side. One that's easy to find in any discount store or drug store is Centrum Performance.

Licking Your Chops Before a Race

The day and night before your marathon, you want to consume complex carbohydrates, lean proteins, and some good fats. You also want to drink plenty of water and a noncarbonated sports drink after your run. Stop eating by 6:00 at night and don't overeat.

You need time to digest your food before race time the next morning. See Chapter 13 for all the details on pre-race eating.

Drinking to Your Health

Ordinary people — that is, non-marathoners — need to drink eight 8-ounce glasses of fluids per day. You need more than that: a minimum of 80 ounces of fluids (including about 30 ounces of a noncarbonated sports drink) every day — more if you can tolerate it. You absolutely need fluids to push toxins out of your body and rehydrate muscles.

To save money, buy Gatorade powder and mix it up yourself. If you buy the huge cans of powder at price clubs, you can make it about 80 times cheaper than if you buy it already prepared.

Dehydration is a leading cause of injury and illness among runners, especially in cooler temperatures when you still need the exact same amount of fluids as you do in hotter temps but don't feel as thirsty. In addition to water and sports beverages, you can get your fluids from the following sources:

✔ **Juice:** Drink fruit juice in moderation because it's high in calories but doesn't fill you up. Limit yourself to one or two glasses of fruit juice per day. Vegetable juice, however, such as tomato juice or V-8, is low in calories, so drink plenty of this.

✔ **Milk:** One or two glasses of low-fat or fat-free milk is a great source of calcium. If you're allergic to milk but don't like the taste of soymilk, try SunSoy before you give up completely. It's the best-tasting soymilk I've ever had.

✔ **Coffee or tea:** The caffeine in these beverages has been proven to improve running perfomance. (See the "Pumping up your training with caffeine" sidebar in this chapter.) The heat of the beverage and the caffeine in it may tend to dehydrate you, so experiment with what works for you and what doesn't.

✔ **Carbonated sodas and carbonated sports drinks:** Most elite coaches recommend steering clear of carbonated beverages, especially sugary drinks, which contain simple sugars that you want to avoid through your day. Carbonated beverages also contain phosphates, which can interfere with calcium absorption and may lead to bone-density problems. Finally, some research indicates that when you drink carbonated beverages, the oxygen in your blood is partially replaced with carbon, thus reducing the ability of your blood to carry oxygen. You need oxygen to run. These are all still theories, but coaches are seeing better results with runners who give up carbonation. If you can, cut carbonated beverages completely out of your life.

What's hyponatremia?

Hyponatremia hit the news recently when a woman collapsed and died during a marathon and was diagnosed with this condition. *Hyponatremia* is, essentially, over-hydration. The body absorbs too much water, so electrolytes (the good stuff in sports drinks) are diluted, and the body has an imbalance.

Does this mean you shouldn't drink water? Absolutely not. Just don't go overboard. Drink 80 to 100 ounces of water every day and make sure that about 40 percent of that comes from a sports drink, which you want to drink right after your run.

Fending Off Food Allergies

Sometimes, marathoners develop allergies to food and other irritants that they don't experience when not training. This is because running many, many miles stresses your body. If your immune system isn't equipped to deal with that stress — because of your genetic makeup, environmental surroundings, poor diet, poor sleeping habits, stress from work, and so on — your body may respond by reacting badly to certain foods that it should be able to tolerate.

This same thing happens to pregnant women, who may develop diabetes, carpal tunnel syndrome, food allergies, and other medical problems because of the stress that carrying a baby puts on the body. Not all pregnant women develop these symptoms, but nearly all the symptoms disappear when they deliver their babies. Training for a marathon can be as stressful to your body as pregnancy is.

Common food *allergens* (foods you may be allergic to) include dairy products, nuts, chocolate, eggs, corn, wheat, and gluten (found in many grain products). If you find that after eating particular foods you experience any of the following symptoms, consider temporarily cutting out that food to see whether your symptoms disappear.

Typical symptoms include the following:

- ✔ Asthma or trouble taking a deep breath; coughing
- ✔ Fatigue or feeling like you're in a fog
- ✔ Hyperactivity
- ✔ Irritable bowel: cramps (sometimes severe), diarrhea, hard and painful abdomen
- ✔ Itchy, stuffy, or runny nose and/or excess mucus in your chest and throat

If you can't seem to narrow down which food is the offender, you have two choices:

✔ **See a physician for a pinprick allergy test.** Your arm or back is pricked with a needle (this part doesn't hurt), and potential allergens are dropped onto each pinprick. If you have an allergy, the pinprick swells and itches. This is the painful part. If you don't react, you don't have an allergy to that allergen.

✔ **Go on an elimination diet.** For a day or so, you eat only organic brown rice, to which few people are allergic, and distilled water. Each day, you gradually add foods back in, one at a time. When you begin to experience symptoms, you know you've found your offending food.

If you intend to train for one marathon and then substantially reduce your mileage and run for fitness or race only in shorter events, you can simply avoid the foods that bother you for those few months. Be sure to take a multivitamin so that you don't miss any nutrients.

If you're training for a longer period of time, however, you may want to see whether you can beef up your immune system to the point where it no longer sees the offending food(s) as a problem. This means that, for several months, you need to get consistent sleep (8 to 11 hours per night), develop excellent eating habits, reduce your stress, eliminate potential allergens in your home or office, and so on. Keep in mind, however, that, in the end, your symptoms may not change. That's when you have to decide between having the symptoms, giving up the offending food(s) for life, or changing your training.

Some people are allergic not to a food itself but to the pesticides, wax coatings, and other residues found on and in the food. If you can't seem to identify a food culprit or if your symptoms come and go without a pattern, switch to all organic foods for 3 or 4 days to see whether your symptoms improve.

If you can't pinpoint food or residues as the problem, your symptoms may be from environmental allergens, such as grass, pollen, pesticides, mold, dust, cigarette smoke, and so on. If, for example, you have symptoms only after being in your office or house for several hours or only when you run on trails or at parks, you're probably allergic to something in that environment. Because these can be hard to avoid, you may need to take an allergy medication to suppress the symptoms.

Running with the runs

Because running requires that you divert blood from your digestive system to your legs and arms, running and food digestion can't happen at the same time. If you eat too close to your training time, you may just get a cramp — or you may end up with diarrhea. In addition, nerves can make you gets the runs at some of the most inopportune times.

For these reasons, runners tend to suffer from diarrhea more than most people, especially just before or just after races. One or two trips to the bathroom during which you experience diarrhea isn't something to worry about, but if it keeps up for an entire day or longer, you run the risk of dehydration.

To stop diarrhea in its tracks, temporarily change your diet: Switch all your water intake to a noncarbonated sports drink and eat bananas, rice, and dry toast or crackers and little else. If your body tolerates them, lean meats, such as chicken or turkey breast, or roast beef, without any toppings or marinades can also stop the pattern.

Be sure to wash your hands after using the bathroom. See your doctor immediately if you stop urinating, see blood or mucus in your stools, or notice that you have a fever.

Part III
Dealing with Running Injuries

The 5th Wave   By Rich Tennant

"You have to admit, we're more suited
for a 2.62-mile duothon than a
26.2-mile marathon."

In this part . . .

*I*njuries — the very word strikes fear into the heart of every marathoner. But injuries aren't inevitable. Instead, with the information in this part, you find out what causes injuries (so that you can avoid them altogether), how to recover fast, and how to stay in shape while you heal. Chapter 12 tells you how to cross-train so that you stay fit even if you do become injured.

Chapter 10

Pinpointing the Causes of Injuries

In This Chapter

▶ Stretching your limbs into a pretzel

▶ Tossing out tattered and lifeless footgear

▶ Resting, relaxing, and recovering

▶ Drinking enough of Adam's Ale

▶ Working with your unique physique

Getting injured is the most frustrating event in a runner's life. Too often, however, the reason behind an injury is a mystery to the injured runner, as if injuries strike certain people without any cause or warning. Not so. Injuries are always caused by one or more of a small number of risk factors. This chapter tells you what they are so that you can try to avoid them.

So, essentially, this chapter is the one you want to read if you're currently healthy or just beginning to feel a potential injury coming on. Chapter 11 also tells you how to treat injuries, if you have one already.

Focusing on Flexibility

The single fastest way to get injured is to skip stretching. Stretching correctly after you run helps you to run longer and faster, and using the Active Isolated Stretching method to stretch properly is ideal. (For more on Active Isolated Stretching and proper stretching exercises and techniques, see Chapter 5.) What happens if you don't stretch is that you tighten your muscles, ligaments, and tendons, making them more prone to tears and sprains.

An inflexible runner experiences many injuries — or often one nagging injury that reappears year after year — and never really reaches his potential.

For years, I — like many runners — prided myself on being inflexible. "Good runners," I thought, "can't bend down and touch their toes." I'm amazed at how wrong I was! The best runners in the world are incredibly flexible, with the help of an entire team of stretchers and massage therapists, of course. They have long fruitful careers because they make and keep themselves as flexible as they can.

If you're inflexible, get yourself a 10-foot rope that's a half-inch thick. Then spend a half-hour going through Chapter 5 where you'll discover the best way to stretch the areas of your body that you use most for marathon training. And if you can afford the cost and time, consider seeing a massage therapist once or twice a month. Chapter 11 can help you locate a masseur or masseuse in your area.

Wearing Worn Out — or Just Plain Wrong — Shoes

Running shoes are the only padding between your sensitive tootsies and the hard, uneven ground below. Unlike athletes in other sports, you don't have to invest in much gear and equipment to successfully complete a marathon, but you do need good shoes. (See Chapter 2 for information on finding the best running shoes for you.) You need the right shoes, and you need to replace them often.

Buying more shoes than Imelda Marcos

You know how you used to get new shoes every school year, and they had to last until the next school year started? Running shoes aren't like that. Instead of lasting for a year, they last for about 400 to 500 miles, which is anywhere from 5 weeks to a few months, depending on how much you're running. I'm not kidding about the 5 weeks. That's how often I replace my shoes, and I'm not alone among distance runners.

The problem with running shoes is that they often don't *look* worn out, even when they are. In fact, if you place a shoe with 400 miles next to a shoe with 100, you probably won't be able to tell the difference. You may see a little more wear on the bottom of the 400-mile shoe, and the shoe may be a little dirtier, especially if you run on dirt roads or trails, but fundamentally, the 400-mile shoes may look identical to the shoes that have only 100 miles on them.

But running shoes break down inside, and after 400 or 500 miles, they simply don't offer you proper support anymore. So you're essentially running barefoot. This can lead to all sorts of problems. Any time you feel discomfort in your joints (ankles, knees, or hips) or in your shinbones, consider replacing your pair of shoes.

Replace your shoes on a regular schedule. Start planning to replace them every 500 miles. Simply write in your running log, discussed in Chapter 4, when you begin each new pair. If you feel discomfort earlier than that, buy a new pair. The $75 you spend on new shoes is much cheaper than the price of medical treatment and the cost to your running health.

Finding a fit like Cinderella's

What happens if you start to feel discomfort really early — say, a week or two after you start wearing a new pair of shoes? You may simply be wearing the wrong type for you, which is a common problem. You may be a pronator wearing a shoe for a supinator or a lightweight runner wearing a shoe that's made to cushion a heavier runner. If all this sounds like Greek to you, jump on over to Chapter 2 for a primer on running shoes.

Not Getting Enough R & R

The *R & R* in the heading refers to the rest and recovery time you need to be a healthy runner. Marathon training puts your body through incredible stress, especially if you're trying to increase your mileage fairly quickly (see Chapter 6). As a result, you regularly need plenty of sleep, which repairs your body and gets it ready for your next run. In addition, after every hard or long run, you need to allow your body time to recover with an easier and possibly shorter run.

Besides not allowing your body to repair, if you're tired, you also increase the possibility of tripping and falling during your runs. When you're fatigued, you don't lift your feet up as high off the ground as you do when you're rested, so every crack in the sidewalk or tree root ends up tripping you.

Sloughing off sleep

Everyone training for a marathon needs a minimum of 8 hours of sleep, and anyone training above 50 miles per week usually needs from 1 to 4 hours more than that. Sure, getting that kind of sleep is difficult when you have a job, and kids, and a long commute, but if you want to avoid injuries, you have to give your body time to repair the damage you do to it during your training.

If you can't sleep 8 to 12 hours at night, see whether you can take a nap sometime during the day or right after work.

And the sleep has to be regular, too. You can't get 6 hours per night during the week and try to "catch up" on the weekends by getting 12 or more hours, because you leave yourself wide open for injuries during the week.

For years, I've heard a story about Olympic gold medalist Frank Shorter, one of America's premiere marathoners in the 1970s. Over time, Frank noticed that the quality of his racing was declining. He couldn't seem to find the cause of his sluggishness, so he decided to change one habit and one habit only: He went from sleeping 8 hours a night to sleeping 10 to 12 hours. That was it: He didn't change his mileage or workouts or anything else. He did this for several months, and before long, he started running great times again. Think about what a few extra hours of sleep could mean for you.

If you find yourself getting drowsy part way through the day, you're not sleeping enough. You know that you hit the right balance of sleep when you wake up (without an alarm) feeling fresh and then feel rested throughout the day.

Running yourself into the ground

Have you ever eaten something that was so delicious — like a mouth-watering peach or chocolate-covered cheesecake — that you wanted to eat it every day of your life? If you were to make a habit of eating that desired dish, before long, you wouldn't notice what had been so pleasant about it. Something that was delicious *because you ate it only rarely* becomes, well, bland and boring. It gets to be just like a tuna-fish sandwich. You lose the special qualities that the delicacy brought you.

Running hard is just like that. In order for hard runs (that is, fast, hilly, or extraordinarily long runs) to make you faster and stronger, they have to be done only once in a while — once or twice a week, at most. You may be tempted to do them every day, because you feel great when you run hard or you consider how good you could be if you ran more hard runs. But the returns eventually diminish. If you run hard too often, you're likely end up hurt, because you won't give your body a chance to recover between the hard sessions. The cheesecake won't taste good anymore.

Plan out your hard runs (see Chapter 7) and weekly long run (see Chapter 6) in advance. Don't let your training partner (or that voice inside your own head) talk you into running harder than you planned. Stick to your weekly schedule, doing your hard runs as planned and proceeding through recovery runs on other days.

Doing too much, too soon

Another way that you can keep your body from recovering is by pushing yourself too hard when you first start running, come back from an injury, or begin to increase your mileage.

A general rule is that you want to increase your mileage no more than 10 percent per week.

But suppose you get injured in January, take 3 weeks off, and still want to run an April marathon. You may be tempted to push that rule a bit, going from 10 miles your first week to 20 (a 100 percent increase) to 30 (a 50 percent increase), to 40, and so on, until you're back to the 65 miles per week that you were running before your injury. Although that may seem like a good idea, it isn't. Unless you're running very low mileage, such that the 10 percent increases amount to only 1 or 2 miles per week, you can't increase your mileage by more than 10 percent a week without risking an injury.

Be patient. Marathons aren't going anywhere, so if you can't get ready for one in a few weeks or months without risking injury, train for one that's several months later or train for next year's running of that same marathon. Sure, you'd love to finish that marathon next month, but what will likely happen is that you won't finish it anyway because you'll be hobbling around.

Being Unbalanced

Running appears to be a whole-body exercise because you use your arms and your legs, so discussing muscle weaknesses and imbalances may seem silly. But the truth is, most runners are lacking strength in certain muscles.

A *muscle imbalance* occurs when one muscle is quite strong, and the *opposing muscle* (the muscle that's opposite the first one) is, by comparison, weak. Because the strong muscle works extra hard to make up for the weakness of the opposing muscle, the strong muscle may develop an injury.

A great example is the stomach and the back. Most runners have fairly strong backs and weak stomachs, so they often injure their backs. This is why I highly recommend doing sit-ups 4 or 5 days per week (see Chapter 7). The *hamstrings* (along the upper back of your legs) and *quadriceps* (the upper front of your legs) are another example. Many runners have strong hams and weak quads, leaving their hams vulnerable to injury. A few runners also have the opposite problem — strong quads and weak hams — leading to the opposite injury. The calves and shins also tend to have this imbalance: Strong calves and weak shins lead to calf injuries.

Sometimes, your opposing muscles aren't weak, exactly. Rather, they're tight and inflexible. If your muscles are tight, your body isn't using those muscles as effectively as it should. Proper stretching (see Chapter 5) and a good massage therapist (see Chapter 11) may help you get more from seemingly weak opposing muscles.

A similar problem to muscle imbalance is a lack of strength in muscles that are used a great deal in running but simply haven't been developed enough. A great example is the shin muscles, which get plenty of use during distance running. Each time that you take a stride, you roll up on your toes and push off, using your shin muscles, but otherwise, they don't get much use in this sedentary society. So when you first start running or come back from an injury or change your training in any way, such as increasing mileage, starting speedwork, and so on, you may injure your shins, because they simply aren't prepared for the work that you're asking them to do. For a great shin and calf exercise, see the information on toe raises in the circuits section of Chapter 7.

Generally, if you stretch after each run, wear the right shoes, increase your mileage gradually, and take many recovery days, your running muscles will become stronger as you progress with your training. If you do find that you have a weakness, however, pay for a visit to a physical therapist to find out how you can strengthen particular muscles with high repetitions of very light weights.

Graduating from the School of Hard Knocks

Because marathons are held on city streets, many marathoners do all of their training on the same type of surface. Unfortunately, research shows a link between running surfaces and injuries: The harder the surface you run on every day, the more likely you are to develop an injury, particularly a stress fracture (see Chapter 11).

 Run on all different types of surfaces. Find a country road that you can drive to 1 day per week. Run on the trails at a state or city park once or twice a week. Or run on an asphalt bike trail instead of a paved cement sidewalk. Cement is far harder than asphalt — that black surface that gets soft in really hot weather.

Dying for a Drink

As discussed in Chapter 9, you need a minimum of 80 ounces (about ten glasses) of fluids, including about 32 ounces (four glasses) of a noncarbonated sports drink, every day. If you don't hydrate well, you don't push toxins out of your body, and that can lead to injury or illness. In fact, dehydration is a leading cause of injury and illness among runners, especially in cooler temperatures when you still need the exact same amount of fluids as you do in hotter temps.

 Hot, caffeinated beverages are fluids, of course, but because the heat and caffeine tend to dehydrate you, don't count them as part of your 80 ounces. For the same reason, avoid carbonated sports drinks and sodas. (See Chapter 9 for the lowdown on caffeine and carbonation.)

 Get yourself a 32-ounce bottle and fill it up with water in the morning. Drink it throughout the day and fill it up again in the afternoon, drinking it throughout the evening. By using a large container that you refill only twice a day, you'll drink your 80 or more ounces of fluids (at least 50 of water and 30 of a sports drink) much more easily than if you drink out of a glass that you have to refill eight or ten times.

Immediately after a run, drink 32 ounces of a sports drink with electrolytes.

Filling Up with the Wrong Fuel

You heard it before, and you'll probably hear it again: Putting bad food into your body is like putting sugar or mud into your car's gas tank — bad fuel clogs your system, resulting in inefficient performance.

 If you tend to eat an abundance of junk food, keep in mind that you only need a few days to change your food cravings. If you can replace your cream-filled pastries, white bread, and processed meats with fresh fruits and vegetables, rich whole grains, and lean meats and seafood for a just a week or so, your craving for your old diet will disappear. You just have to make it through about 5 days.

 Most people eat poorly because foods that are convenient aren't nutritious. Make nutritious food convenient by spending an hour or so on the weekend cutting up veggies, washing and setting out fruit, and shopping for wholesome foods (see Chapter 9). If you keep nutritious snacks and meals on hand and throw or give away your high-fat treats, you won't be tempted to go back to your previous way of eating.

Running Inefficiently

Because running seems like it comes naturally to kids, few people are ever taught how to run properly. (Notice that no one expects kids to be able to swim without basic lessons, though.) Inefficient running technique puts pressure on muscles and joints, and they respond to that pressure with injuries. Small corrections in technique can result in far fewer injuries over the years.

 Take a close look at Chapter 8, which gives detailed instructions for improving your running technique. And ask someone to take pictures or a video of you while you train and race. You may be surprised at what you see.

Inheriting Bad Genes

 I knew a runner who developed multiple stress fractures, yet stretched well, wore the right shoes and replaced them often, got plenty of rest, and so on. But she made a strange motion with her feet as she ran, flipping them up and to the side after she rolled off her toes. Her mother did the exact same thing. Although she tried to unlearn her genetic inheritance, she just couldn't do it. Before long, she gave up running because she couldn't stand the recurring stress fractures.

The best advice that I can offer is as follows: If you have the misfortune of bad genes, first see a sports medicine physician or orthopedic surgeon to determine whether your problem can be corrected. Then, if you have to live with the problem and are determined to train for a marathon, you have to do everything else exactly right. Never go a day without stretching, replace your shoes *before* they ever wear out, get as much sleep as you possibly can, allow plenty of recovery days between hard runs, eat and drink perfectly, and so on. You may be able to overcome your injury-causing inherited flaws.

Falling Down and Other Misfortunes

Most running injuries are the result of fairly minor problems that, when repeated over time, become a much larger injury. But sometimes, the problem is that you trip over a root and bang your knee or bruise your hip. Although you tend to fall more when you're fatigued, sometimes, you just can't help falling, especially if you run on trails.

The trick then is what you do after the fall. Use the acronym ICE on any painful or bruised areas whenever you have a bad fall:

✔ *I* **stands for ice:** Apply small ice cubes or crushed ice to the area for 10 or 15 minutes. (You want to use small pieces of ice instead of a large ice pack so that you can conform the ice to your injured area. Ice packs, when frozen, tend to be stiff and unyielding.) You can also plunge the area into a cold-water bath into which you've emptied your ice cube trays. If your skin is sensitive to cold, put a wet washcloth between the ice and your skin, but recognize that the icing won't be as effective. Continue icing every 10 to 12 hours until the pain and swelling subside or 3 days pass, whichever comes first. (If pain and swelling continue after 3 days, see a physician!)

Never, ever use heat on an area after a fall. When you experience an injury, your body wants to protect the injured area by flooding it with blood, but that extra blood swells and bruises the injury, extending the healing time. Ice discourages blood from rushing to the area, which allows the injury to heal faster.

> ✔ *C* **stands for compression:** If you wrap the ice tightly around the area with an elasticized cloth bandage, the compression helps to keep the swelling down.
>
> ✔ *E* **stands for elevation:** If possible, raise the affected area to a height above the level of your heart while you're icing. This keeps blood from flowing into and pooling in the injured area.

Also use a pain reliever if you can tolerate it. Avoid using Tylenol or other acetaminophen products, however, because, although they relieve pain, they don't reduce swelling like all other over-the-counter pain relievers do.

Avoid running on trails in late fall when they're covered with leaves. The leaves obscure the undulations in the trail, and you may end up with more bruises than you want. Also, steer clear of really rooty trails or sidewalks that are badly in need of repair.

Chapter 11

Treating Your Injuries

● ●

In This Chapter

▶ Stopping potential injury in its tracks

▶ Checking out common running injuries

▶ Deciding when you should see a physician

● ●

*I*f you find yourself injured or even if you have the slightest sus-
picion that you may be hurt, fast treatment and/or quickly
changing your training regimen may reduce your recovery time
and keep you from having to take time off from your training.
Whatever you do, act fast. Responding quickly to any potential
injury can mean the difference between running in your chosen
marathon and watching from the sidelines.

This chapter shares two types of advice: general treatment methods
that you can apply yourself right now, if necessary, and specific
treatment methods for specific injuries that may or may not need a
physician's expertise.

Taking on Do-It-Yourself Treatments

The methods listed in this section are general; that is, they're not
specific to any particular set of symptoms. However, they are, for
the most part, everything you can try before seeing a physician,
and they work for many distance-running injuries.

Getting the kinks out: Stretching

As Chapter 10 describes, inflexibility is the primary cause of injuries
among distance runners. For that reason, stretching is the primary
way to avoid injuries altogether. If you feel soreness, tightness, or
other discomfort in a particular area of your body, see whether

Chapter 5 has a stretch for it. Sometimes, spending a few extra minutes a day stretching out a tight or sore muscle for 2 or 3 days can mean the difference between it becoming a serious injury and being a faint memory. If inflexibility is a problem for you, consider spending 1 or 2 hours each month with a massage therapist. The last section in this chapter, "Making the most of massage," gives you advice on where to find such a person.

Applying ice

Everyone hates icing his injuries, but nothing's better for treating them quickly and efficiently.

At the first sign of any discomfort, ice the area by applying small ice cubes or crushed ice to the area for 10 or 15 minutes. Although cold packs that you keep in your freezer are convenient, most don't conform well to your injured area while they're frozen. Neither do large ice cubes. Instead, you want small cubes or crushed ice that you can arrange to sit directly on the injured area, with no gaps in the ice coverage. If your skin tends to be sensitive to cold, wet a washcloth with cold water and place it between the ice and your skin.

Now, I'm not going to kid you: Icing is a horrible way to spend 10 or 15 minutes of your life. Although your body gets used to the painful chill of the ice after about 4 or 5 minutes, those first few minutes can be excruciating. On the other hand, it's just 10 or 15 minutes, and the benefits are truly remarkable.

If your area of discomfort is large, say, your entire leg, your best bet is to take an ice bath. Fill your bathtub with the coldest water you can get from the tap and then add several buckets full of ice from your freezer or buy a bag or two of ice from a convenience store. Step in, sit down, and stay there for 15 minutes. Keep the following tips in mind, though:

- ✔ **Don't tiptoe in.** Just get in and sit down. An ice bath is one of the more painful experiences you'll have in your life, and if you try to tiptoe in, you may never actually make it into the tub completely.

- ✔ **Wear a sweatshirt or other warm top,** even if it's 90 degrees Fahrenheit in your bathroom. You'll be absolutely freezing — teeth-chattering, can't-catch-your-breath freezing as you sit in the tub. A sweatshirt (or two) helps keep your entire body from becoming chilled.

Wearing orthotics

Orthotics are custom-made shoe inserts, molded to your foot to make you more comfortable. If your doctor prescribes orthotics, you have to decide whether to wear them in your running shoes. Most people do, but the decision depends on your preferences.

Some runners don't like to wear orthotics while running because the stiff inserts make your shoes less flexible: That is, they don't bend easily when you land and roll up onto your toes. Others don't like to wear them because they can't find shoes big enough to fit the orthotics.

If your orthotics are uncomfortable, talk to your podiatrist, who may have some advice or be able to make you another pair of orthotics from lighter-weight material.

✔ **Arrange a distraction beforehand.** Consider placing a riveting book or magazine next to the bathtub or turning on a radio playing a program or songs you really like. You're going to need to distract your focus from the intense cold of the ice bath.

✔ **Take a warm shower directly after your ice bath and change into heavy, dry, warm clothes.** You need to chase the chill away.

"Take two new shoes and call me in the morning"

Worn-out shoes are a leading cause of injury. At the first sign of discomfort in your ankle, knee, or hips joints, or even in your shin area, get another pair of shoes (that day!) and begin wearing them right away. You can avoid serious injury by replacing your shoes on a regular schedule and at the first sign of discomfort.

Keep an extra, unopened pair of shoes in your closet. That way, the moment you suspect your shoes are worn, you can have a new pair to wear that day.

Popping pills

Don't save pain relievers as a last option. If you can tolerate them, use them at the first twinge of discomfort, provided that you stay at or below the maximum dosages listed on the package labeling. These pills not only relieve pain but also reduce swelling (except for Tylenol and other acetaminophen products, which don't reduce swelling), a condition that may be contributing to your pain.

Changing your running surfaces

As Chapter 10 discusses, hard running surfaces are a leading cause of impact injuries, such as stress fractures. To avoid an injury or steer clear of making one you have worse, try to run from one-third to one-half of your mileage on dirt roads, parks, trails, and other soft surfaces.

Strengthening your muscles

If you think that you have a weak or imbalanced muscle or group of muscles (see Chapter 10) and you don't know how to strengthen it by, for example, doing sit-ups, call a physical therapist and ask whether you can pay for a consultation to find out how to strengthen that area. A massage therapist may be able to offer the same advice.

Aaron Mattes, the inventor of Active Isolated Stretching, has also developed strengthening routines for various muscle groups. You can contact his company at www.stretchingusa.com.

Taking time off

Sometimes, especially if you've been overtraining, a couple of days off may be just the rest your body needs to recoup from an injury. (See Chapter 16 for a list of symptoms of overtraining.) Be sure that you really need it, though, and that you wouldn't benefit even more from stretching, icing, or strengthening muscle groups.

If you take 2 or more days off, be careful on your first run back. Do a slow, easy warm-up and keep your mileage fairly low that day.

Keeping your legs elevated

At the first sign of discomfort in your legs, after you've stretched the area, iced, and purchased new shoes, find something to rest your legs on that elevates your legs above the level your heart. Put a pillow at the foot of your bed, under the sheet and comforter. Also find a way to raise your legs while you watch TV or relax at home. In addition, if your legs rest on the floor throughout your work day, ask your boss whether you can order (and, if necessary, even pay for) a stool for your feet. Your legs won't be above your heart, but they'll feel better if they're elevated even a little.

Examining Everyday Injuries

The injuries discussed in this section, listed roughly from the most common to the least common, are a plague on distance runners. Become comfortable with recognizing the symptoms and acting quickly to either treat the problem or see a professional.

For each injury, you find a tip with insider information on the most common way to reduce your discomfort. These tips certainly aren't the only approaches to these injuries. If you ever believe your injury is serious, don't hesitate to see a physician as soon as possible.

Rubbing up against blisters

Blisters are a build up of water or blood under a thin layer of skin, usually on the feet. Friction between your skin and some other object causes blisters.

- **Probable causes:** Because an object rubbing repeatedly against your skin brings on a blister, they're often caused by poorly fitting shoes (too tight or too loose). Shoes that are too tight rub uncomfortably against the skin; shoes that are too loose allow your foot to slide around ever so slightly inside your shoe, and that sliding causes the blister. Socks that are too thick or long can also cause a blister, because they can bunch up and create an object for your skin to rub against. Not wearing socks also causes blisters because your skin rubs against the seams of the inside of your shoe. Shorts or a shirt rubbing against skin can bring on blisters, too.

- **Usual treatment:** Leave them alone and let them dry out on their own.

If you leave them alone and let them dry out on their own, you may spend several days running in severe pain. Blisters are no joke, and because they're painful, you may end up adjusting your running gait to accommodate the pain, and that may lead to a more serious injury. Follow through on these steps instead:

1. **Go to the store and buy Band-Aid Advanced Healing bandages.**

   These look different from regular bandages: They don't have the cotton pad in the middle the way a normal adhesive bandage does, and the surface of the bandage is quite smooth — almost like skin. These bandages come in several sizes, so choose the one that can cover your blister the best.

Correcting calluses

A *callus* is a thickening of the skin that usually has the same causes as blisters: friction between skin and another object. In fact, blisters can turn into calluses if the water never drains out of the blister and a hard callus forms over the area.

Calluses may seem like a good thing — after all, thicker skin is tougher, and therefore better, than thin skin, right? But they aren't. Calluses on your feet have a way of shearing off during long runs or races, exposing raw skin underneath just at a time when you need your feet the most.

To get rid of your calluses, use a metal callus remover, which looks a bit like a cheese grater. (You may never be able to grate cheese again.) You simply rub the tool against your callus, and within a few days, you grind much of the callus right off. It may not completely remove the callus, however, and it doesn't work for hard-to-reach places. An alternative is a chemical corn and callus remover. Usually, these are small discs that you apply to the area and cover with another layer. Before long, the callused skin dries up and sloughs off.

---

2. **Sterilize the blistered area with rubbing alcohol.**

3. **Open the blister up using nail cutters or a small pair of scissors that you've first doused in alcohol.**

   Cut away all of the puffed-up or blistered skin.

   If you take a shower at this point, you'll end up screaming your head off. For some reason, hot water on an open blister is like hot coals on the bottom of your feet.

4. **Blot the blistered area dry with a clean cloth.**

   You want to get it as dry as possible before applying the bandage.

5. **Apply the bandage to the area, place the palm of your hand over the bandage, and apply pressure to the bandage for about a minute.**

   The heat from your hand helps the bandage seal to your skin. The bandage can stay on for several days through your runs and showers. When it begins to peel off, remove it and allow the area to dry for a while. If your blister no longer hurts, leave the bandage off. If it's still causing you pain, place another Advanced Healing bandage on your blister.

If your blister is in an awkward area or is small (the small ones are sometimes the most painful), use one of two liquid-bandage products available: Band-Aid Liquid Bandage and New Skin Liquid Bandage. After sterilizing the blistered area, opening the blister, and cutting away the skin, apply your liquid bandage product of choice generously to the open wound, using the applicator that comes with either product. And get ready to howl in pain, because the liquid bandage product will feel far worse than the blister for about 2 minutes. Afterward, however, the bandage seals the area and feels just like your regular skin.

Staring at shinsplints

Shinsplints refer to pain in your shins that stays constant or actually feels better as you progress through a run.

- ✔ **Probable cause:** Inflexibility in shins and calves; lack of strength in shins; doing too much, too soon.
- ✔ **Usual treatment:** Time off running; taping the shins.

Shinsplints are actually a cinch to treat. You have to massage the troughlike areas just to one side of your two shinbones. Locate one of your shinbones and move a bit to the right and left until you find a deep trough. Deeply massage that trough with your thumbs and fingers. This hurts. Repeat with the other shinbone and follow up by icing your shin. Do this twice a day for 3 or 4 days, and your shin pain will likely disappear. Be sure to stretch your calves well (see Chapter 5), because they're probably tight, as well. If you have high arches (see Chapter 2), you may also consider switching to a shoe made specifically for your type of foot. And always be sure to increase your mileage no more than 10 percent each week to avoid doing too much, too soon (see Chapter 6).

Looking at leg cramps

Some runners experience cramping during sleep or during runs.

- ✔ **Probable cause:** Lack of potassium; dehydration.
- ✔ **Usual treatment:** Increasing potassium intake; consuming enough water; massage.

Is it shinsplints or a stress fracture?

The only official way to tell the difference between shinsplits and a stress fracture is with a *bone scan,* which is done with a machine that looks like an X-ray machine on steroids. If shinsplint pain doesn't respond to massaging and gets worse the more you train, see a physician to schedule a bone scan.

Eat two bananas a day and drink at least 80 ounces of water every day. Bananas are loaded with potassium. In addition, if you're trying to train for a marathon by drinking only water, it won't work. Add at least 32 ounces of a noncarbonated sports drink to your daily fluids.

Arching away from plantar fasciitis

Your plantar fascia is a membrane that stretches from your toes to your heel. With *plantar fasciitis* (pronounced *plan*-tar fa-shee-*eye*-tiss), this membrane swells, and you feel extreme pain in your feet.

> ✔ **Probable cause:** Inflexibility in the foot and calf; improper shoes.
>
> ✔ **Usual treatment:** Orthotics; surgery.

Take a trip to your local running store and ask for a shoe that can alleviate plantar fasciitis. Seriously, it can be this simple if you go to a running store that has experienced staff (people who take the time to get to know you and your running style — see Chapter 2). At the same time, stretch your calves, feet, and toes twice a day (see Chapter 5) and massage your arch, heel, calves, and toes every chance you get. Consider seeing a massage therapist.

Twisting an ankle

You probably twisted your ankle at least once as a kid. As a runner, you're liable to inflict this trauma to the ligaments and tendons around your ankle again.

> ✔ **Probable cause:** Stepping in a hole or on a tree root or other object.
>
> ✔ **Usual treatment:** Heavy bandaging, icing, time off running.

If you twist your ankle on a run, keep your shoe on and continue running! Huh? No really, this immediate nontreatment treatment makes the most sense. The best thing you can do is to not allow the area to swell. By keeping your shoe on and continuing to run — even for just a little while and even very slowly — you keep the swelling down.

When you get home, plunge your ankle into an ice bath (see the "Applying ice" section, earlier in this chapter), and then stretch your ankle well (see Chapter 5) and keep it elevated. Repeat this twice a day for 3 days. Don't bandage the area.

Not needing knee pain

Runners experience all types of pain in their knees.

- ✔ **Probable cause:** Lack of strength in muscles around the knees; poor shoes; twisting the knee on a tree root or other object.

- ✔ **Usual treatment:** Physical therapy; time off running. Physicians often recommend giving up running completely.

Make the local running store your first stop and buy new shoes. Ice your knee at least once a day and do the following knee-strengthening exercises: single-leg squats (see Chapter 7), toe raises (see Chapter 7), and wall slides. To do wall slides:

1. **Lean against a wall with your feet shoulder-width apart and about 18 inches away from the wall.**

   Your upper legs are at a 45-degree angle to the wall, and your back is straight up against the wall.

2. **Slide down the wall until your knees are bent and your upper legs are completely horizontal, parallel to the floor.**

3. **Push yourself back up to your starting position.**

Do each exercise 12 times and do two sets of each every day. You'll notice a difference in about five days.

Holding off hip pain

You may experience soreness in your hips after an especially hard or long run. But pain deep in your hip that doesn't respond to icing or other measures is a different proposition.

- ✔ **Probable cause:** Inflexibility; muscle imbalance; poor running technique.

- ✔ **Usual treatment:** Time off running.

Before taking time off, do the hip stretches in Chapter 5 and do them faithfully, twice a day. In addition, see a massage therapist or physical therapist for strengthening exercises for your hip: The following is a good one.

1. **Lie on your side with a light weight (one pound) on your upper leg.**

2. **Raise and lower your top leg ten times; rest and repeat.**

Check out another good one:

1. **Lie on the same side but put the weight on the other leg.**
2. **Raise the outside leg (the weightless one) and hold it in the air.**
3. **Bring the lower leg with the weight up to the upper leg and back down again, ten times; rest and repeat.**

Backing away from back pain

Runners often experience back pain and tightness in the lower back.

> ✔ **Probable cause:** Lack of strength in stomach muscles; sometimes also from poor running technique, low-quality bedding, or a poorly designed desk chair.

> ✔ **Usual treatment:** Physical therapy; surgery; time off running.

Some back injuries are very serious. However, before you proceed with any serious treatment, if you can, take a couple of weeks and do sit-ups every day (see Chapter 7 for a description). Eventually build up to 100 to 200 sit-ups per day. Also consider getting a new bed and asking your boss for (and, perhaps, offering to pay for) a state-of-the-art desk chair if you spend most of your work time behind a desk.

Fussing about stress fractures

The most common stress fracture is a hairline bone fracture in the shinbones. You may experience pain in your shin that usually gets worse during a run and doesn't respond to icing.

> ✔ **Probable cause:** Running on hard surfaces; extremely low body-fat.

> ✔ **Usual treatment:** Time off running.

The only way to heal a stress fracture is to stay completely off the affected bone for 6 weeks. If you're diagnosed with a stress fracture, get yourself a pair of crutches and stay *off your leg for 6 weeks!* Many doctors prescribe a walking cast for a month, but if you continue to put pressure on the fractured bone, it will never heal completely.

During the 6 weeks that you're using crutches, run in the pool every day to maintain your fitness (see Chapter 12). Running in water is extremely effective. I've seen runners do nothing but train in a pool for 6 weeks, and a month later, win state and national titles.

Knowing When to See a Professional

If you have a severe injury or even a less-than-severe one that worries you or causes you pain, see a professional as soon as you can.

If you'd rather avoid seeing a medical professional and understand that you may worsen the situation by doing so, keep the following guideline in mind: If an injury continues to get worse after 3 days of intensive self-treatment, make an appointment with a professional. If you haven't taken your self-treatment seriously — you think about taking an ice bath but don't, and you want to stretch but haven't — give yourself 3 days of serious self-treatment and then determine whether your condition is getting better, which means the treatment is working, or worse, which means you need to get professional help.

Finding a sports medicine doctor

A *sports medicine physician* is one who specializes in the injuries of sports. Ideally, you want one who specializes in the injuries of distance runners, but finding a doctor who specializes in sports injuries is a pretty good start. To find a sports medicine doctor in your area, contact The American Orthopaedic Society for Sports Medicine at www.sportsmed.org.

Don't go to your family physician for a running injury! Doctors who don't specialize in sports injuries generally have one answer to your running injury: Stop running for a while and allow it to heal. This is a problem for two reasons:

- ✔ If you take time off of your training, you're not likely to be able to run your marathon. Although this is acceptable if your running injury is severe, if your injury isn't severe, you've wasted precious training time.

- ✔ Most injuries have a specific cause, and running is *not* that cause. Something you're doing in conjunction with your training may be the cause, such as not stretching or wearing the wrong shoes or overdeveloping certain muscles while underdeveloping others, but running itself isn't a bad thing. So if you take time off, the injury is likely to come back as soon as you start running again. This, too, is a waste of precious time.

Instead, see a sports medicine doctor. When you call for an appointment, ask whether she specializes in distance runners. If not, ask whether you can get the name of someone in your area who does.

Making the most of massage

Nearly every professional runner at the elite level uses a massage therapist. That's a pretty powerful endorsement, don't you think? If nearly every elite marathoner in the world wore one particular type of shoe or performed just one particular stretch — heck, if elites ate crushed worms every day — you'd probably figure it was worth a try yourself, right? Even if that shoe cost a bundle or the stretch took you some extra time, you'd likely still consider it.

Consider using a massage therapist. A good therapist — one who works with runners and can combine massage with Active Isolated Stretching (see Chapter 5) — is a fantastic investment in your training.

Massage therapy sounds so wonderful, doesn't it? Perhaps you envision an hour of being lulled to sleep by relaxing music as the tightness in your legs disappears. Hah! Although some massage therapists do gently rub your muscles, that's not what you're looking for. (Massage therapists call that sort of massage a *fluff 'n' buff*.) What a *sports massage therapist* does, instead, is put you through an hour of agony as he untangles the knots in your legs. You want this. You'll leave the office really sore, and you'll need extra fluids throughout the rest of the day, but on the next day's run and continuing for the next 7 to 10 days, you won't believe how loose and comfortable you feel. And if you ask your therapist to focus on a particular area that's causing you pain, you may be able to avoid a serious injury. Just keep in mind that you may have to make several visits before your therapist can work through your inflexibility and alleviate your discomfort.

To find a massage therapist in your area, visit the American Massage Therapy Association at www.amtamassage.org. Then call all those who are convenient to your home or office and ask whether they do Active Isolated Stretching in conjunction with deep tissue massage or sports massage. Keep looking until you find one who does. Or if you just can't find one who meets those criteria, look for one who is experienced in working with marathon runners.

Chapter 12

Cross-Training While You're Injured

In This Chapter

▶ Figuring out how to stay fit while healing an injury

▶ Knowing what can keep you in the best running shape

▶ Understanding how to transition back into running

*B*esides the pain and discomfort of injuries, the most frustrating aspect of being injured is probably watching your fitness disappear. After a few months without running, you're soon in the same shape as your next-door neighbor, the guy with the gut who never ran a step in his life.

Instead of watching in frustration, though, you may be able to engage in some activities while you're injured. This chapter gives you some ideas of what keeps you in the best *running* shape — what can make your transition back to running relatively easy and painless. If you're under a physician's care, however, be sure to ask her about these activities before you begin.

Staying Buff While You're Healing

To stay in running shape while you're injured, you need to find an activity that does all of the following:

- ✔ **Allows the injured area to heal:** Be sure that your cross-training isn't stressing the injury just as much as running would.

- ✔ **Uses the same muscles as running:** Many people believe that exercise is exercise (which is where the myth originates that says you can run 3 days per week, cross-train 2 days per week, take 2 days per week off, and still run a successful marathon). All exercises are not equal: In order to get into running shape, you need to run or find an activity that uses exactly or nearly the same muscles that running uses.

✔ **Keeps your heart rate as high as running does:** Running works your heart better than nearly any other activity, so you want your cross-training activity to produce the same kind of results.

✔ **Keeps you from gaining weight:** If, in addition to transitioning back to running after your injury heals, you also have to lose five, ten, or more pounds, getting back to running will be painful and exasperating. If you have to cut down on your calorie intake while you're injured, do so, but also look for an activity that burns plenty of calories.

Chances are, you won't find an activity that satisfies all your needs. So the following sections discuss a variety of popular cross-training activities with these criteria in mind.

As you begin cross-training, you may not be able to train right away for as many minutes as you had been running. If you're able to, however, try to get back to the same number of minutes — or more — as soon as you're able. Keep in mind, though, that your injury is stressing your body, so you may be more fatigued than you usually are.

Running on water (Or is that "in" water?)

Running in a pool is the number one, most terrific, absolutely fantastic way to stay in shape while you're injured. _Pool running_ (also called _water running_) is not swimming, however. When you run in a pool, you wear a special flotation vest, such as the _AquaJogger,_ available at many large sporting-goods stores. The flotation vest keeps your head and shoulders above the water level, so your feet never touch the bottom of the pool. Then you run vertically, moving your arms back and forth just as you do when you run, lifting one knee and fully extending the other leg on each "step." See Figure 12-1 for an example.

Because you run in a pool in a vertical position, with one leg fully extending as you take each stride, you need to run in water that's at least a foot deeper than you are tall. Even at that depth, you may accidentally touch the ground with your toes if you're tall enough. The best place to pool-run is in the diving well of a community or school pool.

Figure 12-1: Running in a pool is ideal while you're healing.

Pool running is such a great cross-training activity because you don't ever land on the pool floor; instead, the flotation vest keeps you afloat. In addition, because the water provides resistance against your running motion, your heart rate gets nearly as high as with running on land. And, because you use the exact same motion as you do while you run — including pumping your arms — you're using the same muscles that you use while running on land.

Because of the resistance of the water, you may at first feel more fatigued running 40 minutes in the water than you did running 40 minutes on land. In fact, your arms may be so fatigued that you have trouble pulling yourself out of the water at the end of your workout.

In order to maintain your fitness, however, you have to run _more_ minutes than you have been running on land. In the pool, your feet don't hit the ground, and it's that contact that creates and maintains strong muscles in your legs. To compensate, you need to water-run about one and a half times as long as you would on land to maintain the same fitness level. So, after spending a couple of days or weeks getting used to running in the pool and gradually building up your minutes, try to run 50 percent more in the pool than you did while land running. For example, a 40-minute land-run becomes a 60-minute pool run. This allows you to transition easily back to land running when you're healed.

Many runners try to do a combination of running and swimming — perhaps it could be called *swunning*. What they do is lean forward at a 45-degree angle, so they're not vertical like they're supposed to be to run and not horizontal as they should be to swim. And instead of using a running motion, they cup their hands and move their arms from side to side — sort of a modified swimming motion. The problem with swunning is that it doesn't do you any good. This cross between running and swimming is much easier than swimming because of the flotation vest, and it's much easier than pool running because instead of the water resisting your forward motion, you're moving easily through the water.

To be an effective water runner, be sure to stay vertical, keeping your back straight and use a running motion with your arms. Using this proper motion, you do move forward a bit as you water-run, just not very fast. Have you ever run into a driving wind and had trouble making much of a forward motion because the wind kept driving you back? That's how water running feels: The water allows you to move forward slightly, but your forward progress isn't impressive. You won't be running in place, though, so be sure to run around the perimeter of a diving well or stake out a swimming lane.

Being a tortoise for a while: Walking

Walking — especially speed walking — is another good alternative to running. The difference between walking and running is that when you're walking, you're never really airborne. Instead, one foot is always on the ground while the other is in the air. Your heart rate doesn't usually get as high while walking as when running, unless you're able to walk fairly fast: 14 or 15 minutes per mile, and even at this pace, you're not mimicking the way you utilize oxygen when you run.

If your injury is due to the high impact of running, walking may allow your injury to heal while using many of the same muscles that running uses.

Don't weigh yourself down

Don't ever run with weights in your hands or wrapped around your wrists or ankles. Even weights as light as one pound put a tremendous amount of pressure on your joints and can quickly lead to an injury. If you decide to weight train, keep the two activities separate: First run, then lift.

You may need to walk for more time in order to achieve the same fitness level and burn the same number of calories as you did while running. If you measure your mileage in miles, walk the same number of miles that you've been running. If you measure your mileage in minutes (see Chapter 4), add 50 to 100 percent to your runs (making a 40-minute run a 60- or 80-minute walk) as soon as you adjust to the new activity.

Practicing aerobics, yoga, Pilates, or Tae-Bo

Chances are, you won't be able to do high-impact aerobics, power yoga, or Tae Bo when you're healing from an injury. High-impact aerobics uses high-knee or stepping motions, which could circumvent your body's efforts to mend its injury. Similarly, power yoga, a combination of aerobics and yoga movements, requires too much high-impact movement to be much use in healing injuries. *Tae Bo* is aerobic kickboxing — *not* a self-defense program — that involves kicking, punching, and dancing moves, which can shock your joints and thus undermine the healing process when you're injured. But if you can cross-train this way (that is, if your doctor tells you not to run but suggests that these activities are okay), great! Join a class or get yourself a good videotape or DVD and after 1 or 2 weeks of getting used to the activity, train at or above your running minutes. You can increase your heart rate, use many of the major running muscles, and burn calories.

In lieu of the high-impact activities, you may be able to cross-train with low-impact aerobics, yoga, or Pilates (pah-*lah*-teez), a method that uses a specific apparatus (a Pilates class or video can introduce you to this apparatus) to perform slow, precise movements that tone your body.

These activities may keep you flexible and fairly toned during your injury, but they won't keep you in running shape. If these are the only activities you're able to do, spend plenty of time and energy working through them. Your transition back to running may still be difficult, but at least you'll be used to exercising.

Biking, blading, skating, and skiing

Biking, rollerblading, speed skating, and cross-country skiing aren't ideal cross-training activities. I group all these activities together because they all use the same muscle groups, which happen to be different muscle groups than runners use. If you don't believe me, look at an elite speed skater and an elite marathoner: Notice any differences in, say, the size of their legs and butts?

These activities do, however, get your heart rate up and burn plenty of calories. Biking, especially, is low impact enough to allow most running injuries to heal.

Like many other cross-training activities, plan to spend more time doing these activities than you did running. You want to bike, blade, skate, or ski about 50 to 100 percent longer than you ran. So a 40-minute run becomes a 60- to 80-minute bike, blade, skate, and/or ski.

Missing the mark on a machine

Using workout machines — such as Nordic Track, rowing machines, the Ab-Doer, and so on — is much like biking, blading, skating, and skiing in the preceding section. No one doubts that, as general exercise, these are top-notch activities. But they're so dissimilar to running that they're not effective ways to cross-train while you're injured, unless you plan to forget about your marathon and enter a 4-hour Ab-Doer competition instead.

Swimming upstream

Swimming isn't a great cross-training activity for running. The muscle groups that you use while you swim are different, your heart rate doesn't usually go nearly as high as it does while running, and you don't burn many calories while swimming.

If you're able to swim as a cross-training activity (and unless you have a cast on, your doctor will probably say it's okay to), run in the pool instead. See the "Running on water (Or is that 'in' water?)" section, earlier in this chapter.

Training with weights

Weight training isn't a great alternative to running. Your heart rate barely bleeps on the screen, you use exceedingly different muscle groups, and you barely burn any calories. While you can weight train and stay off your feet (that is, you can weight train from a seated position), another seated activity, biking, is probably more appropriate.

If you're interested in training with weights as a part of your regular (that is, non-injured) marathon training, consider doing circuits, which combine running with light weight lifting, push-ups, sit-ups, and so on. Chapter 7 explains circuits in detail.

Getting physical — therapy, that is

Physical therapy, while often a necessary part of rehabilitating your injury, is not exercise. Even if you sweat while doing your therapy, it still is so little like running that it's not worth considering as an alternative. If you're scheduled for physical therapy, do it in addition to a workout routine.

Transitioning Back to Running

Depending on how well you're able to mimic running, your transition back to running can be anywhere from a snap to excruciating:

✔ **Pool running and swimming:** Because pool running mimics land running so well, you may have stayed in decent running shape throughout your injury. Swimming, on the other hand, doesn't use the same muscles as running, so as you transition back to running, you may feel extremely sore and out of shape. In addition, no matter which pool activity you've been doing, the environment in a heated indoor pool is much more sheltered than the outdoors, so you're likely to experience some labored breathing as you transition back to running. This passes in a week or so.

✔ **Walking, aerobics, Pilates, Tae Bo, and yoga:** How well you transition to running after doing these activities depends on how fast you walked or how intensely you worked at aerobics, Tae Bo, or yoga. If you walked slowly or did low-impact aerobics, yoga, or Pilates (which may have been great for healing your injury), you may now find that your heart rate didn't get high enough to keep in you in good cardiovascular shape, and your muscles weren't challenged enough to stay in good muscular shape. However, if you walked fast or did the more intense versions of the other disciplines (which usually isn't great for healing an injury but can keep you in terrific shape), you may find that you're comfortable with running again in just a week or so, because these activities use many major running muscles.

✔ **Biking, rollerblading, speed skating, cross-country skiing, and workout machines:** Biking, rollerblading, cross-country skiing, rowing, and so on can keep you in great shape if you do them intensively enough for long enough periods. The problem is that they don't keep you in great *running* shape, which means that you're likely to have a few days or even weeks of soreness as you get back to running. Your breathing (if you did an outdoor activity) and heart rate, however, are likely to weather the transition well.

✔ **Weight lifting and physical therapy:** If these are the only activities you participated in for several weeks, get ready to start running from scratch. These activities don't raise your heart rate even close to the level that running does and don't use the major running muscles. Treat yourself as though you've been off running completely and start from square one (see Chapter 4).

If you've been off your legs for more than 2 or 3 weeks and you haven't been able to cross-train, as is often the case if you're in a cast or have had serious surgery, consider yourself a beginning runner and start from scratch. Don't even think about the training you were doing before you got hurt and don't dwell on the marathon you're going to miss. Instead, start over. Chapter 4 takes you through your first run back and though a sample 5-week training plan. And keep the tips in Chapter 10 in mind to prevent injuries in the future.

So how do you know how long and how many days to run as you transition back? Follow these steps:

1. **The first day, run for one-half of the average number of minutes that you've been cross-training every day.**

   For example, if you've been cross-training for 60 minutes, run for 30 minutes. If you have to stop and walk, that's okay, but start running again as soon as you can.

2. **For the rest of the week, run every other day and cross-train on the day you don't run, running for one-half of your cross-training minutes and cross-training at the same daily level you were before you started running again.**

   Take at least 1 day off the first week.

3. **The second week, increase your running from 3 days to 4 and increase the mileage by 10 percent.**

   Continue cross-training the other two days. Still take 1 day off.

4. **The third week, increase your running from 4 days to 5 and again increase your mileage by 10 percent.**

   Continue to cross-train on the other day, taking 1 day off.

5. **The fourth week, either drop your cross-training completely or cross-train on your day off, still increasing your mileage by 10 percent.**

6. **For the remaining weeks until your marathon, consult Chapter 6 for a variety of training plans.**

   Be sure to add strides and drills, circuits, and workouts, as appropriate.

Part IV
Planning Racing Strategies

The 5th Wave   By Rich Tennant

"I used to think,'running for the endorphins' was a charity race for an endangered sea mammal."

In this part . . .

*R*acing strategy isn't something you're born with; it's something you develop over time. This part cuts down the racing learning curve. Chapter 13 helps you to choose your marathon, enlist in tune-up races to get you comfortable with racing, establish race goals and plans, and visualize your race. Chapter 14 tells you about eating right before your race, picking up your race packet, warming up and stretching before your race, and finding a place at the starting line.

Chapter 15 gives some ideas about what to do after your race, from cooling down and rehydrating to dealing with aches, pains, and post-race blues. You find out not only when you can schedule another marathon but also how you can make your next one even better.

Chapter 13

Easing Into Marathon Racing

- -

In This Chapter

▶ Selecting the best marathon for you

▶ Racing in advance of your marathon

▶ Preparing yourself mentally

▶ Investing in racing clothes and shoes

- -

*I*f you haven't done much road racing, you need a primer on racing basics. This chapter gives you those basics, from choosing which marathon you want to enter to preparing yourself by running tune-up races to developing a racing strategy for any race you enter. If you've done much racing before, this chapter is likely to be a review for you — feel free to skip it. But if you've never raced, this chapter contains information that can calm your nerves and make you as comfortable with racing as you are with your oldest and dearest pair of running shoes.

Picking and Choosing Your Marathon

Selecting your marathon may be simple for you because you want to run the one that your town hosts every year. But remarkably, many marathoners travel across the country (and world) to race because their towns don't offer one or because other courses offer more appealing amenities, such as the time of year that the race is scheduled, whether the course is rumored to be fast, and so on.

Running with the elites or the locals

Marathons are grouped into two categories:

✔ **Runners' marathons:** These marathons share a number of features that make them appear more serious than their community-based counterparts:

- **Aid stations:** A fancy way of supplying water and sports drink, you can find an *aid station* at every 1 or 2 miles along the course. They may even offer energy gel (see Chapter 9) and fruit, such as oranges or bananas, along the course.

- **Big:** They're often quite large with an many as 35,000 entrants.

- **Clocks:** They almost always have huge clocks that show your per-mile *split* (that's another word for "time") or have volunteers reading splits. This feature is helpful if you're trying to race a particular time.

- **Downtown venue:** Held in large cities, major streets are closed off so that you can run through downtown areas.

- **Elitist:** Runners' marathons invite hoards of elite runners, who can be fun to watch before and after the race. The elite winners (male and female) may take home more than $250,000 for winning the race and setting a world record, and those who finish in the top 10 or 15 (nearly always professional runners) may also make a pretty penny.

- **Fanfare and celebration:** They offer a partylike atmosphere from the moment you arrive at the race headquarters until hours after the marathon is over. The marathon may offer an expo, a running clinic, celebrity singers or other performers, visits by famous runners, and hundreds of thousands of spectators to cheer you on. All this excitement can help you survive a marathon that you may otherwise be tempted to quit.

- **Fast:** Often designed to be fast, they have long straightaways, few turns, and few hills.

- **Lottery registration:** These races usually close their registration early and may have a *lottery* registration system. (With the lottery system, even if you register early, your entry may still not be chosen from among all the registrants.) They may also require a qualifying time in another marathon before you can run them.

Marathons may begin registering runners as much as a year before the marathon. One day, you may not be able to register yet, and the next day, the race may be full. Just because you want to run in a particular marathon doesn't mean you'll be able to. Before you make hotel reservations or buy airline tickets, register for the race you have in mind and wait for verification, usually by e-mail or postcard. Some runners' marathons don't verify entries, but you can check on your status by calling or e-mailing the race director. This contact information is usually on the race Web site.

- **Reliable distance:** Usually exactly 26.2 miles, these races are certified by USA Track & Field (USATF), the governing body of track and field and distance running in the United States. (In other countries, local governing bodies usually certify courses.) You can use a time you run on a certified marathon course to qualify for other marathons.

Chapter 18 lists roughly 25 of the largest and most famous runners' marathons around the world.

✔ **Community marathons:** On the small side (2,000 people or less), *community marathons* are often held in small towns or suburbs rather than in large downtown areas and aren't designed to be especially fast. The staff invites zero or few elite runners, but these marathons may offer delightful scenery or other unusual amenities. They're often not USATF-certified. Community marathons do, however, offer aid stations throughout the course, just as runners' marathons do.

Consider running in a community marathon if you don't want to go far from home, want to register shortly before or on the day of the race, don't want to hassle with thousands of people at the starting line, and aren't looking for an abundance of hoopla on race day. The entry fee may also be a bit lower than a runners' marathon. You can find out about a community marathon in your area by visiting your closest running store and browsing their road race information or asking store employees about a local marathon they can recommend.

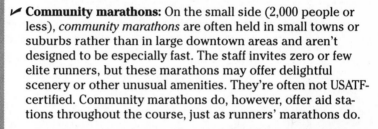

Pre-register or register the day of?

Most marathons close their registrations months before race day, so registering for the marathon on race day isn't an option. Some marathons, however, do allow race-day registration but don't guarantee that registrations won't have filled up by then or don't guarantee a T-shirt on that day. And all marathons charge extra for registering the day of the race.

The only benefit of registering on race day is that you have up until race day to decide whether you want to run. Ultimately, though, this isn't a benefit, because it gives you an out if you don't feel absolutely perfect on race morning.

Ideally, you want to choose your marathon months in advance and register for it right away. By registering early, you assure a spot in the race and also pay less than those who register later (sometimes as much as 50 percent less). You also don't leave yourself an easy way out when you start to get nervous about running 26.2 miles.

Finding the right frequency

Most coaches recommend running no more than two marathons per year, simply because of the wear and tear the race puts on your body. Elite runners usually follow this advice, too, although they may enter shorter races every 1 to 4 weeks in between each marathon.

I recently heard about a guy who runs 30 marathons per year — more than one every 2 weeks — and has done this for years. I also just read about a man who ran three marathons in 3 weeks on two continents. These stories don't necessarily nullify the standard advice to run no more than two per year, however. After all, these two men may have part-time jobs or other unusual situations that you can't duplicate, but they do suggest that no rule is hard and fast.

After your first marathon, don't race another for 6 months. After that, decide whether running marathons more frequently works for you. Perhaps you want to do three or four per year and are willing to make sacrifices in your personal life to do that. If you enjoy this schedule and don't get injured doing it, keep it up.

Tuning Up with Tune-Up Races

A *tune-up race* is one that gets you ready for (that is, tuned-up for) your marathon. Every tune-up race gets you used to racing and makes the day of your marathon that much easier. Chapter 19 gives you a list of about 50 of the largest tune-up races in the United States and Canada (plus a few others from around the world), and your local running store plus the resources in the Appendix can help you find more.

I suggest that you run from three to eight tune-up races in the 10 to 20 weeks before your marathon, depending on how much time you have to train for your marathon. Give yourself at least 6 to 8 weeks to build a mileage base (see Chapter 6), and run at least some strides (discussed in Chapter 8) or a few workouts (see Chapter 7) before running your first tune-up race.

Tune-up races vary in length from 5K (3.1 miles) — which I recommend for your first race and your last one before your marathon — to a half-marathon (13.1 miles) or even longer. Longer races are great preparation for your marathon, but you don't want to do one any closer than one month before your marathon — 6 to 8 weeks before is even better, because, like a marathon, long races from 13 to 20 miles are hard on your body, and you need time to recover from them.

What's your PR?

PR stands for *personal record* — your fastest time at a given distance. Runners like to trade PRs the way that sixth-graders trade baseball cards. After you finish a race at any distance, you can answer the running world's most common opening line: "What's your PR?"

For each race, follow the suggestions in Chapter 14 for preparing yourself the day before and morning of the race: Figure out when and what to eat for your pre-race dinner. Establish a system for setting out your racing clothes the night before the race. Maintain a consistent bedtime and wake time before each race. Develop a race-morning routine, including whether and what you eat for breakfast. Do a warm-up run and stretch before every race. Begin clearing your head of distractions during the race. (Again, details are in Chapter 14.)

Each race also requires a racing strategy, which is discussed in the following "Getting a Handle on Your Strategy" section. Even for your first race ever, you want to create a race strategy that includes an overall goal for that race.

In every way, try to make your tune-up races previews of your marathon. Use your tune-up races to establish a routine that will seem natural by the time your marathon rolls around. A marathon isn't a time to try something new.

Getting a Handle on Your Strategy

Every race needs a strategy, which includes establishing a goal, developing a race plan, and visualizing the race in your mind. Just as you don't set off on a road trip without a map, don't start a road race without a strategy.

Going for a goal

The first step in any racing strategy is developing a goal for every race you enter, including your marathon. Most race goals center around the time you want to finish in; if you make your goal your finishing place — coming in first or among the first ten finishers, for example — you place too much of the burden for your success on other runners. If the race is particularly fast, you may have the best race of your life but finish farther back than you intended. On the other hand, if the race is quite slow, you may finish high with a relatively poor performance.

Goals that focus on your finish time may need to be adjusted if you encounter bad weather on race day, especially if the day is particularly windy. But don't use bad weather as an excuse not to meet your goals: Keep in mind that British marathoner Paula Radcliffe set a world record (2:17:18 — 2 hours, 17 minutes, and 18 seconds) on a 42-degree day with 12 mile-per-hour winds at the 2002 Chicago Marathon.

I assume that you want to finish. No one has ever entered a marathon with a goal of dropping out before the end, except for a few elite athletes who were asked to act as *rabbits;* that is, they paced a friend or teammate for a portion of the race, usually half way, and then intentionally dropped out. So don't make your goal "to finish," because that's a given.

Instead, consider the following sample marathon goals:

- ✔ Finish in under 5 hours, running the entire way. No walking.

- ✔ Run each mile in under 9 minutes.

- ✔ Beat my last marathon time (say, 4:27:50) by 5 minutes.

- ✔ Cross the line before the marathon course closes (6½ hours) by walking no more than 10 of the 26.2 miles.

- ✔ Qualify for the Boston Marathon. (For a 42 year-old man, for example, that's finishing at 3:20 or under — see Chapter 16.)

You can modify these sample marathon goals to work for any race distance. If don't have a clue how fast you may be able to run your first marathon, see Chapter 7 for workouts that help you gauge your potential race pace.

Writing a race plan

A *race plan* is a step-by-step strategy for your race that takes your goal and describes how you plan to achieve it. Like any good plan, make it as specific as you can, detailing the way you intend to run the race, portion by portion.

Consider the following examples of race plans from all sorts of marathon competitors.

✔ **Finish in under 5 hours, running the entire way; no walking.**
Run each mile in 11:16 or under, which is 4:55 pace. Go through
the 10-mile marker in 1:52:36 and 20 miles in 3:45:12. (If you
want to see how to figure your time, see the Cheat Sheet at the
front of this book.)

✔ **Run each mile in under 9 minutes.** Go through the 10K in
55:37, the 10-mile mark in 1:29:42, the half-marathon in 1:57:50,
and the 20-mile mark in 2:59:24. In my last marathon, my mind
started to wander at about 15 miles, and I slowed down, so at
that point, I need to remind myself to keep my focus on the
race and keep watching my split times for 9-minute miles.

✔ **Beat my last marathon time (4:27:50) by 5 minutes or more.**
Work, especially, on the middle 10 miles (miles 9 through 18),
where I started to hurt and thought about dropping out last
time. Hit 10 miles at or under 1:40:00. Hit 18 miles at or under
3 hours.

✔ **Cross the finish line before the marathon course closes by
walking no more than 8 of the 26.2 miles.** Run the first 6
miles and then walk until the 8-mile marker. Run until the half-
marathon marker and walk for 2 miles. Run until the 20-mile
marker and walk for 3 miles. Run the rest of the course.

✔ **Qualify for the Boston Marathon.** Go through the first mile
in 7:40 and maintain that pace for the first 8 miles. Take my
energy gel at the 5-mile mark. At the 8-mile mark, shift gears a
little and begin running 7:35s until the half-marathon mark,
taking another energy gel packet at 10 miles. After I hit that
half-marathon mark, don't let anyone pass me the rest of the
race. Take my third gel-pack at 15 miles. Start focusing on the
backs of people and reeling them in. Maintain 7:35s or speed
up a little. Come through the 20-mile mark in 2:32:00 or under,
which gives me 48 minutes to run the last 6.2 miles (7:49-pace),
a nice cushion. Take my fourth and final gel pack. Really push
those last 6 miles to see what I can do.

The majority of distance-running world records are set with *negative
splits,* which means that runners ran *faster* the second half of the
race than in the first half. To do this in your own marathons, practice it before you ever get to the starting line. Negative-split your
long runs and do a tempo workout occasionally (see Chapter 7) in
which you speed up on each subsequent mile as you run the tempo
portion. Negative split in your tune-up races and plan your
marathon race around a negative split.

Visualizing your race

Visualizing your race means that you go through the entire race in your mind, as though you're watching a movie of yourself in your race before it actually happens. Many elite runners visualize their races beforehand, because it helps them prepare mentally for the race better than just about anything else.

To visualize, work through the following steps:

1. **In the weeks and months leading up to your race, write a race plan.**

2. **Review your race plan a few times.**

3. **Close your eyes and imagine the start of the race, focusing on yourself.**

   Some people like to imagine that they're watching themselves. Others like to imagine the race from their eyes, looking outward at everyone else. Either way is fine.

4. **Imagine the race starting; imagine yourself beginning to follow your race plan.**

   Try to envision what you'll be feeling as you run the first few miles: discomfort that's tolerable; steady, efficient breathing (see Chapter 8); quick and efficient steps.

   You have to be ready to endure some discomfort in a marathon, and envisioning that discomfort prepares you psychologically.

5. **At certain milestones along the race course, picture yourself going through those points in the times you outlined.**

   Imagine a race clock showing the time you plan to run for each portion of the race, as outlined in your race plan. Imagine yourself going by the race clock, looking up at it, and realizing you're hitting your goal pace. At each point, try to be realistic about how you may be feeling physically at that time.

6. **Imagine yourself gutting out the last few miles of the race and crossing the line just as the finish clocks shows your goal time.**

7. **Repeat every week or so.**

Visualization isn't something you begin doing the day before your races. Instead, it's a habit you get into soon after you begin training. Each visualization session may take 5 or 10 minutes and may be difficult at first, but you get better at it the more you do it.

Some sports psychologists specialize in helping you with visualization. Yes, they're expensive, but if you're serious about marathoning and have trouble performing well in races (assuming your physical preparation is everything it needs to be), a sports psychologist may help you get over the hump. You can probably find one by looking in your phone book or searching the Internet for sports psychologists in your area. (Some rural areas may not be well populated with sports psychologists.) Before making an appointment, be sure to ask whether race visualization is something she specializes in.

Deciding Whether to Invest in Racing Gear

If you've run a marathon or have entered tune-up races, you may notice that some runners wear special, lightweight running shoes or sport odd-looking carriers for water and energy gels (see Chapter 9). Still other runners wear perfectly fitted sunglasses or color-coordinated racing outfits. At some point, you may wonder whether you should be spending money on these items.

For your first race, don't bother buying much fancy stuff. Wear the shoes you train in, although I do suggest switching to a new pair of the same brand and model of your current training shoes about 2 weeks before your marathon. Then get yourself a comfortable pair of running shorts and choose a *singlet* (a fancy way of saying tank top — see Chapter 2) that doesn't *chafe* (rub areas raw after running for a number of miles), and leave it at that.

A rundown of your racing-equipment options for future races is as follows:

- ✔ **Sunglasses:** Squinting for 26.2 miles — in addition to all the hours that you spend training — isn't good for your eyes or your face. If you choose to wear sunglasses, check out Chapter 2 to make sure that you get ones that are meant especially for running.

- ✔ **Gel carriers:** As far as gel carriers go, you do need something to carry energy gel packs. Chapter 9 gives you several suggestions.

- ✔ **Color-coordinated singlet and shorts:** This is strictly a matter of choice. If you feel better wearing matching clothes made by a major running-shoe or clothing manufacturer, go for it. All you really need, though, is something light and comfortable.

Elite runners always match and look good in their uniforms, but they rarely pay for them. Elites are usually *sponsored* by shoe companies, which provide them with all the training and racing equipment they need (including shoes and matching uniforms), and may also provide travel money, a salary, and bonuses for performing at certain levels. The top sponsored runners around the world make about $250,000 per year in salary. They also make money from race directors for winning races and setting records. And they never pay for running shoes, racing outfits, hotel rooms, airline tickets, or race entry fees. It's a pretty good gig, if you can get it.

✔ **Racing flats:** Of all that you can buy to race in, I'm least enthusiastic about marathoners wearing *racing flats,* which are lightweight, less-supportive running shoes than the ones you train in. In shorter races, I'm all for wearing racing flats, because the race isn't long enough for the lack of support in the shoe to affect you. But when you're running 26.2 miles, you need a supportive shoe.

The reason runners wear racing flats is because they get to carry less weight around over the duration of the race. If you really want to do this, I recommend that, instead of racing flats, you purchase lightweight training shoes, which are often worn by lightweight, forefoot-striking, efficient runners (see Chapter 2) for everyday training. These types of shoes are probably lighter than your training shoes but still offer good support over the length of a marathon.

Why do elite women wear bunhuggers?

Bunhuggers are just like they sound: shorts that hug the buns of the person wearing them. This variation on running shorts looks just like bikini bathing-suit bottoms and are sometimes worn by elite women (never men!). The question is, why?

The main reason is comfort. No, the shorts themselves aren't really that comfortable to wear in public (no more than wearing underwear in public is comfortable), but racing makes you sweat, and when sweat collects in regular running shorts, those shorts become heavy and stick to your body. Bunhuggers are so light that sweat doesn't weigh them down. This doesn't make much difference to most people, but when you're counting on seconds to help you qualify for races or set records, a little less weight can make a difference.

So perhaps the question should be, why don't elite men wear them?

Chapter 14

Marathon Countdown: T Minus 24 Hours

In This Chapter

▶ Planning your pre-race meals

▶ Getting your race number, timing chip, and T-shirt

▶ Lining up your clothes, shoes, and other gear

▶ Sleeping peacefully the night before

▶ Knowing how to warm up

▶ Getting set at the starting line

*T*he day before and morning of your race are nerve-racking times. Before you ever get to this day, establish a routine for your long runs, tune-up races, and workouts if you choose to do them (see Chapter 7), and then continue that routine for the marathon.

Whatever you do, don't establish a new routine. Continue the same habits — eating, sleeping, running in pre-race runs (the day before a race), warming up and cooling down before a race or workout, and so on — for your marathon. Keep to your routine and don't tweak or change any details at the last minute.

This chapter tells you what a traditional pre-race routine looks like.

Dining the Day Before

The day and night before your marathon, don't pig out on junk food or high-sugar carbohydrates (see Chapter 9). Instead, drink plenty of water (not beer) and eat veggies, whole grains, lean proteins, and some fruits. Stop eating by 6:00 at night and don't overeat. You need plenty of time to digest your food before race time the next morning.

Many big marathons now offer a pasta dinner the night before the race. I suggest staying away from these for three reasons:

✔ They often may serve greasy breadsticks and desserts, and you want to avoid eating any greasy foods the night before your marathon. Many people feel queasy during a marathon, and greasy or fatty foods only add to this discomfort.

✔ Usually dinner doesn't *start* until around 6:00 at night, which is about the time you want to *stop* eating.

✔ They're often all-you-can-eat dinners, which encourage you to overeat. You can eat all you want tomorrow, after your marathon is over, but you're better off eating too little the day before the marathon than eating too much.

If you want to go to the pasta dinner because you can find few other restaurants near your hotel or because you want to participate in every event offered at the marathon just for the experience, go see what it's all about. Try to be one of the first people in line, though, and choose your food carefully. See Chapter 9 for all the specifics about good nutrition for marathoners.

Picking Up Your Packet

One or two nights before your marathon, you're required to pick up a *race packet,* which may include any or all of the following and may even be presented in a nifty bag:

✔ **Your race number (also called a *bib* number) and safety pins:** Pin the number to the front of your race shirt. Nearly every race requires a race number. Pack some extra safety pins, in case your packet doesn't include them.

At most large races, you can't pick up your packet until you know what your race number is. To find this out, you first visit a large board that lists every registered runner by last name. Find your name and read across to your race number. Then proceed to the table that's distributing your number in a range of race numbers. At smaller races, you pick up your packet by telling the race volunteer what your last name is.

✔ **Timing chip:** This chip records when you start the race, at what time you finish, and potentially, whether you crossed certain mile markers. (This last feature keeps people from cheating by jumping in the race partway through.) You attach the chip to one of your shoes by lacing through it or using a tie-down that's in your packet. Race volunteers collect the chip at the end of the race. If you don't finish and don't turn in your chip, you may be charged $30 for the chip.

Smaller races don't usually utilize timing chips.

✔ **Final race instructions:** This may be as fancy as a glossy brochure or as simple as a handwritten sheet of paper, but it contains information that you need to know, such as a course map and any last-minute instructions. Review this carefully. If your packet doesn't contain this information, review the entry form or online information that you first saw when deciding on this marathon, just so you're doubly sure of the starting time and other details.

✔ **T-shirt:** Some larger races have stopped offering T-shirts to racers, but if your marathon does give them out, you probably have to stop by a special T-shirt table, show your race number to the volunteer sitting at the table, and then receive your shirt.

Many people choose to wear their race T-shirts during the marathon. I don't really understand this, because new T-shirts are often unshrunk, itchy, and heavy. You want to be ultra comfortable during your marathon, so plan in advance what to wear in the race and save your race T-shirt for the following week or the trip home.

✔ **Information about other races:** Keep, toss, read, or do whatever with this information that ranges from local, shorter races to other marathons across the country.

✔ **Information about or free samples of products and/or free giveaways from sponsors:** These products range from sample products that relate to running (bandages for blisters, lubricants to help with chafing, energy gels and bars, and so on) to marketing giveaways, such as pens, pins, shoelaces, and sweat bands.

You may decide to try sample products at some later time, but don't use them for this marathon. Don't eat an energy bar that you never tried before or use a lubricant that's new to you. A marathon isn't the time to try anything new, but you can use the information and products in the future if you think they'll help you.

Many marathons don't allow you to pick up your packet the morning of the race nor do they mail packets. If you live far from the marathon and are planning to drive in on race morning, contact the race director to verify whether a friend who lives closer can, in fact, pick up the packet for you. A better bet is to pay for a hotel room near the race start line, pick up your packet the night before, and avoid fatiguing your legs with a long drive on race morning.

Getting Your Ducks All in a Row

The night before your race, attach your race number to your singlet/tank top, running bra, or whatever other top you plan to race in (and not remove during the race). Don't wait until the morning of the race to do this.

Then set out your morning running clothes in the order that you'll put them on. I usually use the back of a chair for this. First lay out your outer layer that you'll wear on your warm-up: running pants, long-sleeved T-shirt, and jacket (if the weather will be cold enough to require a jacket). Next, lay out your singlet or other top, running bra (if that applies to you), and racing shorts. The next morning, you won't have to think or rush around trying to find what you need but can put these items on, in order, while you're still waking up.

Have your shoes ready and laced with your timing chip. (See the preceding "Picking Up Your Packet" section for information about chips.) Place your socks on top of your shoes so that you don't have to look for those, either.

Place the items that you're going to need right before the race starts in a bag. If you plan to change tops after warming up, add your singlet or other top to the bag along with your stretching rope, sunglasses, inhalers (if you have asthma), and so on. Also set out your car keys and wallet or hotel key, so that you don't have to look for them.

 If the race has a *gear check* or *bag check,* use it. The process works like this: You bring the bag you packed the night before with you to the race and keep it close by until you no longer need it (maybe 10 to 15 minutes before the race begins). At that point, you stand in line at the gear check and then hand them your bag. They mark it in some way, usually with your race number, and have it available for you to pick up after the race.

 Don't get caught standing in line at the gear check when the race starts! Plan to check your gear at least 10 minutes before the race starts.

If the race doesn't have a gear check, you have a few options:

> ✔ **If you drive to the race and can park close to the starting line, keep the gear you need in your car.** Lock your car before you head to the start. Allow yourself enough time to get back and forth to your car before the race begins.

Remember to take your car key with you and string it through your shoe laces or put it in the key pocket that's standard in most running shorts.

✔ **If you stay in a hotel that's right at or very near the starting line, use the room as your own gear check.** Leave what you need in the room, go for a warm-up, and then revisit your hotel room to stretch with your rope, get rid of your warm-up gear, go to the bathroom, and so on. Do, however, allow time to get up and down the elevator, which can be time-consuming in a large hotel.

✔ **Ask someone to help you.** This is by far the easiest route. You simply have someone along to whom you hand off your stuff before the race starts and who delivers it to you at the end of the race. If no one you know will do this out of the goodness of his heart, consider paying someone.

✔ **Plan to throw away everything you use before but not during the race.** This means that you don't wear your expensive running pants (see Chapter 2) to warm up in but wear cheap sweat pants that you don't mind losing. You wear your least-favorite long-sleeve shirt and bring an old piece of rope to stretch with. You then leave this stuff at the starting line, knowing that it'll be tossed out by race officials after the start or get picked up by someone looking for another long-sleeve T.

Getting Plenty of Shut-Eye

Whether you're sleeping in your own bed or a hotel room, go to bed early and try to get a good night's sleep.

If your sleeping and training schedules are quite different than the marathon start time allows, spend the week before your marathon getting the two in sync. Suppose, for example, you're running a marathon with a 7:30 a.m. start time. Now, suppose you go to sleep around 11:00 at night because you don't have to be at work until 9:00 the next morning, and you run after work at 6:00. In the week or two before your marathon, start going to bed earlier (say, 9:30), and getting up earlier (say, 6:30), so that you're used to both getting up at that time and running that early. During that week or two, also switch your training schedule and start running in the morning, so that you're used to performing well at that time of day.

Slumbering long enough

If you ran high-school track or cross-country, you may remember your coach telling you that getting plenty of sleep the night before your big race was critical. Well, technically, it wasn't.

The truth is, the amount of sleep you get in the weeks and months of training leading up to your marathon is far more important than how much you get the night before. In fact, many great runners do nothing but toss and turn the night before the race, but they're so well rested that the one bad night of sleep doesn't matter.

Regardless of whether you think you'll get any sleep, plan to be in bed for 10 hours the night before your race. This way, even if you don't sleep well, you may still get 6 or 7 hours of rest. If you're at home, ask everyone in advance to plan to go to bed early or engage in quiet activities after you go to bed. If you're in a noisy hotel (many race hotels turn into party towns the night before a marathon), stuff a thick towel at the bottom of your door before you go to sleep. If you're an especially light sleeper, before you make your reservation, ask whether you can get a room on the top floor, where you're less likely to hear people walking (or dancing) overhead.

When making your reservation, ask on which floor the elite runners are housed and whether you can have a room on that floor. The elite floors are always quiet the night before races.

Setting your alarm

The night before your race, set three alarms for the following morning. Three may seem excessive, but if you miss a race you've been training months for just because you slept through an alarm, you may never forgive yourself.

Set one alarm on your running watch and place it on a bedside table. Get up when you hear that alarm: Sit up and place your feet on the ground. Set another, 3 or 4 minutes later, using an alarm clock. You should already be getting ready when you hear it. To "set" a third, use the hotel wake-up service or ask someone in your family to check in on you 5 or 10 minutes after your alarm clock. This is just a precaution, in case you miss the others.

Get up 20 to 45 minutes before you need to leave for your warm-up, depending on how long your morning routine takes. (See the "Warming Up and Stretching" section, later in this chapter.) This allows you time to put in your contacts, wash your face, brush your teeth, get dressed, and so on without constantly watching the clock. Don't get up earlier than you need to, though: That just gives you extra time to be nervous.

Skipping a Square Breakfast

I don't recommend that you eat anything the morning of the race. You'll have plenty of opportunities to refuel during the race. (See the "Guzzling and Gobbling on the Run" section, later in this chapter.) You'll be awake for less than an hour before you start warming up, so you won't get hungry. No one ever died of starvation from not eating but plenty of people have thrown up during races because they ate when they shouldn't have.

If you feel that you must eat, some people have luck with dry toast or half a plain bagel. You may also want to consider eating an apple or other non-citrus fruit. (Citrus can cause heartburn, especially when you're nervous.)

Although you want to drink plenty of water during your training months, including the day before the race, drinking water the morning of your race only makes you have to go to the bathroom just before or during the marathon. Instead, take a few small sips of water as you go through your morning routine, just to wet your mouth. And if the race offers water near the starting line, have a few more sips there. But don't guzzle water at this point.

Warming Up and Stretching

Before every race, I warm up with a 20-minute run, stretch for about 10 minutes, and do some strides. Invariably, someone in the crowd yells, "You're tiring yourself out," which always makes me laugh. Although running too much before a race (say, 10 miles) would tire anyone out, running 1 to 3 miles and doing a few strides before a race allows your muscles to get ready for the difficult task at hand. And stretching helps you find tight spots and relax them before they cause problems in the race.

I recommend the following routine before your marathon:

1. **About 50 minutes before the race is scheduled to begin, go to the bathroom.**

   The portable bathrooms near the start line often have endless lines, and those lines get longer the closer you get to race time. If the lines look long before your warm-up, try to find a bathroom *during* your warm-up. If you must wait in line, do some stretching while you wait. Plan on this step taking about 10 minutes.

2. **Go on a 10- to 15-minute jog.**

   Start out at whatever pace you need and gradually increase to your marathon race pace.

   Be sure to wear running pants or sweats and a long-sleeve T-shirt, sweatshirt, or running jacket to warm up in, no matter how hot it is. If you're not convinced that this clothing is necessary and you're tempted to wear shorts and a tank top for your warm-up, take a look at the elite runners at your next race. They all wear running pants and a long-sleeve T at a minimum. Elites do this to stay warm and sweaty up until race time. If you warm up, get sweaty, and then get chilled, you've done more harm than good to your muscles.

   Never wait in line to go to the bathroom after you warm-up and remove your warm-up clothes. You'll get freezing cold, and all your leg muscles will tighten.

3. **Get out your stretching rope, find a place to lie down, and stretch each leg for 5 minutes.**

   Even a 20-minute warm-up run is a run, and I advocate stretching after *every* run. (I often do my stretching in a dirty, oily parking lot, but at that point, I don't care.)

   Keep a close eye on your watch at this time, because you don't want to get so into stretching that you forget how close you are to the start time.

4. **Get rid of your rope and warm-up clothes.**

   See the "Getting Your Ducks All in a Row" section, earlier in this chapter, for ideas on what to do with racing paraphernalia. Plan to spend 10 minutes or so getting rid of your gear. If you stand in line at the gear check, leave most of your warm-up clothes on until you're close to the front of the line, so that you don't get chilled.

5. **Make your way to your place in line, doing a few strides on your way, if you like.**

Pulling Strings at the Start

The bigger your marathon, the more trouble you may encounter getting a good position near the starting line. At larger marathons, people have been known to wait 5 or more *minutes* to start running after the gun goes off. Generally, the slower you plan to run your marathon, the more time you're going to wait after the starting gun goes off before you start moving. This is because you must line up according to your race number. Smaller numbers are assigned to people who have or think they will run a faster time, and numbers are increasingly larger for people who have or think they will run slower. Some races ask entrants to line up according to their per-mile race time. Volunteers carry big signs that say, "8:30 per mile," "11:00 per mile," and so on, for runners to see and line up near.

The problem is many people aren't honest: Some runners put a fictitious time on their entry forms or ignore the per-mile signs. Then these runners start out slower than the people behind them, causing a traffic jam. The front of the starting area is for people who plan to run 5- or 6-minute miles. If you're planning to run 10-minute miles, you don't belong in the front. If you're concerned that you'll stand for too long after the gun goes off and mess up your time, I have this advice for you: Run in a small marathon, where this isn't an issue. If you choose to run in a large marathon, follow the rules and help everyone have a pleasant experience.

Although your *finish time* (the time you see as you cross the line and the time printed in the newspaper) doesn't reflect all the time you may wait at the starting line, your chip time will. Your *chip time* registers on the *timing chip* that you wear on your shoe. (To review the features of the timing chip, see the "Picking Up Your Packet" section, earlier in this chapter.) Your timing chip records the time when you cross the timing pad at the starting line and subtracts it from the time you cross the timing pad at the finish line. A chip time is, therefore, much more accurate and can sometimes be used to qualify for other races, such as the Boston Marathon.

Guzzling and Gobbling on the Run

As discussed in Chapter 9, rehydrating and refueling during the marathon is critical. You're given the following options for rehydrating and refueling during your race:

- ✔ **Water:** Most marathons offer water stations about once per mile. I suggest taking advantage of every single one or at worst, every other one. See "Wetting your whistle on the fly" sidebar in this chapter for tips on how to get the water from the cup to your mouth.

At my first long race (15.5 miles) after a long absence from racing, I decided that because I didn't take water on my long training runs, I wouldn't need to take water during the race. In retrospect, I can't believe how silly that thinking was, given that my training runs were run at a slower pace than the race and under much better conditions (on a shaded trail, early in the morning, at cool temperatures). The day wasn't overly hot, but after 8 miles, my calves starting cramping. It felt as though little explosions were taking place in my calves every few steps. This, as you may expect, was incredibly painful. Of course, I started taking water as soon as these cramps started, but it was too late, and I had to finish the second half of the race that way. Sadly, I could have avoided the cramps completely had I just taken a few sips of water at each station.

✔ **High-energy, noncarbonated sports drink:** I personally don't take any sports drinks, such as Gatorade, during a race, but I do inhale it *after* every race. I know many people, however, who do drink it during the race and swear by it. Sports drinks can cause cramping, so if you have a sensitive stomach, stick with water, instead. If you decide to take a sports drink during a race, take water every other time.

Wetting your whistle on the fly

One of the reasons you want to run a few tune-up races before your marathon (see Chapters 13 and 19) is to practice drinking water while you run. It isn't easy, but the following technique may help:

1. **When you approach the water station, aim for one particular cup of water, hold out your hand, and grasp it tightly as you run by.**

2. **With your pinky, ring finger, and middle finger, crush down one half of the top of the cup.**

   This leaves an oval-shaped area on the other side of the cup from which you can drink.

3. **Open your mouth, tilt your head back a bit, and pour the water from the cup into your mouth through this oval-shape, small opening.**

   Don't throw the water back into your throat — you'll just choke on it. Instead, pour the water in and swallow in small sips.

4. **Throw the cup on the ground, not worrying about litter.**

   Volunteers clean up all the cups after all the runners come by.

You often can't tell the difference between water cups and sports-drink cups at the stations. Listen as the volunteers yell out what they have or which comes first, "Water in front, Gatorade in back!"

 ✔ **Energy gels:** *Energy gels* are sugar and fruit goop in a sealed plastic container that you can carry along with you during your marathon. I highly recommend that you practice carrying and taking energy gels during your long runs so that you're used to doing this during your race. Chapter 9 gives you all the information you need about energy gels.

Knowing What to Think About During Your Marathon

People frequently ask me, "What do you think about for hours and hours of running?" The answer: Nothing. That's right: I try really hard during my long runs, workouts, and races to think about absolutely nothing. In fact, I often have to repeat to myself early in a race, "Don't think, just run," whenever random thoughts start to creep in.

The truth is, you have to focus your mind and body completely on your race. Look ahead at the people in front of you and think about trying to catch them. Don't look down or look around; don't read the signs as you go by streets or billboards; don't think up stories about other people in the marathon; don't rehearse what you'll tell others about the race when you're done; don't start justifying why you need to slow down or drop out. Just run and focus exclusively on that.

Banishing thoughts from your mind takes practice, so start early in your training. Running without thinking is much like praying or meditating: When random thoughts creep in, you have to recognize them, let them go, and refocus on the task at hand. Practice not thinking on your long runs and tune-up races, and it will come naturally to you during your marathon.

Chapter 15

After Your Marathon Is Over

In This Chapter

▶ Knowing what to do directly after the race

▶ Recovering in the first week after your marathon

▶ Easing your way back into training

▶ Planning for your next marathon

*T*his is a chapter that you don't want to spend too much time reading before you run your marathon. Yet you don't want to wait until the morning after your race to read it because it contains information that you need to know as soon as you finish.

I suggest reading this chapter 1 or 2 weeks before the marathon and then visiting it again after your marathon. You'll remember enough to know what to do right after the race; you don't want to focus on post-race details when you need to focus on the race itself.

Right after Your Race

Chances are, right after your marathon, you'll feel like doing any or all the following:

- ✔ Crying
- ✔ Drinking anything, from a noncarbonated sports drink to beer
- ✔ Eating anything you can get your hands on
- ✔ Laughing
- ✔ Lying down and taking a nap
- ✔ Never running again
- ✔ Throwing up
- ✔ Wrapping your feet in soft cotton

Although you can't predict how you'll feel after your first marathon, you can plan a few activities that can help you to heal and, perhaps, look forward to your next one.

Immediately following a marathon, you can see plenty of runners who take a seat and then eat and drink. Don't think that because so many people do this, that you should set yourself down to a meal after your big run, too. You won't see those people later that night or for the next 3 or 4 days, when they can barely walk. Stretch a little, walk a little, and get plenty of sugar into your body as discussed in the "Rehydrating and refueling" section, later in this chapter, and you'll be amazed at how great you feel (sore, but not in extreme pain) during the days right after your marathon.

Cooling down

After most shorter races (5K or 10K), you want to spend a few minutes cooling down before you eat anything substantial. For a marathon, however, especially your first one, get plenty to eat and drink (while standing or walking around), and then take a walk.

Try to walk for at least a mile. If you enter any of the larger marathons, the walk back to your car or hotel is likely to be at least that long. But if you're running in a smaller marathon, go a few extra blocks out of the way before heading to your car. And if you're planning to stick around and enjoy the post-race festivities (which can last for hours after the race), change into dry clothes, do a little stretching (see the "Stretching" section, later in this chapter), and then hang out at the event area.

Rehydrating and refueling

The first action you want to take after you finish a marathon is as follows:

1. **Eat one or two packets of energy gel.**

   You can carry an extra packet or two of energy gel or have someone bring them to you at the finish line. A third alternative is to keep some packets in your car, but this helps only if you can park really close to the finish line because you want to consume the gels as soon as possible after finishing your race. See Chapter 9 for more on the benefits of energy gels.

2. **Drink several cups of a noncarbonated sports drink.**

   Sports drinks are better at rehydrating your body after a marathon than water is. You may decide to drink one or two cups of water, too, but at this point, you want to make sure you don't end up in the medical tent due to dehydration. Even if you feel great at the finish, if you don't drink up at this point, you may feel the effects of dehydration within 30 minutes.

3. **Gather up as much fruit and bread as you can hold in your hands and gobble it up.**

    Even if you don't feel like eating, eat! The better you refuel your muscles, the less you'll experience cramping, soreness, and fatigue in the hours ahead. In your food choices, focus on simple carbohydrates (see Chapter 9).

Keep walking while you eat. If you don't feel comfortable walking while you eat, lean up against a wall as you munch. Whatever you do, just don't sit down until you've had a chance to walk and stretch a little. If you sit for a long period right after your race, your leg muscles may cramp and take on a life of their own — a painful life.

Stretching

You absolutely, positively must stretch after your marathon. Before you change out of wet clothes, take a shower, join the post-race party, or drive home, go through at least one set of all your stretches (see Chapter 5). If you don't do this, you'll be so sore the next day that you may not be able to get out of bed.

Okay, I'm not going to lie to you: The day after your marathon, you're going to be sore whether you stretch or not. But stretching makes you less sore than you would be otherwise and keeps your muscles loose, which can help you avoid an injury.

Treating blisters

You're likely to experience painful blisters after (and even during) your marathon. No matter how bad they are, though, you can probably get around well enough to get something to eat, walk back to your hotel room or car, and stretch a little. After that, your first step should be to take care of those blisters. Chapter 11 gives you a detailed description of how to treat blisters using some products that you can buy in any drug store.

When you pack your bag before your marathon, be sure to include several sizes of Band-Aid Advanced Healing bandages, alcohol, sterilized gauze pads, nail cutters or small scissors, and Band-Aid Liquid Bandage or New Skin Liquid Bandage. Chapter 11 tells you when and how to use these products.

Planning a shake-out run or walk

A *shake-out run* is a short run that you take the afternoon or evening after a morning race. (This short run can also be a *shake-out walk* — a brisk walk.) You may begin to tighten up from 4 to 6 hours after your race is over, especially if you've been riding in a car or have taken a nap. A shake-out run loosens you up again and keeps you from being as sore the next day. Run or walk anywhere from 10 to 20 minutes — no more than that.

If a short run or walk just isn't possible the day of your race, try to do *some* sort of activity for 10 to 20 minutes: Ride a bike, swim, do some aerobics in front of the TV, and so on.

The Week after the Marathon

The week after your marathon, and especially the day after, is critical to your recovery. This section helps you get through what can be a painful week.

If you run a Sunday marathon, I suggest taking the following Monday off work. You can sleep in, hobble around, take a nap, and eat, and eat again without having work interfere.

Dealing with aches and pains

Chances are, you're going to be sore — maybe even really sore. You may feel some soreness in your back and arms, but your legs are probably going to be your main tormentor. Many runners have trouble walking down the stairs after a marathon and may have trouble even getting out of bed the morning after.

To manage soreness, do the following:

- **Keep stretching.** Even if you take a few (or more) days off running, keep stretching every day. See Chapter 5 for the lowdown on stretching.

- **Drink plenty of fluids.** In the week after your marathon, don't go anywhere without a water bottle. (And occasionally, substitute a non-carbonated sports drink for water.) Drink as much or more than you did before the marathon.

- **Take cold baths.** Cold baths are initially painful — perhaps even more than the soreness in your legs! But because they heal small tears in your muscles, they relieve soreness better than almost anything else. Chapter 11 gives you specifics about taking a cold bath.

Whatever you do, don't use a hot pad or any other source of heat on your legs. Heat tends to pool your blood, causing microscopic bruises and more soreness.

✔ **Keep running, walking, or running in the pool.** One of the best ways to relieve soreness is to continue activity. This seems backward, but it's true. The more that you move around, the faster your soreness dissipates. If running seems too painful, try walking. Or better yet, spend some time running — not swimming — in a pool, as discussed in Chapter 12.

Knowing how much (or whether) to run

Deciding how much or even whether to run the week after your marathon is really up to you. Continuing to run offers the following benefits:

✔ **Diminish soreness.** Continuing to run dissipates soreness far more effectively than taking time off.

✔ **You maintain your training habits.** Often, the key to consistent training is never getting out of the habit of running every day.

✔ **Even if you overeat, you probably won't gain weight.** Because you're likely to eat too much in the week(s) after your marathon, you may gain a bit of weight if you choose not to run.

✔ **You can get ready for your next marathon that much more quickly.** Even if you run easy the week after your marathon, you'll be ready to get back to your old mileage and workouts faster than if you take time off.

Taking time off, however, also offers benefits.

✔ **Your body gets a physical break** that it may need to heal and recover, especially if you developed blisters or some other minor injury during the marathon.

✔ **You also get an emotional break** from day-in, day-out training that can make future training more palatable.

✔ **You lead a more normal life** for a week or so, with more time for friends, family, and other hobbies.

You don't have to make this an either/or proposition. If you don't feel like running for the first day or two after your marathon, take time off. If you then feel like venturing out for a run, do so. If you want to take another day off after that, go right ahead. Do whatever feels best to you, keeping the benefits of each approach in mind.

Getting plenty of rest

Sleep is essential for getting rid of soreness and getting back into running. I highly recommend taking a nap the afternoon of the marathon. The next day (if you can take time off work or can go to a late church service), sleep in as long as you can and take a nap later that day, too.

For the week following your marathon, you're likely to need as much or more sleep as you need in the weeks leading up to it. Plan on a *minimum* of 8 hours of sleep per night, recognizing that you may need as many as 10 or 12 hours for a while. Soon, however, your body will adjust and return to a more normal schedule.

Eating well

In 2001, U.S. Olympian Deena Drossin finished her first marathon in 2:26:58 — 2 hours, 26 minutes, and 58 seconds. When asked what she planned to do next, she said she wanted to sit on her couch and eat junk food for a month. (Okay, that's not an exact quote, but you get the idea.) Drossin, an elite runner the likes of which hasn't been seen in the United States in years, experienced what every marathoner feels: the need to eat every bad food you can get your hands on the week after a marathon. It's probably a psychological need more than a physical one, but it's still very real, nonetheless.

Give yourself some time to eat all the junk you want but don't take it too far. Eating well is largely a matter of habit, so if you pig out on junk food for too many days in a row, you may have trouble feeling satisfied by foods that are good for you. In addition, if you're combining poor eating with time off from running, you can quickly gain weight that you may struggle to lose in the upcoming months. Establish a deadline for eating junk food, say, 3 days. Then return to the healthy eating regimen described in Chapter 9 as quickly as you can.

The Next Month

What the month following your marathon should look like depends entirely on your running goals: If you never intend to run again, you may choose to fill the next month with weekly knitting classes, never venturing near a running store or even thinking about going for a run. But if you're planning to run another marathon or enter other, shorter races, how you approach your next month of training is important.

If you ran your marathon as a one-shot deal, think about continuing to run for fitness for the rest of your life. You developed a great training regimen, you're fit, and you know plenty about running, so why not continue to keep yourself healthy with this activity? You can always knit some other time.

Working through the post-race blues

If you aren't sure what comes next on your running calendar, you may experience a unique psychological phenomenon: the post-race blues. (See the following "Deciding what comes next on your racing calendar" section.) Marathon training is all about setting a goal and working to reach it. But as soon as that goal is gone, you may feel disconnected and flounder, even more so if the marathon didn't go as well as you planned or if you trained with a group of people that has now disbanded.

The longer you train for your marathon, the more likely you'll experience the post-race blues. Your response may range from simply not knowing what kind of training to do without having a specific marathon to shoot for to not having any energy to pervasive sadness that lasts for days or weeks.

The key to eradicating the post-race blues is to set a new goal, hook back up with some of your training partners (if you had any), and establish a new training routine. Your next goal doesn't have to be another marathon — you may decide to race a half-marathon or a 10K (6.2 miles) — but if you're aiming for a marathon again, you may decide to run the next one 5, 10, or 30 minutes faster! You may decide to add in some of the training ideas discussed in Chapter 7 or increase your mileage to a higher level than you did before or work on your running technique (see Chapter 8).

Whatever you decide, remember that your training never has to be short-term, even if your goal is. Running is an activity that you can do for the rest of your life, even when you're 90 years old. If you continue to stretch, practice taking 1 or 2 recovery days for every hard day (see Chapter 6), and hydrate and eat well, you can run — without injury — for the rest of your life. And that life will likely be a long one that's not plagued by disease and obesity.

Deciding what comes next on your racing calendar

If you're interested in running a marathon again, sit down with a calendar and a pencil, review a list of marathons like the one in Chapter 18, and decide which one you want to enter. (Keep in mind that some marathons close their entries as much as a year before the marathon, others have lotteries to choose who will make it in, and still others require a qualifying time.) Pencil this race in on your calendar.

I recommend waiting 6 months before tackling your next marathon. Although people do wait less time than this, 6 months gives you time to build a base again, especially if you didn't have enough time to build a decent base for your last marathon (see Chapter 6). Try adding some speedwork (see Chapter 7), running in a few tune-up races (see Chapters 13 and 19), and so on.

After deciding on a marathon that you think you'll be guaranteed entry to, peruse the list in Chapter 19, along with entry forms from your local running store, to determine which tune-up races you want to enter in the 2 or 3 months before your marathon. Pencil these in your calendar. Then review Chapters 6, 7, and 8 to determine how much of your training time you want to spend building a base and when you want to do speedwork, hills, circuits, and strides/drills. Start from scratch, just like you did for your last marathon, with an eye toward adding any portion that was missing from your training before.

Building your base again

Even if you aren't sure exactly when you want to race again, begin building your base anyway (see Chapter 6). A solid base (an accumulation of weeks or months of consistent training at pretty high mileage) is what's missing from the training regimens of most people who are new to marathon training. The lack of a solid base is not through any fault of their own, but by the time they decide to run a marathon, they have only a few months to train for it. This time, spend 4, 6, 8, or even 12 months doing nothing but running distance runs, stretching, and (possibly) doing circuits, strides, and drills. Throughout this time, see whether you can gradually decrease your pace per mile, so that you're running each mile faster.

Knowing when to add speedwork

Speedwork (see Chapter 7) can wait. First, get back into training and build your mileage base again.

On the other hand, circuits (see Chapter 7) and strides and drills (see Chapter 8) don't take much out of you and are a perfect complement to a base. Your base, especially if you eventually increase your longest days to 24 or 26 miles, guarantees that you'll complete the entire 26.2 miles with relative ease. Circuits make you strong and able to bear down in difficult moments of a race. And strides/drills help improve your running technique and keep you flexible. I'll even go as far as to say that you can run a successful marathon on just mileage, circuits, and strides/drills, without ever doing the tempo runs, intervals, repetition workouts, and so on discussed in Chapter 7. (But do stretch after every run — see Chapter 5.)

Chapter 16

Reducing Your Finish Time Next Time

●●

In This Chapter

▶ Examining what you did to prepare

▶ Training too much or too little

▶ Changing a little makes a big difference

▶ Coming to terms with your lack of improvement

●●

*Y*ou've finished your first marathon and experienced the intense pain and the incredible satisfaction. And even though you swore this was a one-time event, now you're not so sure.

Maybe the race went just as well — or even better — than you expected, and now, instead of just trying to finish a marathon, you want to see how fast you can run, maybe even qualify for Boston. Or you may be thinking about making this marathon an annual event through which you can raise money for charity. Or perhaps your first marathon didn't go as well as you had hoped, and you'd like another chance to do it better.

Whatever your reasons, this chapter offers ideas of how you can make your second, third, fourth, or twentieth marathon an even better experience than your first.

Peering into Your Past Training

If you want to improve your next marathon's finish time, the first question to ask yourself is whether you did enough training in the weeks and months leading up to your last marathon. Ask yourself whether you could have done any of the following but didn't:

✔ Started weeks or months earlier?

✔ Run more miles per week?

✔ Taken fewer days off?

✔ Run faster or more consistently on your longer runs?

✔ Lengthened your longer runs?

✔ Done speed or strength workouts regularly and with great effort?

✔ Made strides and drills a regular part of your training routine?

✔ Circuit trained?

✔ Stretched after every run?

If you answered, "Yes," to any of these questions, chances are, you can train more or train harder for your next marathon. Peruse Chapters 6, 7, and 8 for ideas on how you can pump up your training. Also, review the two sections that follow, "Adding more speed workouts" and "Bumping up your mileage," which give you a brief overview of some of the concepts in those chapters.

Adding more speed workouts

If the training for your first marathon consisted of running the same pace for approximately the same distance for 4 or 5 days per week, you may have simply underprepared yourself to run a fast strong marathon.

This time around, consider following a training routine such as what follows:

✔ Do strides and drills three times every 2 weeks just after a distance run. Do them twice one week and do them once the next week.

✔ Do circuits three times every 2 weeks. Do them twice one week and do them once the next week.

✔ Once a week, do a workout. (See Chapter 7 for the lowdown on all four types of workouts.) About 6 weeks into your training, start with a tempo run and for the next 6 weeks, switch off between tempo runs and fartlek, doing each every other week. Then, for the next month or so, stop doing tempo and fartlek and switch to interval training one day per week. Finally, for the last 3 weeks leading up to your marathon, switch to repetition training.

✔ At least one other day per week, plan a run over a hilly route.

You're doing circuits or strides/drills after an easy run for 3 days per week, and 2 other days per week, you're doing a workout and a hill run. That leaves 1 day for your very long run and 1 day for a very short run or a day off. Any of the 3 days that you're doing circuits or strides/drills can also be short days, and any of those 3 days can also be your hilly run.

Bumping up your mileage

If you ever read articles about how elite marathoners train, you probably saw that they run between 70 and 120 miles per week. And even though many elites get paid to train and don't have to worry about pesky day jobs, they still wouldn't run that kind of mileage unless they thought they had to.

Qualifying for Boston

If qualifying for the Boston Marathon is one of your goals, keep the following qualifying times in mind. (A *qualifying time* is a time you run in an earlier marathon than the Boston Marathon, and you have to run your qualifying time in a certified marathon. In other words, the marathon you qualify in has to be legit — it can't be an all-downhill marathon, for example. And it can't be put on by your cousin Lenny, with you as the only participant!) Make a mental note, though, that these times change from time to time, so periodically check the marathon's Web site at www. bostonmarathon.org to find out whether the times have been updated.

Age	Men	Women
18-34*	3:10:00	3:40:00
35-39	3:15:00	3:45:00
40-44	3:20:00	3:50:00
45-49	3:30:00	4:00:00
50-54	3:35:00	4:05:00
55-59	3:45:00	4:15:00
60-64	4:00:00	4:30:00
65-69	4:15:00	4:45:00
70-74	4:30:00	5:00:00
75-79	4:45:00	5:15:00
80 and over	5:00:00	5:30:00

*Also bear in mind that you must be at least 18 years old to run in the Boston Marathon.

The biggest difference between elite marathoners and someone just starting out (besides the big, fat checks elites get for setting course records) is in their weekly mileage. Sometimes, 70 or more miles per week is just too much to fathom when you're struggling to finish a 3-mile run. And running that many miles makes you tired, forces you to get more sleep, and takes time away from your family and friends, so you may decide that you don't want to make that sort of commitment to your marathon training. In addition, to get from 40 miles per week to 70, 80, or 90 requires many, many weeks of patience, because you increase your mileage no more than 10 percent each week. So getting from 40 miles per week to 70 miles per week takes at least 7 weeks, and that's assuming everything goes perfectly. (I spent 3 months getting from 40 to 70 miles.)

Training on Your Last Legs

Although less common than undertraining, if you want to run your next marathon even faster, look for the following signs of overtraining:

- ✔ Your *quadriceps* (thigh muscles) and/or *hamstrings* (upper backs of your legs) are *always* sore and tired.

- ✔ One or more nagging injuries just won't go away.

- ✔ Although you feel like you *should* go out on a run, you rarely feel like you *want* to.

- ✔ Your legs are restless at night, and you wish you could keep your legs elevated all the time.

- ✔ If sleeping for an entire day were an option, you're often tired enough to do it.

- ✔ You get many colds, have a nagging cough, or frequently experience diarrhea.

- ✔ Writing, reviewing, and counting up the mileage in your running log more than once a day.

- ✔ When filling in your running log, you don't have much of anything that's positive to write about your own training.

- ✔ Shifting into another (that is, faster) gear seems impossible when you do strides, repetition workouts, or hills or when you try to pass someone in a race.

- ✔ You're sick of racing.

If you have just one of these symptoms, you may only be experiencing the difficulties of marathon training. But if you have two or more, you may be due for a break from running. Try switching to a fun activity that keeps your heart rate up, coming back to marathon training only when you feel as though you really miss it.

Understanding the One-Percent Theory

The *one-percent theory* is difficult to prove (and, therefore, not called the *one-percent rule*), but anecdotal information shows that the theory does seem to hold true:

> For every element you add to or improve on in your training, you will improve your race time by 1 percent.

See the following examples of training elements:

- ✔ Stretching (see Chapter 5)
- ✔ Allowing recovery days (see Chapter 6)
- ✔ Doing circuits (see Chapter 7)
- ✔ Doing workouts (see Chapter 7)
- ✔ Using great running technique (see Chapter 8)
- ✔ Doing strides and drills (see Chapter 8)
- ✔ Hydrating well (see Chapter 9)
- ✔ Eating the best possible foods (see Chapter 9)
- ✔ Using energy gels (see Chapter 9)
- ✔ Getting enough sleep (see Chapter 10)

Doing some of these (such as stretching, circuits, or strides) can improve your time by far more than 1 percent, but the idea is that they all add up. So if you do all ten of them, you can improve your marathon time by 10 percent. Not sure that's worth it? Well, if you ran your last marathon in 4:30, a 10-percent improvement is a 27-minute improvement! That's phenomenal. And in reality, if you aren't doing *any* of the elements listed, your improvement is likely to be far more than 10 percent, because some of them are so fundamental to marathon training.

Making Peace with Plateaus

Occasionally, distance runners find themselves on a *racing plateau*. They see improvement, more improvement, and then more improvement, and then, finally, the improvement levels off, such that every race time is essentially the same or, perhaps, even slower than the one before.

What's going on? Well, probably one of the following four factors figures in:

- ✔ Sometimes, runners do just plateau — without any reason — for a short while. Usually, however, with continued good training, sleep, eating, and so on, you soon find yourself improving again. If this is the case with you, waiting it out while rededicating yourself to your training may be just what you need.

- ✔ Often, runners plateau because of overtraining or undertraining. Examine the two earlier sections of this chapter, "Peering into Your Past Training" and "Training on Your Last Legs," for signs and symptoms of both problems and then see what you can fix in your own training.

- ✔ If you find yourself losing interest in distance running, your heart may not be in your races. Take a break by getting involved in another activity and go back to running when you really miss it.

- ✔ After a certain age, which is different for everyone, you may find that you don't improve anymore. If that's the case, you have to find other elements of distance running — besides race times — to motivate you. And also consider adding circuits to your training regimen to combat the loss of muscle mass that occurs as you age.

Don't immediately assume that as you get into middle age your times will slow down.

- • Priscilla Welch, who *started* running at age 34, won the New York City Marathon in 1987 at age 42.

- • Carlos Lopes won an Olympic marathon gold medal in 1984 at age 39.

- • Regina Jacobs, one of America's premiere distance runners has performed on an international level at 1,500 meters throughout the entire decade of her thirties.

Your 30s and 40s don't have to slow you down. Weight gain in middle age isn't inevitable if you eat the right number of calories (see Chapter 9), nor is inflexibility if you stretch well (see Chapter 5). What happens, though, is that people get busier in middle age, so they begin to compromise on what they eat, how much they train and stretch, and so on, and then want to believe that slowing down at middle age is inevitable!

Part V
The Part of Tens

The 5th Wave By Rich Tennant

FITNESS SCHED.
MONDAY

SKIP ROPE
WEIGHTS
CRUNCHES
SQUATS

"I **AM** following the schedule! Today
I skipped the rope, then I skipped
the weights, then I skipped the crunches..."

In this part . . .

*L*ike every Dummies book, this one ends with a Part of Tens that gives you ten (or more) fun nuggets of information in each chapter. You find out how to keep your training enjoyable, where you can find the biggest marathons, and which tune-up races have the most to offer you.

Chapter 17

Ten Ways to Keep Running Fun

In This Chapter

▶ Finding ways to make running more interesting

▶ Staying motivated as you train for your marathon

*O*kay, I'll admit it. Even though I've been running for a long time, it hasn't always been fun. In fact, at times in my running life, I dreaded the thought of having to go on my next run. But I never — in all those times that I didn't think I could run another step — regretted going out to train. After I get out there, even if I don't feel great, I'm grateful for the opportunity to run.

If you're looking for some motivation for your own running, look no farther than this chapter. It gives you ten ways to make you look forward to running day in and day out.

Creating a Club

An alternative to running with one training partner is to start a running club at work or in your community. (See Chapter 4 for more on clubs.) Running clubs can be ultracompetitive, professional racing clubs or can just be a group of people trying to train for local races. I suggest the latter.

Keep rules to a minimum in your club. As soon as you start making attendance mandatory, requiring steep annual fees, or forcing runners to attend races that they don't want to go to, your club won't be much fun anymore. Let people commit to the club as they're able and keep the entire experience enjoyable.

If you want to run with someone else but aren't interested in joining or starting a club, consider setting up a regular training time with a training partner.

Be sure your partner trains at about the same pace you do (see Chapter 6) and has similar goals. You certainly won't be having any more fun if you're training partner is constantly leaving you in the dust or if you're the one doing the dusting.

Don't train with your partner every day, or soon, you'll need a break from that, too.

Galloping with Your Dog

If you have (or are thinking of getting) a dog, and she likes to run, take the dog with you and experience running from a whole new perspective. Watch your dog running with wild abandon — eyes wide, tongue out, paws and ears flying — and you'll find yourself smiling and laughing. That's just the antidote you need for your running blahs.

Make sure that you allow your dog an opportunity to build up his mileage (just as you've done or are in the process of doing), going from 1 or 2 miles of walking and running the first few times up to 8 or 10 miles of running several months later. And don't take a puppy running until he's 20 or more weeks old. Puppies' bones are soft and still growing, and training during these first few months of life can change his bone structure.

Leaving Your Watch Behind

Chapter 4 suggests that you run for time instead of mileage, so that, for example, you're running 70 minutes, not 9 miles. This is a wise course of action, but if you find that running isn't so much fun anymore, take your watch off and just go for a run — anywhere! Don't think about how far or how fast you're running, just run, explore, feel the sun, wind, rain, or snow on your face, and think about how lucky you are to be healthy enough to be out running.

Playing Games

Whether on your own, with one or more training partners, or with your dog, you can play running games that make running more fun.

Game ideas include creating a route that goes past all the historical markers in your town and stopping to read each one (running in place, of course, while you read), playing soccer or Frisbee (without stopping running for any reason) instead of running a distance run, or doing what high schoolers used to call (very politically incorrect) *Indian runs*, in which you and at least one other person run single-file, the person in front throws a baton or ball out as far out to the side as he can throw, the person in back goes to fetch it and comes back to the group at the front of the pack, and the whole thing repeats.

Running in the Rain

Nothing perks up a run as much as running in the rain. Why? Because everyone will think you're nuts, which makes you feel special and different. And you *are* special and different: How many people do you know who are nutty enough to train for a marathon? Get on your Gore-Tex jacket or vest (see Chapter 2), put on a baseball cap, and (as long as you don't see lightning) get out there in that rainstorm!

Setting a New Goal

If you're becoming bored with running, consider revisiting your running and racing goals. If your goal during the last few years has been to finish your local marathon in less than 6 hours, consider raising the bar: Perhaps you can try to do it in less than 5.5 hours next time. (See Chapters 6, 7, and 8 for tips on improving your training so that you can race faster.)

Your new goal can be anything from running more miles per week to racing a different marathon than the one you've done the last few times to being able to train with a friend who runs faster than you do.

Starting Speedwork

Speedwork (see Chapter 7) doesn't exist just to make your running more fun. It exists to make your running more productive, but it can actually be fun. If you've been doing nothing but long runs for weeks and weeks, spending time doing hill repeats, a track workout, circuits, or any other type of special workout can ease the boredom.

Workouts are hard! You'll be tired after you finish and may be sore the next day. But just because they're hard doesn't mean they can't be fun.

Taking Days Off

If you haven't taken a day off in a while and you're feeling stale, plan for a day off. (See Chapter 6 for a discussion on whether taking a day off is a good idea.) Don't do it today, because you'll miss the opportunity to look forward to it. Instead, decide that next Saturday, you're going to take a day off. Then relish it. Wake up that morning and *don't* go running but do whatever else your heart desires. By the next day, you'll feel differently about your training.

You may decide, on your one day off, to cross-train. Chapter 12 has some ideas for you: The cross-training activities listed in Chapter 12 are meant to keep you fit while you're injured, but for one day, they may be fun.

Whatever you do, don't take 2 days off in a row. Two days of not running can quickly get you out of the habit, and you may find the second day turning into a third, and a fourth, and a fifth. Keep in mind that in just 4 to 6 weeks of not running, all your fitness goes down the drain.

Taking the Scenic Route

If you know of a great country road or trail to run on — even one that's a bit of a drive away — plan to spend a weekend morning driving out to run it.

Check the Internet to see what trails, parks, or roads may be nearby. Type in the name of your geographic area followed by the words *trails* or *running routes*. Some industrious runner in your area has probably outlined all sorts of great new routes.

Spending even one run on a beautiful, peaceful trail can eliminate boredom in a flash.

Varying Your Route

If you're running the same route every day, until you just can't stand the thought of going down that same street, past that same house, where that same man yells the same stuff to you every time you go by, don't throw in the towel — just change your route!

If you usually take a right out of your driveway, take a left. Or drive to a neighboring town and take an *adventure run,* where you really don't know where you're going, but you investigate new streets in a new area. If you're worried about getting lost, take a cellphone with you. The best adventure runs are through historic districts or areas with unusual architecture.

Chapter 18

The Ten Biggest Marathons

• •

In This Chapter

▶ Running in marathons from New York to Paris

▶ Looking at many other choice marathons

• •

*R*esearchers who track marathon participation often break marathons down into two categories: runners' marathons and community marathons. A *runners' marathon* is considered to be one that's fast (not many twists and turns), flat (no hills), certified by the USA Track & Field (USATF) (see Chapter 13), and big — many people enter or watch the race. These are good marathons to attend if your main interest is running fast, and you don't mind paying a bit of money to travel to and from the race and stay at the race hotel, which is usually located right at the starting line and is pretty expensive. Beginning with the largest, this chapter lists the ten biggest runners' marathons — many of which close their registrations very early, and some of which use a lottery system for entrants.

This chapter also suggests a few more marathons at the end of the chapter that may be a bit easier to get into. These marathons, called *community marathons,* are much smaller races that you choose because they're a close drive to your house or because they offer something special — a climb up a huge mountain, beautiful scenery, trails, and so on. The courses tend not to be USATF certified, which means that your time may not be recognized as qualifying time. If you do run fast enough to qualify for Boston, for example, your time may not be recognized by the Boston Marathon race organizers. Community marathons also tend to be slow and, perhaps, hilly. Far fewer people run in community marathons than in runners' marathons, which means that you don't stand in a traffic jam at the starting line. A smaller race, though, also means that you don't get as much hoopla, such as a runners' expo the day(s) before the marathon, famous bands playing at the start and finish, tens or hundreds of thousands of spectators along the course, and a day-long celebration after the race is over. All that hoopla can be very motivating, so if you want to get pumped up, consider a runners' marathon. If you just want to be able to wake up, drive over to a marathon, run it, and go home, a community marathon is for you. To find a community marathon in your area, visit your local running store or visit www.marathonguide.com and peruse the Marathon Directory of U.S. Races or international races.

The number of entrants who finish the race — not the number that sign up — is what makes the ten largest marathons in this chapter big. And because many marathons grow substantially each year, don't be surprised if next year's numbers are far greater.

Flora London Marathon

In mid-April, nearly 32,000 people flood onto the streets of London to run in the largest marathon in the world. The course, which boasts 80 pubs, crosses the Thames and goes through nearly every famous and historic portion of the city. Find out more at www.london-marathon.co.uk. The entry closing date is usually in mid-October and involves an entry-form system that's complicated for foreigners. (See the Appendix for information on taking tours to foreign countries to run marathons.) Entrants are drawn by a lottery and informed in December whether they made it into the race.

New York City Marathon

Held in early November, almost 30,000 run in the New York City Marathon, but over 2,000,000 line the streets to cheer. Applications and instructions are available online at www.nycmarathon.org from January through May. A lottery is held in mid-June.

LaSalle Bank Chicago Marathon

This marathon, which many consider the fastest in the world, is held in mid-October, with just under 28,000 runners. Registration runs from January through August or until the total number of entrants reaches its limit. Register online at www.chicagomarathon.com.

Paris Marathon

Held in early April, with just under 28,000 runners, registration for this race opens in early September and goes until mid-March. This event also includes a half-marathon (*semi-marathon* in French). The official Web site is at www.parismarathon.com, but unless you know fluent French, click on the U.S./U.K. flag on the right side of this Web site's home page to bring up the English-language version.

Berlin Marathon

With about 23,000 runners winding through this historic and beautiful city in late September, the Berlin Marathon is one of Germany's largest athletic events. Unlike most marathons, inline skating is allowed during the race. Registration begins in December or January preceding the race and goes until the race is full. Register online at www/berlin-marathon.com/world/E.

Honolulu Marathon

Held in early December, with almost 23,000 runners, the Honolulu Marathon is unique among the biggies because it doesn't limit registration: You can register until the day before the race, but to save money and hassle, register online at www.honolulumarathon.org.

The City of Los Angeles Marathon

The L.A. Marathon, held in early March, draws a crowd of a little over 17,000 runners. Registration begins in July and goes through the week before the race, although you take your chances at that point of not getting in. Visit the marathon's Web site at www.lamarathon.com.

Marine Corps Marathon

Held in late October in Washington, D.C., the Marine Corps Marathon caps the field at 16,000 runners. Registration begins in mid-March, and a lottery drawing begins in mid-April. Visit the Web site and register online at www.marinemarathon.com.

Suzuki Rock 'n' Roll Marathon

In early June, nearly 16,000 people gather at Balboa Park to run 26.2 fast and flat miles past most of San Diego's famous attractions: the San Diego Zoo, the Gaslamp District, Sea World, and so on. In addition, this hip, happening marathon always features a post-race concert by a famous artist in an honest-to-gosh amphitheatre that, if held anywhere else, would cost you as much as your $65 entry fee to this marathon. You also get 26 other bands playing along the course, a health and fitness expo in the days leading up to the race, and Suzuki products given away at random. Early registration ends in late October of the preceding year. Visit www.rnrmarathon.com for all the details.

Boston Marathon

Held on a Monday in the third week of April (Patriot's Day in Boston), a little over 15,000 runners finish this race. The Boston Marathon is the only major marathon to require a qualifying time in a USATF-certified marathon. You must have run the qualifying time (which varies based on your age and sex) between late September of the preceding year and early February in the race year. Register early, because if the marathon limits the field and if too many people qualify in a given year and you register late, you may not get in. Visit www.bostonmarathon.org for qualifying standards (also given in Chapter 16), information, and online registration.

Other Marathons to Consider

The following marathons are additional races that you may consider. They're a little smaller than the ten preceding marathons, yet most would be an exceptional marathon experience. I list them by calendar date, but the races that have a musical theme are left for the very end of the list.

- ✔ **Hops Marathon (Tampa Bay):** Race in early January without the misery of snow and ice; visit online at www.tampabayrun.com/hops.

- ✔ **Disney World Marathon (Orlando):** Held in a magic place in mid-January; registration is limited and closes early; go online to www.disneyworldsports.com.

- ✔ **hp Houston Marathon:** Held the third week of January; check out the Web site at www.hphoustonmarathon.com.

- ✔ **San Diego Marathon:** Held the third week in January; limited to 3,000 people; visit online at www.sdmarathon.com.

- ✔ **Las Vegas International Marathon:** Combine gambling with racing in early February; see the race Web site at www.lvmarathon.com.

- ✔ **Mercedes Marathon (Birmingham):** An Alabama marathon to try in early to mid-February; visit the marathon Web site at www.mercedesmarathon.com.

- ✔ **Florida Gulf Beaches Marathon (Clearwater):** See the race Web site at www.floridamarathon.com. This race takes place in mid-February.

- ✔ **Nokia Sugar Bowl Mardi Gras Marathon (New Orleans):** Boasts the longest name among marathons; held in mid-February; flat course; visit online at www.mardigras marathon.com.

- ✔ **Big Sur International Marathon:** This slow and hilly California race takes place in late April; check out the Web site at www.bsim.org.

- ✔ **Cincinnati Flying Pig Marathon:** The logo (a rotund airborne pig) alone is worth the trip; held in early May; visit the Web site at www.flyingpigmarathon.com.

- ✔ **Vancouver International:** Early May; dips into the United States for a time; visit online at adidasvanmarathon.ca.

- ✔ **Lake Geneva Marathon (Lake Geneva, Wisconsin):** Early to mid-May, this race is another alternative to the LaSalle Bank Chicago Marathon. Visit online at www.lakegenevasports.com/marathon_index.htm.

- ✔ **Bayshore Marathon (Traverse City, Michigan):** Held Memorial Day weekend in Traverse City, Michigan; fast and flat; visit online at www.tctrackclub.com.

- ✔ **Grandma's Marathon (Duluth, Minnesota):** Mid to late June; a late-season marathon that's still cool; fast and flat; visit www.grandmasmarathon.com.

- ✔ **Mayor's Midnight Sun Marathon (Anchorage):** Gorgeous scenery; held in mid to late June on the longest day of the year; visit online at www.muni.org/parks/mayor.cfm.

- ✔ **Chronicle Marathon (San Francisco):** Held in late July in a beautiful city; go online to www.chroniclemarathon.com.

- ✔ **Quad Cities Marathon:** If you're looking for a marathon in the Chicago area that's a little smaller than the LaSalle Bank Chicago Marathon, try the Quad Cities Marathon (held the third week in September) in Moline, Illinois. Get information and register at www.qcmarathon.org. The event also includes a half-marathon.

- ✔ **Maui Marathon:** If the Honolulu marathon is too big or offered at a bad time for you (although I have trouble believing that Hawaii in December would be a problem for anyone), consider the Maui Marathon, held in late September. You can start registering online about a year before the marathon date at www.mauimarathon.com; late registration fees begin around June 1.

- ✔ **Portland Marathon:** Held in early October; visit the race Web site at www.portlandmarathon.org.

- ✔ **Detroit Free Press International:** Held sometime in October (depending on when the Detroit Lions have home games); crosses into Canada for about 5 miles; check out the Web site at www.detroitfreepressmarathon.com.

- ✔ **Canada International Marathon (Toronto):** Held in Toronto, a city definitely worth the visit; late October; visit online at www.runtoronto.com.

- ✔ **Columbus (Ohio) Marathon:** Held in late October; visit online at www.columbusmarathon.com.

- ✔ **Mercury Interactive Silicon Valley Marathon:** Run fast on flat surfaces in late October at this California marathon. Check out the Internet site at www.svmarathon.com.

- ✔ **Citizens Bank Philadelphia Marathon:** If you're looking for a race close to New York City but don't want to join (or weren't picked in the lottery to enter) the New York City Marathon, consider this race, which has about 10,000 runners. It's in late November, and you can register online until a week before the marathon at www.philadelphiamarathon.com or until the day before race day in person.

- ✔ **Seattle Marathon:** Race held in early December; check out the Web site at www.seattlemarathon.org.

- ✔ **Rocket City Marathon (Huntsville, Alabama):** Another rare mid-December marathon; go to their Web site at www.huntsvilletrackclub.org.

If the timing of the Suzuki Rock 'n' Roll Marathon doesn't work for you, but you're interested in running a musically oriented race, check out the following:

- ✔ **Rock 'n' Roll Arizona Marathon and Half-Marathon:** Beginning in 2004, this marathon will be held in Phoenix in mid-January. Go online at www.rnraz.com.

- ✔ **Country Music Marathon and Half-Marathon:** Held in Nashville, Tennessee, in mid to late April; go online to www.cmmarathon.com.

- ✔ **Rock 'n' Roll Half-Marathon:** Held in Virginia Beach in late August. See www.rnrhalf.com on the Internet.

Chapter 19

Best Tune-Up Races in North America

In This Chapter

▶ Reviewing tune-up races by region

▶ Finding a race at the right distance

▶ Seeing what fun features are offered

*B*y definition, a *tune-up race* is any race that gets you ready for (or tunes you up for) your chosen marathon. Although some people do choose to run a marathon as their first race ever, you have a greater chance of success in your marathon if you get yourself used to racing by entering one or several tune-up races in the months leading up to your marathon.

Your best source of local road race information is at your local running store. Most carry brochures from even the smallest races; some high-tech stores also sport a Web site that features local races.

This chapter lists the longest, biggest, and most-popular races for four different regions of the United States, plus races in Canada, Mexico, and the Caribbean. In each region, you can find several cities that host the Komen Race for the Cure. The races are offered throughout the year to raise funds for and awareness about breast cancer, and each is 5K (3.1 miles). Visit the Komen Web site at www.komen.org/race.

If you're looking for races in Europe, Australia, or other parts of the world, search any of the sites listed in the Appendix or search on the name of the country or city followed by the words *road race* or *running race*.

Some races listed in this chapter have a *lottery entry,* in which tens of thousands of people submit entry forms, and race directors then draw a predetermined number of names (say, 10,000) from among the entries. For most races, your odds of getting in are about 1 in 3 or 1 in 2. The cutoff date for sending your entry is usually quite early — as much as 10 months before the event.

Note: Within each section, races are listed in order by race length, beginning with the shortest.

Northeast and Mid-Atlantic United States

You won't find many winter races in this region, which runs from Maine to Washington, D.C., but between early spring and late fall, you can find plenty of opportunities to race.

Falmouth Road Race

Named "Best USA Road Race" by *Runner's World* magazine, Falmouth is a treat for participants. The course is hilly near the end and hot from the third mile on, but the 15-minute bus ride to the starting line, scenic Atlantic coastline, and festive atmosphere make the tough course worthwhile.

Distance: 7.1 miles; **Location:** Falmouth, Massachusetts; **Race date:** Early to mid-August (lottery registration); **Web site:** www.falmouth roadrace.com

Utica Boilermaker 15K Road Race

Nearly 12,000 runners start this fun, friendly, upstate New York race that also includes a 5K.

Distance: 15K (9.3 miles); **Location:** Utica, New York; **Race date:** Mid-July; **Web site:** www.boilermaker.com

Army Ten Miler

This race, with nearly 12,000 finishers, is in a perfect vacation town. Run a 10-miler, tour the Smithsonian, take a romp through the White House, and head home.

Distance: 10 miles; **Location:** Washington, D.C.; **Race date:** Mid to late October; **Web site:** www.armytenmiler.com

National Cherry Blossom Festival 10-Mile Run

This 10-miler is part of the National Cherry Blossom Festival, a nearly 100-year-old festival that marks the celebration of a gift of 3,000 cherry trees by the city of Tokyo to the people of Washington, D.C. The smells and sights are breathtaking.

Distance: 10 miles; **Location:** Washington, D.C.; **Race date:** Early April; **Web site:** www.nationalcherryblossomfestival.org

New Haven 20K Road Race

New Haven offers an unusual race distance on a day when you know you'll be off work. The fall colors aren't in full bloom, but the area is beautiful nonetheless.

Distance: 20K (12.4 miles); **Location:** New Haven, Connecticut; **Race date:** Labor Day; **Web site:** newhavenroadrace.org

New Bedford Half-Marathon

Although New Bedford is chilly, it offers an opportunity to tune-up for the Boston Marathon, which is held about a month later.

Distance: 13.1 miles; **Location:** New Bedford, Massachusetts; **Race date:** Mid-March; **Web site:** www.rixsan.com/nbvisit/events/marathon.htm

Philadelphia Festival of Races

The Philadelphia half-marathon allows you to kill two birds with one stone: run a race and tour the city via this scenic, historic route.

Distance: 13.1 miles; **Location:** Philadelphia, Pennsylvania; **Race date:** Mid-September; **Web site:** www.philadistancerun.org

Southeast United States

The southeast — from northern Virginia to Florida and over to the Texas border — offers the most tune-up races, and many are held in the dead of winter when few other locales can offer a fast road race.

Crazy 8's 8K Run

This event really is crazy, given that the race starts at 9:58 p.m. Although your body may balk at running a race that late at night, you get to run a race in the south during the hot summer months.

Distance: 8K (4.96 miles); **Location:** Kingsport, Tennessee; **Race date:** Mid-July; **Web site:** www.crazy8s.org

Azalea Trail Run

This is one of the flattest, fastest courses in North America, with the added bonus of being beautiful, too.

Distance: 10K (6.2 miles); **Location:** Mobile, Alabama; **Race date:** Late March to mid-April; **Web site:** www.pcpacers.org/atr/

The Peachtree Road Race 10K

With 55,000 entrants — a number that would fill many football stadiums — Peachtree is wildly popular. The race entry closes early and includes a lottery.

Distance: 10K (6.2 miles); **Location:** Atlanta, Georgia; **Race date:** July 4; **Web site:** www.atlantatrackclub.org

Bank of America Gasparilla Distance Classic

This early winter road race in sunny Florida also features a 5K.

Distance: 15K (9.3 miles); **Location:** Gasparilla, Florida; **Race date:** Has varied from early January to mid-February; **Web site:** www.tampabayrun.com/gasparilla

Gate River Run

This race takes you across the mile-long Hart Bridge and features some of the best elite runners in the country.

Distance: 15K (9.3 miles); **Location:** Jacksonville, Florida; **Race date:** Early March; **Web site:** www.1stplacesports.com/rrinfo.htm

Anheuser-Busch Colonial Half-Marathon

Any visit to historic, beautiful Williamsburg is worth the trip, and if you can also run a half-marathon, your vacation can be doubly fun.

Distance: 13.1 miles; **Location:** Williamsburg, Virginia; **Race date:** Mid to late February; **Web site:** www.racepacket.com

Kiawah Island Half-Marathon

A half-marathon, great weather, and a beautiful island: That's a recipe for a great race, which also offers a marathon and a 5K.

Distance: 13.1 miles; **Location:** Kiawah Island, South Carolina; **Race date:** Mid-December; **Web site:** www.kiawahresort.com/marathon

News and Sentinel Half-Marathon

This race offers a hilly, challenging course — and I do mean hilly. (Don't look up during the race, or you may get discouraged!) It's a great event, though, that can test your mettle.

Distance: 13.1 miles; **Location:** Parkersburg, West Virginia; **Race date:** Mid to late August; **Web site:** http://newsandsentinel.com/halfmarathon/index.html

Rock 'n' Roll Half-Marathon

The focus is on music and a whole lotta fun, but it offers good timing for a fall marathon tune-up.

Distance: 13.1 miles; **Location:** Virginia Beach, Virginia; **Race date:** Labor Day weekend; **Web site:** www.rnrhalf.com

Walt Disney World Half-Marathon

Who doesn't love Disney World? The Magic Kingdom has offered a marathon and half-marathon in January for a number of years, and participation keeps growing. The race has a lottery and early cutoff date.

Distance: 13.1 miles; **Location:** Orlando, Florida; **Race date:** Mid-January; **Web site:** www.disneyworldsports.com

Midwest United States

The Midwest offers a wide variety of races across this vast region. You can find few in the winter, but plenty of races take place from late spring through late fall.

Quad-City Times Bix 7

Races in Iowa don't come up all the time, so this is a rare treat if you live in the heartland.

Distance: 7 miles; **Location:** Davenport, Iowa; **Race date:** Mid to late July; **Web site:** www.bix7.com

Crim Festival of Races

Crim offers terrific crowds and almost too many events to count (and an 8K, a 5K, and a host of kids' races). The course has just three hilly miles.

Distance: 10 miles; **Location:** Flint, Michigan; **Race date:** Late August; **Web site:** www.crim.org

Chicago Half-Marathon

This half-marathon offers a great tune-up for the Chicago Marathon, which is usually held about 6 weeks later.

Distance: 13.1 miles; **Location:** Chicago, Illinois; **Race date:** Early September; **Web site:** www.chicagohalfmarathon.com

Indianapolis Life 500 Festival Mini Marathon

As part of the Indy 500 Festival, the Mini is a fun, flat, friendly half-marathon. Entries close early.

Distance: 13.1 miles; **Location:** Indianapolis, Indiana; **Race date:** First Saturday in May; **Web site:** www.500festival.com/mini_marathon

Kentucky Derby Festival Half-Marathon

You, too, can run for the roses by participating in this Kentucky Derby Festival event.

Distance: 13.1 miles; **Location:** Louisville, Kentucky; **Race date:** Late April; **Web site:** www.kdf.org

Lincoln Half-Marathon

Nebraska isn't a road race Mecca, which makes the Lincoln Half-Marathon and Marathon a great event. Look for cool temperatures and a flat course.

Distance: 13.1 miles; **Location:** Lincoln, Nebraska; **Race date:** Early May; **Web site:** www.lincolnrun.org

Fifth Third River Bank Run 25K

This race, which used to be called Old Kent, is one of the longest races you can run short of a marathon. It's a great test of your training and plenty of fun for participants. Look for cool temperatures.

Distance: 25K (15.5 miles); **Location:** Grand Rapids, Michigan; **Race date:** Early to mid-May; **Web site:** www.riverbankrun.com

Western United States

The west region, covering everything west of the Midwest, offers far more races than those listed. This section gives you the biggest and best known, however.

Wharf to Wharf

This race, run from Santa Cruz to Capitola, offers gorgeous scenery.

Distance: 6 miles; **Location:** Santa Cruz/Capitola, California; **Race date:** Late July; **Web site:** www.wharftowharf.com

Celestial Seasonings Bolder Boulder

The Bolder Boulder is a hilly, challenging course run at high altitude. If you've been training at sea level, don't be surprised if you have a bit of trouble breathing and run a relatively slow time.

Distance: 10K (6.2 miles); **Location:** Boulder, Colorado; **Race date:** Memorial Day weekend; **Web site:** www.bolderboulder.com

Bay to Breakers 12K

Somehow, way back when, race participants started dressing up in goofy costumes. The tradition continues today and makes this race one of the most unique in the United States.

Distance: 12K (7.44 miles); **Location:** San Francisco, California; **Race date:** Mid to late May; **Web site:** www.baytobreakers.com

Lilac Bloomsday Run

True to its name, this race is lined with the beautiful sights and scents of lilac bushes.

Distance: 12K (7.44 miles); **Location:** Spokane, Washington; **Race date:** Early May; **Web site:** www.bloomsdayrun.org

Great Aloha Run

Hawaii in winter? 'Nuf said.

Distance: 8.15 miles; **Location:** Honolulu, Hawaii; **Race date:** Mid-February; **Web site:** www.greataloharun.com

3M Half-Marathon

This rare winter half-marathon is a great tune-up for a spring marathon.

Distance: 13.1 miles; **Location:** Austin, Texas; **Race date:** Early February; **Web site:** www.3m.com

Gatorade Half-Marathon

This warm-weather winter race also features a 5K.

Distance: 13.1 miles; **Location:** San Diego, California; **Race date:** Mid to late February; **Web site:** www.rhodyco.com. (San Diego hosts another half-marathon in August; for more on the half-marathon, go online at www.afchalf.com.)

Race to Robie Creek

Robie Creek offers a challenging course in beautiful Boise. Use this race as an excuse to travel to a gorgeous state.

Distance: 13.1 miles; **Location:** Boise, Idaho; **Race date:** Mid-April; **Web site:** www.robiecreek.com

Canada

Canada is road-race crazy, and you can find a number of tune-up races across the country. For more races, visit www.runthis planet.com and search on *Canada*.

Grande Course de Montreal

Montreal is one of the most ethnically diverse cities in North America, yet unlike some cities in Quebec, everyone speaks English. To find additional races in the Quebec Province, visit the Fédération Québécoise d'Athlétisme Web site at www.athletisme.qc.ca/sousmenus/4_calendrier.html.

Distance: 10K (6.2 miles); **Location:** Montreal, Quebec; **Race date:** Early September; **Web site:** www.runnerschoice.com/quebec/grande/grande.htm

Sporting Life 10K DownHill

Billed as Canada's fastest 10K, this race really is downhill!

Distance: 10K (6.2 miles); **Location:** Toronto, Ontario; **Race date:** Early May; **Web site:** www.runnerschoice.com/ontario/sl10/sl10.htm

Times-Colonist Garden City

Victoria, British Columbia is a taste of England in North America, and the weather is temperate year-round. After your 10K, take in high tea offered at many local hotels.

Distance: 10K (6.2 miles); **Location:** Victoria, British Columbia; **Race date:** Late April; **Web site:** www.timescolonist10K.com

Calgary Herald Stampede

Calgary is a good-old cowboy city, and the events surrounding this race include a chuck wagon race and a rodeo. What could be more fun? This race also features a marathon and 10K.

Distance: 13.1 miles; **Location:** Calgary, Alberta; **Race date:** Early July; **Web site:** www.stampederoadrace.com

Pacific RoadRunners First Half Half-Marathon

Beautiful route that takes advantage of scenic views of the Pacific.

Distance: 13.1 miles; **Location:** Vancouver, British Columbia; **Race date:** Early February; **Web site:** www.pacificroadrunners.ca/firsthalf

ScotiaBank Toronto Waterfront Half-Marathon

This half-marathon gives you front-row seats (er, I guess that's front-row feet) for viewing this great Canadian city.

Distance: 13.1 miles; **Location:** Toronto, Ontario; **Race date:** Mid September; **Web site:** www.runnerschoice.com/ontario/stwm/waterfront.htm

ScotiaBank Vancouver Half-Marathon

Billed as the world's most scenic half marathon, this race also features a 5K.

Distance: 13.1 miles; **Location:** Vancouver, British Columbia; **Race date:** Late June; **Web site:** www.runnerschoice.com/western/svhm/vanhalf.htm

Around the Bay 30K

This race is the longest race distance short of a marathon. It's cold, but you won't find a better test of whether you're ready for a marathon.

Distance: 30K (18.6 miles); **Location:** Hamilton, Ontario; **Race date:** Late March; **Web site:** www.aroundthebayroadrace.com

Mexico and the Caribbean

Ready for sun, sand, and sweaty road races? If you live in this area, you already know why it's a great place to live and train. If you live in the United States or Canada, running a road race in Mexico or the Caribbean is a great way to vacation and run in some of the most scenic races in North America.

Cara Suites 10k

Beautiful scenery and a unique location make this a perfect vacation race.

Distance: 10K (6.2 miles); **Location:** Gros Islet, St. Lucia; **Race date:** Mid October; **Web site:** www.runnerschoice.com/caribbean/caribseries.htm (provides e-mail and phone contact information)

Out to Hell 'n' Back 10K

Courses don't get much more scenic than this fast and flat race in the Cayman Islands.

Distance: 10K (6.2 miles); **Location:** Grand Cayman Island; **Race date:** Early November; **Web site:** www.runnerschoice.com/caribbean/caribseries.htm (provides e-mail and phone contact information)

Ufukuzo Midnight 10K

Never thought you could start a race in one year and not finish it until the next? With this race, you can! You start just before midnight on New Year's Eve and finish on the next day and year.

Distance: 10K (6.2 miles); **Location:** Barbados; **Race date:** December 31; **Web site:** www.runnerschoice.com/caribbean/caribseries.htm (provides e-mail and phone contact information)

World's Best 10K

Race directors bill this as the World's Best 10K. Located in beautiful San Juan, who's going to argue with them? The course is stunningly fast and flat.

Distance: 10K (6.2 miles); **Location:** San Juan, Puerto Rico; **Race date:** Late February; **Web site:** www.worldbest10k.com/

Cozumel Half-Marathon

This fast and flat race finishes right on the beach.

Distance: 13.1 miles; **Location:** Cozumel Island, Mexico; **Race date:** Late February; **Web site:** www.cozumelhalfmarathon.com

Run Barbados Festival, ScotiaBank Half-Marathon

This large festival — well attended by elites and amateurs alike — also features a marathon and 10K.

Distance: 13.1 miles; **Location:** Barbados; **Race date:** Early December; **Web site:** www.runbarbados.com

Running Web Sites and Other Resources

· ·

*T*his Appendix gives you several marathon training and racing resources.

Web Sites

The Web is a great way to search for races and get up-to-the-minute news.

www.marathonguide.com

As the best marathon site on the Web, MarathonGuide.com does it all: news, comprehensive marathon results, marathon lists, training information, book sales, and running links. Bookmark this site and check it often.

www.coolrunning.com

Although it offers training advice, news, and useful links, Cool Running is most useful for finding marathons and tune-up races in your area. Search for races by clicking on the Events tab.

www.sportscentral.com/marathon.html

SportCentral's claim to fame is that its marathon page offers a list of marathons by state, so you can quickly find one in your area. The list isn't complete, but it's a great starting point.

www.marathontour.com

If you want to run a marathon in an exotic international location but aren't sure how to get started, check out this Web site. The company specializes in tours to marathons and arranges the entries, airfare, hotels, and more.

www.usaldr.org

USA Track & Field (USATF), the governing body of running in the United States, operates this site. The site posts news items, results, rankings, and statistics that may be of interest to long-distance runners.

Magazines

Running magazines offer advice, training tips, and racing calendars. The two in this section are probably most useful to you.

Running Times

While other magazines are geared toward fitness running *(Fitness Runner* and *Runner's World),* high-tech research *(Peak Running Performance),* or racing results *(Track & Field News), Running Times* is a perfect blend of the three. The magazine is geared toward serious runners who race often and with purpose. It's not available on grocery-store newsstands, but you can find it at running stores and major booksellers. Visit the magazine's Web site at www.running times.com to get news or sign up for a subscription.

Runner's World

Runner's World, the most widely read running magazine in the world and the main competitor of *Running Times,* is a fun magazine that gives you short, well-illustrated articles for everyone from beginning runners to those who have already run a few marathons. Yes, it has plenty of fluff that's meant to attract newsstand readers (nearly every issue has an article about losing weight or getting six-pack abs), but the regional road-race listings alone are worth the price of each issue. Check out www.runnersworld.com for a good marathon calendar (listed chronologically) and other news.

Look especially for Ed Eyestone's column, "The Fast Lane." Each month, Eyestone, a former U.S. Olympian, offers a quick, one-page tip about speedwork, drills, strides, and other ways to improve your running performance. His columns aren't complicated or overly technical, but neither are they so basic that you feel as though you're a third-grader. Instead, Eyestone explains in plain but respectful English how you can try new techniques to breathe life into your training.

Index

• NUMERICS •

16-week training plan
  for beginners, 106–107
  for experienced runners, 107–108
  extending, 108

• A •

aches. *See also* soreness
  caring for, 66
  post-race, 228–229
Achilles stretch. *See also* stretching
  defined, 88
  illustrated, 88
  steps, 88–89
Active Isolated Stretching (AIS)
  Achilles stretch, 88–89
  active stretching, 75
  ankle stretches, 89
  believing in, 77
  butt stretch, 90, 91
  calf stretches, 85–86
  defined, 74
  hamstring stretches, 79–80
  hip adductor (groin) stretch, 84–85
  hip rotator stretch (external), 82–84
  hip rotator stretch (internal), 81–82
  lower-back stretch, 90–92
  quadriceps stretch, 80–81
  results, 76
  soleus stretch, 86–88
  stretch isolation, 75
  stretch setup, 76
  toe stretches, 89
active stretching, 75
aid stations, 204, 205
AIS. *See* Active Isolated Stretching
ankle stretch, 89
ankles, twisted, 188
anorexia, 161
antiperspirants, 59
Appalachian Trail, 45

arm carriage. *See also* technique
  defined, 137
  determining, 138
  hands and, 139
  illustrated, 138
  testing, 139

• B •

back extensions. *See also* drills
  with hop, 142
  illustrated, 141
  steps, 141–142
back pain, 190
backward running, 147
Bayshore Marathon (Traverse City,
    Michigan), 255
belly-breathing, 149
Berlin Marathon, 253
bib number, 214
Big Sur International Marathon, 255
biggest marathons
  Berlin Marathon, 253
  Boston Marathon, 20, 237, 254
  The City of Los Angeles Marathon,
    253
  Flora London Marathon, 252
  Honolulu Marathon, 253
  LaSalle Bank Chicago Marathon, 252
  Marine Corps Marathon, 253
  New York City Marathon, 252
  Paris Marathon, 253
  Suzuki Rock 'n' Roll Marathon, 254
bike paths, 43
biking, 197–198, 199
black ice, 51
blading, 197–198, 199
blisters
  avoiding, 54–55
  causes of, 185
  defined, 185
  liquid bandages and, 186–187
  treating, 185–187, 227

Boston Marathon
  information, 254
  qualification goal, 20
  qualifying for, 237
bounding. *See also* drills
  defined, 147
  illustrated, 148
  performing, 147
Brand-Miller, Jennie (*The Glucose
    Revolution: The Authoritative
    Guide to the Glycemic Index*), 158
bras, 31–32
breathing. *See also* technique
  to beat of feet, 150
  belly, 149
  chest, 148, 149
  habits, 148
  pattern, 150
  practicing, 149
bunhuggers, 212
butt stretch. *See also* stretching
  benefits, 90
  illustrated, 91
  steps, 90

• C •

caffeine
  benefits, 155
  energy gels with, 156
calf stretches. *See also* stretching
  evertor, 86, 87
  illustrated, 86
  invertor, 86
  steps, 85
calluses, correcting, 186
calories, eating additional, 16
Canada International Marathon
    (Toronto), 256
carbohydrates. *See also* eating
  calories from, 154
  complex, 153, 154
  defined, 153
  energy gels, 154–157
  list of, 154
  simple, 153, 154
cellphones, 59
cemeteries, 47
chair dips, 126

challenge, as reward, 12
charity, 13
chest-breathing. *See also* breathing
  defined, 148
  determining, 149
chip time, 221
Chronicle Marathon (San Francisco),
    255
Cincinnati Flying Pig Marathon, 255
cinder tracks, 117
circuit training. *See also* training
  benefits, 120
  chair dips, 126
  crunches, 129
  curls, 122
  defined, 101, 120
  difficulty, 121
  increasing, 236
  punches, 128
  push-ups, 130
  run with weights, 133
  shrugs, 124
  single-leg squats, 127
  sit-ups, 123, 132
  speedwork versus, 112
  stations, 120
  steps, 121
  step-ups, 125
  toe raises, 131
  in training schedule, 134
  upright rows, 132
Citizens Bank Philadelphia Marathon,
    256
The City of Los Angeles Marathon,
    253
city streets, 41–42. *See also* running
    locations
clocks, 204
clothing. *See also* running gear
  base layer, 33
  bunhuggers, 212
  chafing points, 30–31
  fabric, 31
  face masks, 36–37
  as fashion, 30
  gloves, 36, 37
  jackets, 33–34
  mittens, 36, 37
  pants, 36

racing, 211–212
running bras, 31–32
running shorts, 17, 34–35
singlets, 32
size, 30
socks, 37–38
tights, 35–36
t-shirts, 32–33
upper body, 31–33
vests, 33–34, 52
wind and, 33
coaches
    finding, 72
    good, 72
    hiring, 71–72
    warning, 72
cold baths, 66, 228–229
cold weather, 50
colds, 105
Columbus (Ohio) Marathon, 256
combination runs, 58
community marathons. *See also*
        runners' marathons
    aid stations, 205
    benefits, 205, 251–252
    defined, 205, 251
complex carbohydrates. *See also*
        carbohydrates
    before races, 164
    defined, 153
    list of, 154
    protein consumption ratio, 160
compression, 180
construction last, 26–27
conventions, this book, 2
cool-down
    need for, 93
    post-race, 226
    sprinting and, 93
    stretching and, 94
    time, 93
    walking, 93
Country Music Marathon and Half-
        Marathon, 257
country roads. *See also* running
        locations
    benefits, 43
    challenges, 43–45
    dogs and, 43, 44

isolation, 44–45
steep grading, 44
traffic, 43
cramps
    eating and, 55–56
    leg, 187–188
cross-training. *See also* training
    biking, blading, skating, skiing,
        197–198
    days off for, 100, 105
    with injuries, 193–200
    low-impact aerobics, 197
    Pilates, 197
    snowshoeing, 104
    swimming, 198
    Tae-Bo, 197
    walking, 196–197
    water running, 104, 194–196
    weight training, 198
    workout machines, 198
    yoga, 197
crunches, 129
curls, 122

• D •

darkness, running in, 52
days off
    cross-training on, 104, 105
    example, 103–104
    post-marathon, 229
    staleness and, 248
    as treatment, 184
    two, in a row, 248
    warning, 105
dehydration. *See also* fluids
    assistance in, 59
    hot, humid weather and, 49
    injury and, 165
    signs of, 49
Detroit Free Press International, 256
diarrhea, 168
diminishing returns, 175
dirt trails. *See also* running locations;
        surfaces
    Appalachian Trail, 45
    benefits, 45
    disadvantages, 46
    finding, 45, 56

Disney World Marathon (Orlando), 254
dogs
  as potential problem, 43, 44
  running with, 246
drills
  back extensions, 141–142
  back extensions with hop, 142
  backward running, 147
  bounding, 147–148
  defined, 140
  front extensions, 143
  front extensions with hop, 143
  high knee, 144
  increasing, 236
  karaoke, 146–147
  kick butts, 144–145
  performing, 140–141
  plyometrics, 140
  quick feet, 145–146

• E •

eating
  after running, 158
  before races, 164–165, 213, 214
  calories, 16
  carbohydrates, 153–159
  cramps and, 55–56
  fats, 161–163
  food allergies and, 166–167
  habits, changing, 178
  post-race, 230
  protein, 160
  quality, 151
  regime, taking breaks from, 151
  vegetables, 164
  vitamins/minerals supplements,
      163–164
eccentricity benefit, 14–15
elevation. See also compression; icing
  after falls, 180
  as treatment, 184
energy bars, 159
energy gels
  with caffeine, 156
  carrying, 157
  comparison, 156
  defined, 154
  hooked on, 155

during marathons, 223
  popularity, 157
  purchasing, 156
  recommendation, 156
entry fees, 171–178
environmental allergies, 167
equipment. See running gear

• F •

face masks, 36–37
falling down, 179–180
fartlek. See also speedwork
  curves and straights, 115
  defined, 68, 114–115
  examples, 115–116
  pole-to-pole, 115
  6-2-6-2, 115–116
  tempo run versus, 115
  in training schedule, 134
  2-1-1-1-1-30-30, 115
fats. See also eating
  bad, 162
  good, 162
  trans-fats, 162–163
  truth about, 161
feet
  listening to, 25–26
  rolling to toes, 26–28
  striking ground, 23, 24–25
final race instructions, 215
finish time, 221
first runs. See also running
  distance, 66–69
  pace, 64
  pacing, 67–68
  pointers, 53–64
  slow start and, 64–66
  weekly mileage, 68–69
flashlights, 52
flexibility, 74, 171–172
flexible arches, 27
Flora London Marathon, 252
Florida Gulf Beaches Marathon
      (Clearwater), 255
fluids. See also dehydration
  coffee/tea, 165, 177
  on the fly, 222
  juice, 165

during marathons, 221–223
milk, 165
minimum daily need, 165, 177
soreness and, 228
sources, 165
sports drinks, 164, 165, 177, 222–223
water, 177, 221–222
food allergies
common, 166
responding to, 167
symptoms, 166
training and, 166, 167
forefoot striking, 25
front extensions, 143

• G •

Gatorade. *See* sports drinks
gear check, 216
gel carriers, 157, 211
genetics, 178–179
gloves, 36, 37
The Glucose Revolution: The Authoritative Guide to the Glycemic Index (Brand-Miller, Jennie), 158
glutes. *See* butt stretch
glycemic index
defined, 158
food ratings, 158
illustrated, 159
goals
Boston Marathon qualification, 20
examining, 18–20
examples, 18–20
finish line, 208
new, setting, 247
pace and, 67
race, 18–20, 207–208
run entire marathon, 20
under four hours, 20
walk/run finish, 18–19
weekly mileage and, 18
golf courses, 46
Gore-Tex, 32, 33, 34
graded roads, 44
Grandma's Marathon (Duluth, Minnesota), 255
grass course, 117

• H •

half-marathons, 10. *See also* tune-up races
hamstrings
defined, 79
illustrated, 78
inner, 80
outer, 80
stretch variations, 80
stretching, 79–80
hard landers, 25
hard runs, 174–175
high knees, 144
hills, running, 119–120, 134
hip adductor (groin) stretch. *See also* stretching
benefits, 84
steps, 85
hip pain
causes of, 189
defined, 189
treating, 189–190
hip rotator stretch (external), 82–84
with angle, 84
illustrated, 83
steps, 84
hip rotator stretch (internal). *See also* stretching
with angle, 83
illustrated, 82
steps, 82
hitting the wall, 103
Honolulu Marathon, 253
Hops Marathon (Tampa Bay), 254
hot, humid weather, 49–50
Houston Marathon, 255
hyponatremia, 50, 166

• I •

ICE (ice, compression, elevation), 179–180
icing. *See also* treatments
distractions during, 183
falls and, 179
pain, 182
process, 182
tips, 182–183

icons, this book, 4
icy conditions, 51
identification, 59
indoor tracks, 47
inefficient running, 178
inflexibility, 171–172
injuries
  causes of, 171–180
  cross-training during,
    193–200
  dehydration and, 165
  everyday, 185–190
  falling, 179–180
  genetics and, 178–179
  imbalance-related, 175–176
  inefficient running, 178
  inflexibility, 171–172
  physical therapy and, 199
  rest and recovery, 173–175
  running surfaces link, 177
  shoe-related, 29, 172–173
  transitioning back to running and,
    199–200
  treating, 181–192
intervals. *See also* speedwork
  defined, 116
  examples, 116–117
  5-5-5s, 117
  repeat miles, 116–117
  in training schedule, 134
  2-1-2, 117
Ironman triathlons, 10

• *J* •

jackets, 33–34
junk miles, 99

• *K* •

karaoke. *See also* drills
  defined, 146
  illustrated, 146
  warning, 147
kick butts. *See also* drills
  defined, 144
  illustrated, 145
knee pain, 189

• *L* •

Lake Geneva Marathon (Lake Geneva,
    Wisconsin), 255
landing, sound of, 25
Las Vegas International Marathon, 255
LaSalle Bank Chicago Marathon, 252
leg cramps
  causes of, 187
  treating, 187–188
liquid bandages, 186–187
long runs
  length of, 101–102
  in mimicking race conditions,
    102–103
  need for, 102
  planning, 101–103
  support options, 102
long, slow distance (LSD), 99
loop runs, 57
lottery registration, 204
lower-back stretch. *See also* stretching
  illustrated, 91
  steps, 92
low-impact aerobics, 197, 199
LSD. *See* long, slow distance

• *M* •

magazines, 274–275
marathoners
  anorexia link, 161
  eating and, 152
  elite versus beginner, 238
  vitamins/minerals for, 163
marathons
  biggest, 251–254
  charities in conjunction with, 13
  choosing, 203–206
  community, 205, 251–252
  eating before, 213–214
  energy gels during, 223
  finding, 10
  first, 11
  fundamentals, 9–11
  goals, 18–20
  Ironman triathlon, 10
  length, 9, 11
  list of, 252–257

loosing interest in, 240
next, when to run, 232
pasta dinner nights and, 214
rehydrating during, 221–222
rewards, discovering, 12–15
risks for, 11
run frequency, 206
runners,' 203–205, 251
starting position, 220–221
targeting, 105
thought process, 223
marathon-training classes, 69–70
Marine Corps Marathon, 253
massages, 192
Mattes, Aaron L. (kinesiologist), 74, 75, 184
Maui Marathon, 256
Mayor's Midnight Sun Marathon (Anchorage), 255
medium landers, 26
Mercedes Marathon (Birmingham), 255
Mercury Interactive Silicon Valley Marathon, 256
midfoot striking, 24–25
mileage
defined, 97
increasing, 98
increasing, after first marathon, 237–238
measurement devices, 61
recording, 59–60
in running log, 59
in sharpening phase, 98–99
totaling, 98
weekly, 18, 68
mileage base
building, 97–98
speedwork and, 98, 110
tapering, 98
mileage wheels, 61, 100
minerals, 163–164
mini-marathons, 10
minutes
benefits, 63
calculating, per mile, 63
disadvantages, 62
running, 62
totaling mileage in, 98

mittens, 36, 37
muscles
calf, 85
front/rear views of, 78
gluteus maximus, 89
gluteus medius, 90
groin, 84
hamstrings, 79
imbalance, 176
lack of strength in, 176
location of, 76
quadriceps, 79, 80
soleus, 86
tearing, 100

• N •

nasal mucus, 64
neck stretches, 92
negative splits, 155, 209
neutral position. *See also* running shoes
defined, 28
illustrated, 26
New York City Marathon, 252
Nokia Sugar Bowl Mardi Gras Marathon (New Orleans), 255

• O •

odometers, 61
one-percent theory, 239
organization, this book, 2–3
orthotics, 27, 183
out-and-back runs, 57–58
outsoles
blown-rubber, 25
hard landers, 25
medium landers, 26
soft landers, 26
overtraining
breaks and, 239
signs, 238

• P •

pace
chart, 111–112
first run, 64, 67–68

pace *(continued)*
goals and, 67
increasing, 101
learning, 100
per-mile, determining, 100
speeding up, 101
training, 100–101
pain relievers, 183
pants, 36
Paris Marathon, 253
parks, 46
pedometers, 61
personal record (PR), 207
physical therapy, 199, 200
Pilates, 197, 199
plantar fasciitis, 188
plateaus, 240–241
plyometrics, 140
pool running. *See* water running
Portland Marathon, 256
post-race
aches/pains, dealing with, 228–229
blister treatment, 227
blues, 231
cool-down, 226
eating, 230
month after, 230–233
rehydrating/refueling, 226–227
rest, 230
right after, 225–228
running, 229
shake-out run/walk, 228
stretching, 227
week after, 228–230
posture. *See also* technique
back, 136
chin tilt, 137
lean back, 137
lean forward, 136–137
shoulder scrunch, 137
viewing, 135–136
PR (personal record), 207
professional treatments, 191–192
pronation. *See also* running shoes
defined, 27
illustrated, 26
protein
before races, 164
complex carbohydrate ratios, 160

sources, 160
warning, 160
punches, 128
push-ups, 130

• Q •

Quad Cities Marathon, 256
quadriceps
in running, 80
stretch illustration, 81
stretching, 80–81
qualifying time, 237
quick feet. *See also* drills
defined, 145
illustrated, 146

• R •

race countdown
eating, 213–214
gear prep, 216–217
night before, 216
packet pickup, 214–215
setting alarm, 218
skipping breakfast, 219
sleep, 217–218
starting position, 220–221
warm-up and stretching,
219–220
race goals. *See also* strategy
modifying, 208
sample, 208
time, 208
race number, 214
race packet
defined, 214
final instructions, 215
information, 215
picking up, 214–215
race number, 214
timing chip, 214
T-shirt, 215
race plans. *See also* strategy
defined, 208
examples, 209
negative splits and, 209

races
after, 225–233
eating before, 164–165
goals for, 207–210
information on, 215
long runs and, 102–103
strategy for, 207–211
tune-up, 206–207, 259–271
visualizing, 210–211
racing
calendar, 232
clothes, 211–212
easing into, 203–212
frequency, 206
gear, 211–212
plateaus, 240–241
thinking and, 223
racing flats, 212
rain, running in, 51, 247
reader assumptions, this book, 2
rearfoot striking, 24
recovery runs
after tempo runs, 113
in training, 100
reflective vests, 52
refueling, 227
registration
day of, 205
lottery, 204
pre-registration, 205
time period, 204–205
rehydrating. *See also* fluids
defined, 49
hot weather, 49
inability, 50
post-race, 226–227
repeat miles, 116–117
repetition workouts
intervals versus, 118
sample, 118
in training schedule, 134
use of, 118
resources
magazines, 274–275
Web sites, 273–274
rest and recovery time, 173–175
rewards
challenge, 12
charity, 13–14
eccentricity, 14–15
stress relief, 13
training, 12–13
Rock 'n' Roll Arizona Marathon and
Half Marathon, 257
Rock 'n' Roll Half-Marathon, 257,
263–264
Rocket City Marathon (Huntsville,
Alabama), 256
rolling to toes
category determination, 26
illustrated, 26
neutral, 26, 28
pronation, 26, 27
supination, 26, 28
routes
combination, 58
good, 56–58
loop, 57
out-and-back, 57–58
scenic, 248
surface, scanning, 56–57
varying, 58, 249
runners' marathons. *See also*
community marathons;
marathons
aid stations, 204
biggest, 251–254
clocks, 204
defined, 251
downtown venue, 204
elite runners, 204
fanfare and celebration, 204
features, 203–205
lottery registration, 204–205
reliable distance, 205
size, 204
speed, 204
*The Runner's Training Diary For
Dummies* (St. John, Allen), 60
Runner's World magazine, 274–275
*Runner's World Training Diary For
Dummies* (St. John, Allen), 60
running. *See also* runs
antiperspirants and, 59
blisters and, 54–55
for charities, 13–14
colds and, 105
with diarrhea, 168
with dogs, 246
dress and, 54

running. *See also* runs *(continued)*
drills, 140–148
drinking water during, 222
eating and, 55–56, 151–168
fartlek, 68
fun, keeping, 245–249
games, 246–247
hills, 119–120
identification and, 59
inefficiently, 178
intervals, 116–117
mileage, 59–63
minutes, 62
nasal mucus and, 64
with others, 69–72
posture, 135–137
in the rain, 247
routes, 56–58
snowshoe, 104
technique, improving, 135–150
transitioning back to, 199–200
walking and, 65
with weights, 133, 196
running bras, 31–32
running clubs
alternative, 71
before joining, 71
benefits, 70
creating, 245–246
defined, 70
disadvantages, 70
rules, 245
ultracompetitive, 245
running gear
clothing, 30–38, 54
costs, 16–17, 21
finding, 21–22
race prep, 216–217
shoes, 16–17, 22–29
sports watch, 29–30, 54
running gloves, 36, 37
running groups, 71
running locations
alternatives, 40
bike paths, 43
cemeteries, 47
city streets, 40–42
country roads, 43–45
dirt trails, 45–46

golf courses, 46
grass course, 117
parks, 46
sidewalks and, 39
suburbs, 42
tracks, 47, 117
treadmills, 47–49
running logs
defined, 59
recording details, 60
running mittens, 36, 37
running pants, 36
running shoes. *See also* running gear
blisters and, 54
board last, 27
breakdown, 28–29, 173
combination last, 27, 28
construction last, 26–27
cost of, 16, 22
curved last, 26, 27, 28
decision factors, 23
fit, 173
ground striking and, 23, 24–25
injury from, 172–173
motion control, 27
need for, 22
new, as injury treatment, 183
orthotics, 27, 183
outsole, 25–26
perfect, 22
quality, 22
racing flats, 212
replacement distance, 17, 28–29
replacement schedule, 173
saving on, 23
semi-curved last, 26, 27
shape last, 26
shopping for, 54
slip last, 27, 28
straight last, 26, 27
toe box, 54
running shorts. *See also* clothing
built-in underwear, 35
fabric, 35
key pocket, 35, 157
length, 35
number of, 17
soccer/basketball shorts versus,
34–35

running socks. *See also* clothing
   defined, 37
   fabric, 37–38
   recommendation, 38
   size, 38
   SmartWool, 38
   style, 38
   weight, 37
running stores, 22, 54, 70
running tights. *See also* clothing
   baggy, 36
   defined, 35
   when to wear, 35
Running Times magazine, 274
runs
   first, 53–69
   hard, 174–175
   long, weekly, 101–103
   recovery, 100, 113
   shakeout, 228
   short, weekly, 103
   stretching after, 103
   tempo, 113–114

• S •

St. John, Allen
   *The Runner's Training Diary For
      Dummies,* 60
   *Runner's World Training Diary For
      Dummies,* 60
San Diego Marathon, 255
scenic routes, 248
Seattle Marathon, 256
shake-out run, 228
shape last, 26
sharpening phase, 98–99
shinsplints, 187
shoes. *See* running shoes
shorts. *See* running shorts
shrugs, 124
sidewalks, 39
simple carbohydrates. *See also*
      carbohydrates
   after running, 158
   defined, 153
   energy gels, 154–157
   list of, 154
single-leg squats, 127

singlets, 32
sit-ups
   in circuit training, 123, 132
   illustrated, 123
   importance, 90, 132
16-week training plan
   for beginners, 106–107
   for experienced runners, 107–108
   extending, 108
skating, 197–198, 199
skiing, 197–198, 199
sleep
   amounts, 16, 174
   bedtime and, 217
   before race, 217–218
   lack of, 174
   post-race, 230
SmartWool socks, 38
snowshoeing, 104
socks. *See* running socks
soft landers, 25
soleus stretch. *See also* stretching
   defined, 86
   illustrated, 87
   steps, 86–88
soreness
   caring for, 66
   diminishing, 229
   post-race, 228–229
speed
   increasing, 98
   training, 109–118
   walking, 196
speedwork
   additional, 236–237
   circuit training versus, 112
   defined, 109, 110
   fartlek, 114–116
   intervals, 116–117
   mileage base before, 110
   need for, 110
   repetition, 118
   starting, 247–248
   tempo runs, 113–114
   when to add, 233
   workouts, 113
splits
   defined, 17
   negative, 155, 209

sport packs, 157
sports bras, 31–32
sports drinks
  after runs, 177
  before marathons, 164
  carbonated, 165
  during marathons, 222–223
sports medicine doctors, 191–192
sports watches. *See also* running gear
  cost, 30
  defined, 54
  as everyday watch, 30
  finding, 29
  options, 29–30
SportsStretch program, 74–75
starting position
  chip time and, 221
  finish time and, 221
  rules, 221
  wait time, 220–221
step-ups, 125
strategy. *See also* races
  goal, 207–208
  race plan, 208–209
  visualization, 210–211
strength
  benefits, 109
  building, 119–133
  circuit training and, 120–133
  hill running and, 119–120
  as injury treatment, 184
  muscle, lack of, 176
strength-speed phase, 98
stress fractures, 190
stress relief, 13
stretching. *See also* Active Isolated
    Stretching (AIS)
  Achilles, 88–89
  active, 75
  ankles, 89
  before races, 219–220
  butt, 90, 91
  calves, 85–86
  cool-down and, 94
  debate(s), 73–74
  hamstrings, 75, 79–80
  hip adductor (groin), 84–85
  hip rotator (external), 82–84
  hip rotator (internal), 81–82

holding, 74, 75
injury and, 171–172
as injury treatment, 181–182
isolating, 75
low-back, 90–92
muscle location and, 76
neck, 92
old rules of, 73
post-race, 227
quadriceps, 80–81
setting up, 76
soleus, 86–88
soreness and, 66
toes, 89
stretching rope, 76
strides
  defined, 139
  goal, 140
  increasing, 236
  performing, 139
  process, 139–140
  in training schedule, 134
striking
  forefoot, 25
  midfoot, 24–25
  rearfoot, 24
suburban streets, 42
sunglasses, 211
sunstroke, 49
supination. *See also* running shoes
  defined, 28
  illustrated, 26
surfaces
  changing, 184
  concrete, 56
  dirt, 56
  grass, 57
  injury link to, 177
  trail, 57
Suzuki Rock 'n' Roll Marathon, 254
swimming, 198, 199

• T •

Tae-Bo, 197, 199
tapering, 98
technique
  arms, 137–139
  breathing, 148–150

drills, 140–148
improving, 135–150
posture, 135–137
strides, 139–140
tempo runs. *See also* speedwork
breakdown, 113–114
defined, 113
fartlek versus, 115
first, 114
in training schedule, 134
warm-up/cool-down and, 114
thinking, 223
tights. *See* running tights
time
chip, 221
cool-down, 93
finish, 221
qualifying, 237
race goals, 208
training, 15
walking, 197
warm-up, 92
timing chip, 214
toe raises, 131
toe stretches, 89
tracks
cinder, 117
indoor, 47
using, 47
trainers. *See* coaches
training
benefits, 12–13
circuit, 101, 120–133
classes, 69
energy, 15
first five weeks, 68
first week, 66
food allergies and, 167
habits, maintaining, 229
on last legs, 238–239
one-percent theory, 239
pace, 100–101
partners, 246
past, reviewing, 235–236
speed, 109–118
strength, 109
time, 15
with weights, 198

training plan
creating, 105–108
current mileage and, 106
goals and, 106
16-week (beginners), 106–107
16-week (experienced runners),
107–108
time and, 106
24-week, 108
trans-fats. *See also* fats
alternatives, 162–163
defined, 162
travel expenses, 18
treadmills. *See also* running locations
boredom, 47
buying, 48
features, 48
at home, 47–48
TV watching on, 47
using, 48–49
treatments. *See also* injuries
for back pain, 190
for blisters, 185–187, 227
for calluses, 186
days off, 184
do-it-yourself, 181–184
elevation, 184
for everyday injuries, 185–190
for hip pain, 189–190
ice, 182–183
for knee pain, 189
for leg cramps, 187–188
massage, 192
muscle strengthening, 184
new shoes, 183
pain relievers, 183
for plantar fasciitis, 188
professional, 191–192
for shinsplints, 187
sports medicine, 191–192
for stress fractures, 190
stretching, 181–182
surface change, 184
for twisted ankle, 188
triathlons, 10
T-shirts. *See also* clothing
fabrics, 32, 33
long-sleeved, 32

T-shirts. *See also* clothing *(continued)*
  race, 215
  size, 32
  turtleneck, 32
tune-up races. *See also* races
  best, 259–271
  Canada, 267–269
  defined, 206, 259
  length of, 206
  lottery entry, 260
  Mexico and Caribbean, 269–271
  Midwest United States, 264–265
  negative splits, 209
  Northeast/Mid-Atlantic United
    States, 260–261
  preparation for, 207
  as preview, 207
  Southeast United States, 262–264
  strategy, 207
  times to run, 206
  Western United States, 266–267
turnover, 140
twisted ankles, 188

• *U* •

ultramarathons, 10
undertraining, 11
upright rows, 132

• *V* •

Vancouver International, 255
vegetables, 164
vests. *See also* clothing
  cold weather, 33–34
  reflective, 52
visualizing races
  defined, 210
  as habit, 210
  psychologists and, 211
  sessions, 210
  steps, 210
vitamins, 163–164

• *W* •

waist bags, 157

walking
  cool-down, 93
  as cross-training, 196–197
  injuries and, 196–197
  post-race, 228
  ratio, 65
  running and, 65
  speed, 196
  time length for, 197
  in transition back to running, 199
warm-up
  kinks and, 92–93
  moving out of, 93
  race, 219–220
  time, 92
water
  daily, 177
  during marathons, 221–222
water running. *See also* cross-training
  benefits, 195
  defined, 194
  effective, 196
  illustrated, 195
  land running versus, 195
  post-race, 229
  swimming combined with, 196
  in transition back to running, 199
  warning, 196
weather
  cold, icy, 50–51
  hot, humid, 49–50
  nighttime, 52
  rainy, 51
Web sites, 273–274
weight loss, 164
weights
  running with, 133, 196
  training with, 198, 200
The Whartons' Stretch Book (Wharton,
    Jim and Phil), 74
wind pants, 36
workout machines, 198, 199

• *X* • *Y* • *Z* •

yoga, 197, 199

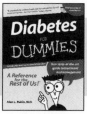

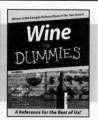

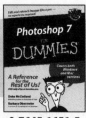

FOR DUMMIES®

The advice and explanations you need to succeed

SELF-HELP, SPIRITUALITY & RELIGION

Sex FOR DUMMIES

0-7645-5302-X

Parenting FOR DUMMIES

0-7645-5418-2

Religion FOR DUMMIES

0-7645-5264-3

Also available:

The Bible For Dummies
(0-7645-5296-1)

Buddhism For Dummies
(0-7645-5359-3)

Christian Prayer For
Dummies
(0-7645-5500-6)

Dating For Dummies
(0-7645-5072-1)

Judaism For Dummies
(0-7645-5299-6)

Potty Training For
Dummies
(0-7645-5417-4)

Pregnancy For Dummies
(0-7645-5074-8)

Rekindling Romance For
Dummies
(0-7645-5303-8)

Spirituality For Dummies
(0-7645-5298-8)

Weddings For Dummies
(0-7645-5055-1)

PETS

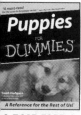

Puppies FOR DUMMIES

0-7645-5255-4

Dog Training FOR DUMMIES

0-7645-5286-4

Cats FOR DUMMIES

0-7645-5275-9

Also available:

Labrador Retrievers For
Dummies
(0-7645-5281-3)

Aquariums For Dummies
(0-7645-5156-6)

Birds For Dummies
(0-7645-5139-6)

Dogs For Dummies
(0-7645-5274-0)

Ferrets For Dummies
(0-7645-5259-7)

German Shepherds For
Dummies
(0-7645-5280-5)

Golden Retrievers For
Dummies
(0-7645-5267-8)

Horses For Dummies
(0-7645-5138-8)

Jack Russell Terriers For
Dummies
(0-7645-5268-6)

Puppies Raising &
Training Diary For
Dummies
(0-7645-0876-8)

EDUCATION & TEST PREPARATION

Spanish FOR DUMMIES

0-7645-5194-9

Algebra FOR DUMMIES

0-7645-5325-9

The ACT FOR DUMMIES

0-7645-5210-4

Also available:

Chemistry For Dummies
(0-7645-5430-1)

English Grammar For
Dummies
(0-7645-5322-4)

French For Dummies
(0-7645-5193-0)

The GMAT For Dummies
(0-7645-5251-1)

Inglés Para Dummies
(0-7645-5427-1)

Italian For Dummies
(0-7645-5196-5)

Research Papers For
Dummies
(0-7645-5426-3)

The SAT I For Dummies
(0-7645-5472-7)

U.S. History For Dummies
(0-7645-5249-X)

World History For
Dummies
(0-7645-5242-2)

Available wherever books are sold. Go to www.dummies.com or call 1-877-762-2974 to order direct.

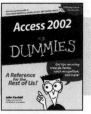